BOOKS IN THE MENUS AND MUSIC SERIES

*Dinner and Dessert*

*Holidays*

*Dinners for Two*

*Nutcracker Sweet*

*Music and Food of Spain*

*Picnics*

*Dining and the Opera in Manhattan*

*Lighthearted Gourmet*

*Rock & Roll Diner*

*The Irish Isle*

*Afternoon Tea Serenade*

*Spa*

*Sharon O'Connor's Menus and Music*

Favorite Recipes from Celebrated Spas

Ideas for Revitalizing Mind and Body

Soothing Classical Piano Music

Menus and Music Productions, Inc.
*Emeryville, California*

Recipes on pages 20 and 49 to 56 adapted with permission by publisher Cal-a-
Vie Spa and Health Resort from *Cal-a-Vie's Gourmet Spa Cookery*, copyright ©
1997 Cal-a-Vie Spa and Health Resort, Vista, California.

Recipes on pages 91 to 100 adapted with permission by author Michel Stroot
from *The Golden Door Cookbook*, copyright © 1997 Golden Door (published
by Broadway Books, New York City).

Library of Congress Catalog Card Number: 98-65843
O'Connor, Sharon    Menus and Music Volume XIII
Spa
    Favorite Recipes from Celebrated Spas
    Ideas for Revitalizing Mind and Body
    Soothing Classical Piano Music

Includes Index
1. Cookery    2. Nutrition and Fitness
I. Title

ISBN 1-883914-24-8 (boxed set: paperback with compact disc)
ISBN 1-883914-25-6 (boxed set: paperback with cassette tape)
ISBN 1-883914-26-4 (hardcover with compact disc)

Menus and Music Productions, Inc.
1462 66th Street
Emeryville, CA 94608
(510) 658-9100

Cover design by Brenda Rae Eno, San Francisco
Book design by Fifth Street Design, Berkeley
Cover food photograph by Frankie Frankeny, San Francisco
Cover food styling by Wesley Martin
Cover water photograph by Gary Crabbe, Mountain Light Photography,
Emeryville, California

Manufactured in the United States of America

10 9 8 7 6 5 4 3 2 1

# CONTENTS

Introduction / 6

A History of the Spa / 8

Cook's Notes / 12

Healthy Eating / 18

Homemade Spa Treatments / 23

The Spa Experience at Home / 37

Music Notes / 43

Cal-a-Vie / 46

Canyon Ranch / 57

Canyon Ranch in the Berkshires / 65

Château Élan / 73

Givenchy Hotel & Spa / 80

Golden Door / 88

Grand Wailea Resort,
Spa Grande / 101

The Greenhouse / 112

The Hills Health Ranch / 125

Hilton Head Health Institute / 134

Ihilani Resort & Spa / 144

The Inn at Manitou / 153

La Costa Resort & Spa / 162

The Lodge at Skylonda / 172

Meadowood Napa Valley / 180

The Peaks at Telluride / 186

The Phoenician Centre
for Well-Being / 195

Rancho La Puerta / 202

Sonoma Mission Inn & Spa / 217

The Spa at Doral / 229

Topnotch at Stowe / 239

Basics / 250

Nutritional Data / 258

Conversion Charts / 259

List of Contributors / 260

Spa Resources / 262

Acknowledgments / 264

Index / 266

# INTRODUCTION

*If I had known I was going to live this long,*
*I would have taken better care of myself.*

—Eubie Blake

Ahh, the spa life! During the past year, I had the chance to take a break from my hectic schedule and experience the pleasures of the spa. Sunrise mountain hikes, circuit training, aerobics, weight-lifting, and stretch classes left me bounding with energy and with a determination to sustain this feeling by including exercise as part of my daily routine. Aromatherapy facials and exfoliating body scrubs made my skin glow, and disciplined yoga sessions gave me a tension-relieving technique to use at home. I attended lectures on nutrition, fitness, and stress management, and was introduced to the momentary eternity of meditation as well as deeply relaxing massages that go beyond language. And three times a day I was astonished by how flavorful and highly satisfying spa cuisine can be—I vowed to keep eating this low-fat, nutritious food when I returned home! Relaxed and happy, I was energized enough to take on the challenges of writing this book and finding music that would create a peaceful mood for healthier dining and home-spa pampering.

A week at a spa is a time to step back from the stress of daily living and to see life from a different perspective. Many of the spa guests I met were trying to find balance in their lives, rethink priorities, or make changes that would lead to a healthier lifestyle. To help meet these goals, each of the spas in this book provides a nurturing environment focused on fitness, healthy eating, relaxation, and renewal.

Whether you go to a spa every year, are thinking about a spa vacation, or simply want to take more responsibility for your own well-being, this volume will help you create the spa experience for yourself. The contributors to the book have provided you with a sampling of cuisine that has pleased guests at some of the best spas in North America. I asked the chefs to choose recipes with the home cook in mind, so you don't need to be a highly skilled cook to prepare any of these dishes. Some of my favorites are Breakfast Bread with Cranberries and Apricots (page 207), Mediterranean Vegetable Bisque (page 224), Grilled

Swordfish with Papaya-Kiwi Salsa (page 97), and Chilled Melon Balls with Warm Ginger Sauce (page 249). This kind of food proves you don't have to choose between good taste and good health. It reflects a variety of international and regional cuisines and is not soul-depriving diet food—healthful and fresh, it provides energy and gives your body the nutrients it needs. I have enjoyed making these dishes in my own home and hope the recipes will spark your creativity and increase your enjoyment of good food.

I have also included recipes for facials, masks, body scrubs, aromatherapy baths, and other spa-style treatments that can be reproduced at home with natural, readily available ingredients. Go ahead and treat yourself to some relaxing, luxurious pampering. By making time to take care of yourself, you'll look better, feel better, and be more capable of handling whatever comes your way. During some of your treatments, I hope you will enjoy the elegant and calming piano pieces that accompany this book.

I believe the beauty of the music recorded here has the power to bring us into a garden of earthly delights, such as can be experienced at any one of the spas in this book. While visiting Cal-a-Vie and Rancho La Puerta, I kept hearing passages of enchanting music by Chopin, Debussy, Ravel, and Satie in my mind. While gazing at Cal-a-Vie's gentle gurgling stream and later, after finding myself lost in the beauty of a garden at Rancho La Puerta, I realized that these composers have given us musical impressions of clouds, gardens, water, and dreams. My intense happiness while listening to classical music during Phyllis Pilgrim's Inner Journey classes at Rancho La Puerta made me realize how much this tender, luminous music can add to the spa experience. The program of music I have selected will create a restful ambience for your home spa and set a gracious mood for dining or relaxing after a wonderful meal.

To discover renewed health, energy, and well-being, perhaps you can plan a visit to a spa and experience its abundant pleasures for yourself. In the meantime, I hope this volume helps you to enjoy the spa experience at home. Take some time to treat yourself or someone special and enjoy a few moments that let you soar above your everyday routine. To your health and happiness!

—*Sharon O'Connor*

7

# A History of the Spa
## From Ancient Roman Baths to Today's Fitness Retreats

Although today's emphasis on health, fitness, and stress-relief may seem directly related to our nonstop lifestyles and toxin-filled environments, people have gone to spa retreats for centuries to ease their nerves and renew their energy. The word *spa* is an acronym derived from the Latin *solus per aqua*, meaning "health by water," and such healing waters have long been the focus of pilgrimages, miracles, therapeutic regimens, and pure pleasure.

## Roman Baths

Both ancient Greeks and Romans used bathing and massage as part of their athletic and cosmetic routines, and the Romans built bathing stations at natural hot springs throughout their empire. Many of the medicinal waters were discovered by observing injured animals, who instinctively searched out mineral springs to heal their wounds. Workers digging canals also noticed that when they found themselves standing in thermal waters to work, any ailments they had healed much better. Bathing became a popular social event for the vast Roman leisure class, and they began building elaborately designed baths that included libraries, galleries, and entertainment. Many of these ancient Roman baths evolved into the grand resorts that are the basis of the European spa culture.

In the first century, Romans turned the small town of Bath, England, into a resort that has ever since been famous for its hot springs, which still gush out of the earth at a constant temperature of 120°F (49°C) and contain thirty minerals and elements. A small town in Belgium was given the name Spa, and for centuries after famous people went there to "take the waters." Queen Christina of Sweden, Peter the Great, and Victor Hugo all sipped and bathed in the waters, which were thought to cure heart disease, rheumatism, and respiratory inflammation. Kaiser Wilhelm II even selected the town as the site for his abdication.

# European Spas

During the eighteenth and nineteenth centuries, European spas flourished. Fashionable spas included Baden-Baden in Germany, with its fabulously ornate gambling casino and hot radioactive waters; Bad Ischl in Austria, where emperors, the aristocracy, artists, composers, and writers congregated to take healing saltwater baths; Karlsbad in Czechoslovakia, which was visited by Bach, Beethoven, Tolstoy, Gogol, Paganini, Chopin, and Liszt; Brighton in England; Aix-les-Bains in France; Lake Balaton in Hungary; and many others. The desirable attributes of these great spas, in addition to their famous water treatments, included a beautiful location, clean air, a large park, a gambling casino, and an aura of glamour.

No spa was better than its reputation, which often depended more on frequent visits by crowned heads and celebrities than the quality of its thermal springs. The socially ambitious, as well as the socially secure, were attracted to the healing waters, and so were creative geniuses. Turgenev, Balzac, and George Sand wrote and took the waters at Baden-Baden; Goethe spent thirteen summers at Karlsbad; and the French town of Evian-les-Bains played host to Nijinsky, Isadora Duncan, Greta Garbo, and Marcel Proust.

European spas were not just high-end vacation spots, however. Before the advances of medicine, doctors often sent the chronically ill to such spas. As we North Americans begin to appreciate the influence of mental states on our physical well-being and to understand the limits of medicinal drugs, the "spa cure" of centuries past no longer seems so quaint and ineffectual. Today, many Europeans take restorative bath treatments as part of yearly, doctor-prescribed spa visits. At home they use an array of bath treatments, such as those developed by Father Sebastian Kneipp, that are available in pharmacies throughout the continent.

# Spas in North America

In 1774, Saratoga Springs, New York, became the first pleasure resort in America. The area, where abundant mineral waters issue from a geological fault in the rock, had been known to the Mohawk Indians for many centuries.

*Saratoga* is an Indian word meaning "the place of the medicine waters of the great spirit." Among the first visitors to the resort were George Washington, Alexander Hamilton, and Governor Clinton of New York, who enjoyed the beneficial effects attributed to the different springs. The waters were even bottled and sold throughout the United States. In 1863, the Saratoga Springs racetrack, now the oldest in the United States, became a fashionable attraction.

Another early spa resort was the city of Hot Springs in West Virginia. Located in an area of many thermal springs, originally along a Native American game trail, it was one of two original springs (the other is Warm Springs) to be developed by white settlers. Compared to bustling Saratoga, the early Hot Springs had a sleepy, Southern feel, and guests followed a regime traditionally consisting of bathing in a warm pool while sipping mint juleps. The resort became popular at the end of the last century, and Henry Ford, John D. Rockefeller, and Andrew Mellon all went there regularly.

The oldest continuously run fitness spa in North America is Rancho La Puerta in Tecate, Mexico (see page 203). Founded in the late 1930s, this spa was not based on location next to a hot springs, but was run according to the owners' philosophy that well-being is founded on physical exercise, mental stimulation, and an organic diet. Their vision was the basis of the spa industry as it now exists. Since the 1960s, the number of spas in the United States has grown from a handful to nearly three hundred today.

## Spas Today

Studies have shown that 75 percent of all diseases are lifestyle inflicted—a statistic that leaves many wanting to take responsibility for their own well-being. Over the past four decades, there has been a gradual fitness revolution, and an increasing number of North Americans are visiting spas, incorporating the spa experience into their daily lives, and maintaining their bodies at optimum levels. People are making time for good nutrition, regular exercise, relaxation, and beauty care, which are all parts of overall personal health and increase the enjoyment of life.

Incorporating the classic water treatments of the traditional European spa, but also including more modern elements, North American spas today typically focus on good nutrition, fitness training, weight control, sports conditioning, preventive medicine, holistic health, stress management, and even spiritual awareness. The idea at many spas is to balance the latest mind-body fitness techniques with traditional European pampering and treatments, such as thermal waters, hydrotherapy tubs, and seaweed wraps.

In addition, just as great North American chefs are using local ingredients to cook regionally, the best spas now offer beauty and body treatments that take advantage of indigenous elements. Hawaiian spas offer ti leaf wraps, lomi-lomi massage, and papaya enzyme baths, while Southwestern spas offer body treatments using Indian hot rocks, aloe vera, jojoba, clay, and sage. Modern spas also provide educational programs for people who want to get in shape, eat better, combat the effects of aging, and look and feel their best.

If you are interested in going to a spa, you have three different types to choose from: destination spas, resort spas, and day spas. *Destination spas* are usually designed around a seven-day program, with all-inclusive packages most typical. Programs include three meals a day, and guests are usually assigned a full schedule of daily activities, including exercise classes, body treatments, and mind-enrichment seminars. *Resort spas* are located within a larger vacation resort; their services typically are à la carte or designed for day and half-day programs, but may also include longer programs. *Day spas* are retreats that offer revitalization over a period of a few hours to all day. They often provide a selection of face and body treatments, use of a workout gym, and a spa lunch. The spas in this book are either destination or resort spas, and many of the resorts have day-spa offerings.

# Cook's Notes

## What Is Spa Cuisine?

In this cookbook, talented and creative chefs provide you with a sampling of the tasty dishes served at some of the best spas in North America. Making use of fresh, wholesome foods, their recipes retain the flavors, textures, and presentation of gourmet cuisine, while minimizing fat, salt, refined sugar, and excessive calories. This type of cooking is based on natural ingredients cooked in simple ways to highlight their flavor and inherent goodness.

Although eating the small portions of spa cuisine typically served at spas is, of course, a good way to lose weight, eating slightly bigger portions of the same dishes works as a healthful maintenance diet to help you feel better, lighter, and more energetic. A poor diet, on the other hand, can leave you feeling heavy, bloated, and logy and can manifest itself in skin problems, headaches, digestive discomfort, and other physical conditions. While I researched this book, many spa chefs told me how much better they looked and felt just from eating their own food!

Spa cuisine emphasizes whole grains, lean protein, low-fat dairy products, fish, and the freshest vegetables and fruits, while avoiding artificial colorings, flavorings, preservatives, overly processed foods, and unhealthy cooking techniques such as deep-frying. Guests at spas find that the meals are naturally delicious, and they soon lose their taste for rich, fatty, salty foods. After a visit to any one of the spas in this book, you will be inspired to keep eating this way when you return home. And although it may take some adjustments in your kitchen and eating habits, you can easily learn to prepare these palate-pleasing dishes yourself.

In general, a healthy diet is based on balance, moderation, and variety—it does not mean deprivation or eliminating entire categories of foods from your diet. In your home kitchen, you can cook fresh low-fat foods and establish a healthful eating pattern that will benefit the entire family. Remember, it's the foods you eat on a daily basis, not the splurges and exceptions, that help to determine the state of your health!

# *Preparing Spa Cuisine at Home*

Today there are so many demands on our time that it is tempting to rely on the wide variety of "convenience" foods—but if overprocessed, nutrient-poor food leads to lower energy and more health problems, how convenient is it in the long run? While spa cuisine may take more time to prepare in the beginning—since you will be making more meals from scratch—once you've started the process you'll find it becomes quicker and easier. For example, if you poach chicken for dinner, save the broth for another meal and use leftover cold chicken in a salad for lunch the next day. Vegetable stock may be made and frozen in cubes for easy future use, and stir-fries and other mostly vegetarian dishes are usually simpler and faster to make than meat-based dishes.

In today's hectic world, cooking can play an important role in the quality of our daily lives. A home-cooked evening meal makes a pleasurable transition between a busy day and a more relaxed evening. Cooking with fresh flavorful ingredients becomes an *enjoyable* way to promote health. Of course, if you're especially busy one day, you can make simpler dishes or just add some fresh ingredients to already prepared food.

## Shopping Lean

Cooking spa cuisine begins with the choices you make at the market. In general, choose lean meat and poultry, fish, low-fat dairy products, and minimally processed foods such as fresh vegetables and fruits, whole grains, and dried beans. These foods contain fiber, vitamins, and minerals and are rich in phytochemicals (antioxidants that protect against many diseases). Studies show that low fiber intake is associated with a higher incidence of colon cancer and coronary artery disease. Besides the supermarket, try shopping for ingredients at natural foods stores, ethnic markets, and farmers' markets.

**Fruits and Vegetables** Choose the freshest possible—let availability be the guide to what you'll be cooking rather than a rigid shopping list made out ahead of time. Ideally, purchase fruits and vegetables that are organic and in season, as they are usually tastier and more nutritious. When purchasing frozen vegetables, choose ones without sauce or cheese.

13

**Poultry**   Reduce fat by serving skinless chicken and turkey breast (about a third of the fat is in, and immediately under, the skin; white meat has less fat than dark). Free-range poultry has more flavor and less fat.

**Fish**   Try to include fish (which reduces the risk of coronary heart disease) in your diet at least once a week. When buying canned fish, make sure it is packed in water.

**Meat**   Choose lean beef cuts such as top round or sirloin, lean pork cuts like tenderloin and center loin roast, and lean ground meat like sirloin. Avoid organ meats such as liver, kidney, and sweetbreads. Whenever possible, purchase naturally raised meats.

**Beans and Grains**   Purchase lots of grains, pastas, rice, and dried beans. (Beans are high in complex carbohydrates, fiber, and protein, and only 2 to 5 percent of their calories come from fat.)

**Dairy**   Choose low-fat or nonfat milk and yogurt; reduced-fat or nonfat cheese, sour cream, and cream cheese; low-fat or nonfat cottage cheese. Avoid nondairy substitute creamer and whipped toppings that contain coconut and palm oil, which are saturated fats.

**Desserts**   Good choices are sorbets, fresh fruit, light ice cream or ice milk, and angel food cake.

**Snack Items**   Choose dried fruit, bread sticks, rice or popcorn cakes, fig bars, gingersnaps, graham crackers, raisins, pretzels, bagel, fresh vegetables and fruits, snack-sized canned tuna, fruit juice popsicles, string cheese or other low-fat cheese, and crackers such as Melba toast, Wasa, Finn crisps, Ry Krisps, or water crackers. Read the nutrition labels and select mostly low-fat foods that have 3 grams of fat or less per serving. Avoid crackers and other foods made with partially hydrogenated oils.

**Beverages**   Choose bottled water, fruit juices, low-salt V8 juice, sparkling waters (plain and flavored), and teas in place of soft drinks.

# Cooking Light

Spa cooking delivers flavor without the high-calorie and saturated-fat count of many gourmet meals. Here are some of the methods and techniques developed by spa chefs to create satisfying, tasty, and attractive dishes. (*Note:* Be sure to consult your physician before beginning a low-fat diet.)

- Cook without adding fat by grilling, baking, broiling, steaming, poaching, and microwaving.

- Use nonstick pans and vegetable-oil cooking sprays or small amounts of olive oil or organic canola oil. High-quality cooking sprays (including olive oil spray) are now available in many markets; if you want to spray your own favorite oils, purchase a sprayer for the purpose at a cookware store.

- If you cut back on the amount of oil in a recipe, reduce the cooking temperature to avoid burning.

- If onions begin to stick to the pan when sautéing, add a small amount of water and continue cooking until the water evaporates.

- To retain moisture, braise rather than fry by using a small amount of oil combined with a little water, chicken or vegetable stock or broth, or wine.

- Serve each person a total of no more than 6 ounces (185 g) of cooked lean meat, poultry, or fish each day. Fill up the rest of the plate with vegetables and a carbohydrate side dish such as rice or pasta.

- When cooking meat, trim all visible fat. Remove the skin from poultry.

- Serve no more than 3 to 4 egg yolks per week (egg whites don't have to be limited).

- Store foods in the refrigerator in their whole form rather than cutting them up to retain maximum nutrients and flavor.

- Never soak produce for a long time, as nutrients will leach out.

- Bring cooking water to a boil before adding vegetables to it so they will retain more of their vitamins and minerals.

- Cook vegetables only until crisp-tender.

- Make your own salad dressings using olive oil, vinegar, lemon juice, herbs, and garlic to avoid additives and saturated fats.

- Showcase fresh seasonal fruits to make tempting desserts, and substitute fruit sorbets and low-fat or fat-free frozen yogurt for ice cream.

Finally, remember that part of eating well is the visual experience of beautiful, tempting food. Use low-fat garnishes, such as fresh herb sprigs, chopped tomatoes, slivered red and yellow peppers, and chopped red and green onions. You can even garnish with fresh edible flowers such as nasturtiums, borage, rose petals, garlic flowers, and zucchini blossoms. Slices of lime, fresh berries, and mint sprigs add flair to desserts, and drinks can be garnished with a slice of lemon, lime, or orange, a sprig of mint, strawberries frozen in ice cubes, a few fresh raspberries, or a celery stalk. Be creative!

## Low-Fat Ways to Add Flavor

- herbs and spices, both fresh and dried
- onions, garlic, and shallots
- homemade stocks and canned low-salt broths
- balsamic vinegar and flavored vinegars
- Dijon mustard
- salsas
- relishes
- barbecue sauce
- horseradish

- chutneys
- low-salt teriyaki sauce, soy sauce, and steak sauce
- small amounts of flavorful cheeses, such as grated Parmesan, feta, sharp Cheddar, and Swiss
- citrus zests
- tomato juice
- lemon and lime juice
- wine and sherry
- chilies, pepper flakes, and cayenne

# Adapting Your Favorite Recipes

Make changes gradually and turn your tried-and-true favorites into healthy, energy-enhancing meals. Add two onions or bell peppers instead of one, use less sugar, substitute poached chicken for fried—this is the kind of experimenting that makes cooking fun! Use your sense of taste, smell, and feel rather than precise measurements and the rigid acceptance of exact ingredients. Some of the most delicious dishes are created when you adapt a recipe to emphasize an ingredient that sounds best to you that day or is freshest at the market. Here are some ideas for turning your favorite recipes into spa cuisine:

- Add fresh in-season fruits and vegetables to dishes you routinely prepare—for instance, add sautéed onions, garlic, bell peppers, and even shredded carrots to burritos.
- Top your morning cereal with fresh fruit, raisins, wheat germ, or low-fat cottage cheese.
- Add spinach, lettuce, and tomato slices to your sandwiches, and onions, garlic, mushrooms, bell peppers, and fresh herbs to your pasta sauces.
- Cook with cremini, shiitake, portobello, and chanterelle mushrooms instead of white cultivated mushrooms for added flavor.
- Poach, broil, or grill chicken or fish instead of frying it.
- Use low-fat milk or buttermilk instead of whole milk.
- When making cakes, cookies, or muffins, use yogurt, nonfat sour cream, mashed banana, or applesauce for half the called-for amount of butter or other fat.
- You can usually reduce butter or oil by 25 percent without a noticeable change in taste or texture.
- Try part-skim or low-fat cheeses.
- Instead of whipped cream, serve yogurt cheese (see Basics) or nonfat plain yogurt mixed with vanilla and either honey or maple syrup.
- Substitute 2 egg whites for 1 whole egg. (*Note:* This may not work if eggs provide the only fat in the recipe.)
- Substitute 3 tablespoons cocoa powder for 1 ounce (30 g) baking chocolate (if chocolate is not the only fat in the recipe).

17

# Healthy Eating

## Tips from the Experts

*Choose nutrient-rich foods, and eat a wide variety of them.* No one food offers the more than forty different nutrients that scientists have identified as essential. By eating a wide variety of foods, you can decrease the possibility of consuming an unhealthy amount of any nutrient and avoid exposure to a concentration of toxins that any single food might harbor.

*Limit your consumption of fat to 30 percent of your total daily calories,* as recommended by the American Heart Association and the American Cancer Society. This doesn't mean every dish has to be less than 30 percent fat, just the daily total. To decrease the risk for heart disease and cancer, it is also recommended that you limit your intake of saturated fat to only 10 percent of total daily calories. Saturated fats increase blood cholesterol levels and are found in the greatest amounts in animal products and some tropical plant oils, such as coconut and palm. Consider becoming a part-time vegetarian or eating less red meat and more poultry and fish.

*Keep near your ideal weight, but avoid calorie-restricted diets.* For weight reduction, concentrate on decreasing the amount of fat in your diet, eating smaller portions, and exercising rather than obsessive calorie counting. Too few calories means not enough fuel and nutrients, which can cause a lack of concentration, impaired judgment, and poor memory. Long-term food restrictions can also result in tiredness, depression, and decreased energy. Remember, you burn calories faster when you are more active physically.

*Eat regularly.* Skipping a meal sets you up for an energy slump and can lead to eating unhealthy (but readily available) food or to eating too much. Spreading your intake throughout the day, on the other hand, stabilizes your blood-sugar level and keeps you in balance. Pay attention to your body's natural eating pattern and make sure you eat when you need to: some people do best on three well-rounded meals a day, while others require an afternoon or mid-morning snack.

*Drink eight to twelve glasses of pure water a day,* as suggested by most nutritionists, exercise physiologists, and doctors. Getting enough liquid is especially important if your diet is high in fiber (to avoid constipation), if you are sick, or if you are dieting, since dieters need to flush away more waste by-products.

*Minimize salt in the diet* to avoid water retention and the possible development of high blood pressure. The American Heart Association recommends limiting your sodium intake to less than 2,400 milligrams per day. Tastebuds will gradually adjust to a lower salt level, and herbs, spices, and lemon juice make good salt substitutes. (Note that recent studies have found that only about 8 percent of the population is salt sensitive in terms of blood-pressure problems.) When you cook your own meals, you can control the amount of salt in your food, as most of the salt in the average North American diet comes from canned, frozen, and packaged foods. In fact, you may be eating more salt than you realize!

## Breakfast

Your breakfast affects your metabolism all day long, and people who skip it often have energy swings and weight problems. Skipping breakfast, or any meal, lowers your basal metabolic rate, which means your body burns calories at a slower rate. Your breakfast should help you function at your best and keep you from getting hungry again for at least three hours. If it doesn't, include more protein, such as low-fat yogurt, eggs, cheese, or low-fat milk with a whole-grain cereal. You'll be less likely to be ravenous at lunch and will have added energy and improved concentration. (*Note:* If you consume a lot of fiber at breakfast, don't take vitamin pills or supplements with this meal or they won't be digested.) For a quick spa breakfast, try one of the granolas, cereals, or breads in this book that can be made a day or two in advance. For a more leisurely breakfast, enjoy an omelette, French toast, waffles, pancakes, or freshly made muffins with fruit butter.

## Lunch

Take time for your lunch. Make it an important break in your day, rather than a rushed bite to eat at your desk or in the car. If you need to be alert after lunch, eat more protein and fewer carbohydrates, which raise the level of the amino

19

acid tryptophan and can lead to a sleepy feeling. Overeating at this meal can also make you feel lethargic—it's better to eat less and make up the difference with a light snack in the afternoon. Most of the lunch menus in this book are for weekends, entertaining, and when you have a little more time to cook. To bring a healthy spa lunch to the office, try a risotto, soup, chowder, pasta, or other single-dish meal that can be made the day before.

## Snacks

Have healthy snacks available both at home and at work (see the list on page 14 for suggestions). Accompany them with plain pure water, fruit juice, vegetable juice, smoothies, mineral water with lemon slices, or tea—or just have a refreshing beverage on its own. Many spas serve smoothies or fresh vegetable or fruit juices as mid-morning and afternoon snacks. Here are two favorites.

### ≈ Cal-a-Vie Revitalizer ≈

*After morning exercise classes, this refreshing drink is a favorite with Cal-a-Vie guests. Delicious hot or cold.*

6 cups (48 fl oz/1.5 l) fresh or bottled tomato juice

3 cups (24 fl oz/750 ml) water

2 cups (8 oz/250 g) assorted sliced vegetables,
such as roots, onions, bell peppers, and chard

2 celery stalks, chopped

1 large carrot, peeled and chopped

4 tomatoes, chopped

1 bunch parsley

2 bay leaves

$1/2$ to 1 teaspoon red pepper flakes

2 teaspoons minced fresh rosemary,
or 1 teaspoon dried rosemary

$1/2$ teaspoon fennel seeds

2 tablespoons chopped fresh basil
or 1 tablespoon dried basil

In a large nonreactive saucepan, combine all the ingredients and bring to a boil. Reduce heat to low, cover, and simmer for 40 minutes. Drain in a sieve set over a bowl, pressing firmly with the back of a large spoon to extract all the juices, or process through a food mill. Discard the pulp. Serve the revitalizer hot or cold. If you wish, freeze it in 1-cup (8-fl oz/250-ml) measures for later use. Makes 10 cups (1$^1$/4 qt/1.25 l).

PER 1 CUP (8 fl oz/250 ml)

*Calories 50 • Carbohydrates 12 g • Cholesterol 0 mg • Fat 0 g • Protein 2 g • Sodium 40 mg*

---

## ≈ *Aveda Pear-Ginger Smoothie* ≈

*This recipe is by chef Jim Kimberg of the Aveda Spa Retreat
in Osceola, Wisconsin.*

**4 ripe pears, preferably Anjou
2$^1$/2 cups (20 fl oz/625 ml) carrot juice
2 teaspoons grated fresh ginger
1 cup (8 fl oz/250 ml) low-fat milk**

In a blender or food processor, combine all the ingredients and purée until smooth and frothy. Makes four 10-ounce (310-ml) servings.

PER SERVING

*Calories 180 • Carbohydrates 42 g • Cholesterol 5 mg • Fat 1.5 g • Protein 4 g • Sodium 110 mg*

---

# Dinner and Dessert

Sit down and enjoy a satisfying evening meal. Before and during dinner, establish a pace that encourages dining rather than just consuming food. Meals eaten on the run often result in more overall consumption of food and poor eating habits because they leave us still looking for satisfaction. Try stretching your dinner out over several courses, from hors d'oeuvres to dessert, and increase your awareness of what you are eating.

If food is to be properly digested, it should be eaten in a calm environment. Medical studies show that listening to soothing music during meals causes people to consume smaller portions, eat fewer forkfuls per minute, chew their food more thoroughly, and have longer conversations with each other. Dining with beautiful music sets a leisurely tempo and adds to the gracious enjoyment of good food, so play your CD or cassette and enjoy the health benefits!

Most of the dinner menus in this book include an appetizer, soup, or salad; a fish, poultry, or vegetarian entrée; and a delicious spa dessert. For a lighter or more casual dinner, try one of the lunch menus.

## Losing Weight

If you are trying to lose weight, consider trying some of the following suggestions:

- Take the edge off your hunger by starting dinner with a light appetizer and a low-calorie beverage such as tomato juice, sparkling water with a twist of lime, or a blend of herbal tea and fruit juice.

- You are more likely to recognize the physiological response to fullness by eating slowly and mindfully. When we eat, receptors perceive a rise in the glucose level of the blood and signal the brain that the body has consumed enough food. It takes about twenty minutes for this signal to reach the brain, so it's easy to pass the point of satiation without realizing it. If you eat quickly, it's more likely that you will consume more food than you need.

- Limit eating to only a few places in your home. Try portioning out your food on plates in the kitchen rather than from serving dishes on the table.

- Take a walk after dinner to help digestion and provide an alternative activity to more eating.

- Keep low-calorie snack items readily available to replace snack foods that are high in fat, sugar, and salt (see page 14 for ideas).

# Homemade
# Spa Treatments

Cares melt away when you're pampered with luxurious beauty treatments at a spa—and many of them can be re-created at home using readily available ingredients. The following recipes for soaks, scrubs, masks, and soothing baths are fun to prepare and let you control what you put on your skin. Using them will make you look and feel better, while promoting the delightful sense of relaxation that comes with such pampering.

All the recipes in this section make one generous application, unless otherwise noted. You can double or triple any of the recipes and keep extra portions in clean glass or plastic containers.

*Note:* These recipes are not meant to replace diagnosis and treatment by a qualified medical practitioner and are not intended for those with skin conditions. Make sure to test a small patch of skin for allergic reactions to any mixtures in this book twenty-four hours before applying a full treatment. Essential oils should not be taken internally or applied directly to the skin. If you are pregnant or have a medical condition, consult a doctor before using essential oils.

## Facials

Facials are one of the most enjoyable and relaxing treatments at any spa. Giving yourself a facial at home can be a soothing session of pampering that gives your complexion a fresh look and brings a glow to your skin. Before you begin a facial, first determine your skin type. Leave your skin free of makeup or creams overnight and in the morning use a clean tissue to swipe your skin, especially around the nose, brow, and chin.

- If the tissue is clear, you have *dry* skin, which usually has fine pores, is easily chapped, and shows early signs of aging.

- If the tissue is lightly marked with oil, your skin is *normal* (neither oily nor dry).

- If the tissue is stained, you have *oily* skin, which usually has visible pores and won't age as fast.
- Many people have *combination* skin, with blemishes and oily and dry patches. This type of skin is often sensitive.

When you have the time, treat yourself to a complete facial. Begin with a mild cleansing and an exfoliating scrub followed by steaming to open the pores and hydrate the skin. When finished, apply a toner, followed by a mask and finally a moisturizer. Set a relaxing mood by playing the music that accompanies this book or another recording that you enjoy, and dim the lights or light some candles.

## Cleansing

First, clean your face with warm water and a cleanser that is appropriate to your skin type.

## Scrubs

Exfoliating facial scrubs are recommended, at least occasionally, for all skin types except hypersensitive and acne-prone skin. The purpose is to slough off dead and dry skin that makes skin look dull and flaky in order to bring a luster to the complexion. This can also be accomplished with natural chemical peelers, such as alpha hydroxy acid or papaya enzyme.

### ≈ *Scrub for Normal, Dry, and Oily Skin* ≈

**2 tablespoons oatmeal**
**1 to 2 tablespoons hot water**
**2 to 3 drops olive oil**

In a blender or food processor, process the oatmeal until it is finely ground. In a small bowl, mix all the ingredients together to form a paste. Moisten your face with warm water, apply the scrub, and gently massage. Rinse with warm water and pat dry.

### ≈ *Scrub for Oily Skin* ≈
*You can use this oil-free scrub every other day.*

**$^1/_3$ ripe banana**
**2 tablespoons cornmeal**

In a bowl, mash the banana and stir in the cornmeal until well blended. Moisten your face with warm water, apply the scrub, and gently massage; leave on for 1 minute. Rinse with cool water and pat dry.

## Steaming

Steaming your face unclogs pores and stimulates blood flow to the skin. It is recommended for most skin types, except acne-prone skin. Be careful never to scald your skin, and use steam only once or twice a week at most. Dried mint, camomile, lavender, and rosemary are excellent choices for herbal steams. Before steaming, apply a thin layer of skin cream around your eyes and a moisturizer on your lips.

### ≈ *Herbal Steam* ≈

In a large covered pot, heat 4 cups (32 fl oz/1 l) water and $^1/_2$ cup (1 oz/30 g) dried herbs until almost boiling. Pour the mixture into a large bowl and lean your face over the bowl, at least 12 inches (30 cm) from the water. Drape a towel over your head and the bowl and relax while breathing deeply. If your skin is dry or sensitive, steam for only 2 to 3 minutes, keeping your face far enough away from the water so that moisture accumulates on the skin but little heat is felt. If your skin is oily, steam for 3 to 5 minutes. Normal skin may be steamed for up to 10 minutes.

## Masks

Soothing and relaxing, masks deep-clean and moisturize and are recommended for all skin types once a week. For best results with any facial mask, steam your face first. Never apply a mask to the area immediately around your eyes. After applying the mask, lie back and relax. This is a perfect moment for listening to music or meditating.

### ≈ *Moisturizing Mask for Dry Skin* ≈

**¹/₂ ripe avocado, peeled and pitted
1 tablespoon olive oil or clear sesame oil**

In a bowl, mash the avocado and stir in the olive or sesame oil. Apply the mask evenly to your face and leave on for 3 to 5 minutes. Rinse off with warm water and pat dry.

### ≈ *Cucumber and Yogurt Mask for Dry or Sensitive/Combination Skin* ≈

**¹/₄ cucumber, peeled and chopped
1 tablespoon plain yogurt**

In a blender or food processor, blend the ingredients together until smooth. Massage the mask evenly onto your face and leave on for 10 minutes. Rinse off with warm water and gently pat dry.

### ≈ *Papaya Mask for Oily Skin* ≈

*Papaya exfoliates, and egg white tones the skin; be especially careful not to get this mask close to the eyes.*

**¹/₂ ripe papaya, peeled and seeded
1 egg white, lightly beaten**

In a bowl, mash the papaya and stir in the egg white. Apply the mask evenly to your face and leave on for 15 minutes. Rinse off with warm water and pat dry.

### ≈ *Oatmeal Mask for Normal Skin* ≈

**¹/₄ cup (2 oz/60 g) cooked oatmeal
1 egg
1 tablespoon almond oil**

In a blender or food processor, blend all the ingredients together until smooth. Massage the mask evenly onto your face and leave on for 5 to 7 minutes. Rinse off with warm water and gently pat dry.

# Toning

Toners remove all traces of cleanser, close pores, and restore the pH balance of the skin; they should be alcohol-free.

### ≈ Cider Vinegar Toner for All Skin Types ≈

*The acidity of the vinegar restores the shield
that protects the skin.*

**1 cup (8 fl oz/250 ml) filtered or spring water
2 tablespoons cider vinegar**

Mix the water and vinegar together. Soak a cotton ball with the mixture and gently apply to your face and neck, avoiding the eye area.

### ≈ Milk Toner for Sensitive Skin ≈

**¹/₄ cup (2 fl oz/60 ml) milk**

Use milk straight from the refrigerator and apply it to your face with a soaked cotton ball. Rinse with cool water.

### ≈ Lavender Toner for Normal to Oily Skin ≈

**2¹/₂ cups (20 fl oz/625 ml) boiling water
2 tablespoons dried lavender flowers**

Steep the lavender flowers in the water for 1 hour off heat. Strain through cheesecloth into a bottle, seal, and refrigerate. Apply to your face and neck with a soaked cotton ball.

# Moisturizing

Moisturizers, which hydrate and protect natural oils in the skin, are recommended for most skin types, except acne-prone skin. Many excellent products are available—read the labels and find one that is right for you. Use at least once a day, especially around the eyes and on the upper lip. If you have oily skin, use an oil-free moisturizer.

## ≈ Easy Moisturizer ≈

*This light moisturizer is easily absorbed. Jojoba oil is excellent for dry skin, and aloe vera for oily skin. The recipe makes several applications.*

**3 tablespoons jojoba oil or aloe vera gel**
**4 to 5 drops essential oil of choice**

In a glass or plastic container, thoroughly mix the ingredients together. Apply the mixture evenly to your face and neck in delicate circular motions.

# Hand and Nail Care

## ≈ Home Manicure ≈

*A home manicure provides relaxation as it beautifies, rehydrates, and repairs your nails.*

Remove any nail polish. Trim your nails and use a good-quality emery board to file them into shape, filing in one direction only. Rinse with warm water. Apply cuticle cream or the cuticle softener that follows and massage it into each nail, especially around the base. Relax while the cream soaks in for a few minutes. Using a cotton ball–covered orange stick (wooden cuticle stick), gently push down each cuticle. Soak your fingers in a bowl of warm water and remove any remaining cuticle cream with a tissue. Moisturize the hands with your favorite hand cream and gently massage. Buff your nails with a commercial nail buffer, or apply a base coat followed by two coats of your favorite nail polish. Seal the polish with a top coat.

## ≈ Cuticle Softener ≈

To soften cuticles and nurture the nail bed, apply a capsule of vitamin E and massage it into cuticles and nails.

# Foot Care

Treating your feet with a bath soak, a scrub, a massage with a soothing lotion, and a pedicure will repay them for all their hard work. If you make your feet feel good, the rest of your body will feel good too!

## ≈ Herbal Foot Soak ≈

**2 cups (16 fl oz/500 ml) boiling water**
**1 cup (2 oz/60 g) dried lavender flowers or chopped fresh rosemary,**
**or a combination of the two**
**1 cup (8 oz/250 g) sea salt or kosher salt**

Pour the water into a medium bowl, add the lavender and salt, and let steep for 5 to 10 minutes. Strain the liquid through cheesecloth or a sieve into a basin large enough for your feet. Add enough warm water to cover your feet, and soak them for 10 or 15 minutes.

## ≈ Soak for Hot, Tired Feet ≈

**¼ cup (½ oz/15 g) chopped fresh rosemary or lemon thyme,**
**tied in a square of cheesecloth**
**8 cups (2 qt/2 l) boiling water, plus 8 cups (2 qt/2 l) cool water**
**4 peppermint tea bags**
**1 lemon, sliced into thin rounds**
**1 tray ice cubes**

Pour the water into a basin large enough to soak your feet and add the sachet of rosemary or lemon thyme, the peppermint tea, and lemon slices; let steep for 10 minutes. Add the tray of ice cubes, plus enough cool water for the desired depth. Slip your feet into the basin and soak for as long as you like.

## ≈ Foot Scrub ≈

**3 tablespoons fine beach sand**
**3 tablespoons olive oil or canola oil**
**3 to 5 drops rosemary or peppermint essential oil**

Stir all the ingredients together to make a paste. Massage the scrub onto your feet. Rinse off with warm water and pat dry.

## ≈ Foot Massage ≈

This will soothe your feet and make your whole body feel relaxed. First, soak your feet in a warm herbal-scented foot bath, which will soften the skin and allow it to absorb lotion more easily. Apply a generous amount of lotion to the palms of your hands and then apply it to your feet, top and bottom. Massage the top of each foot with your fingertips. Place your thumbs in the center of each foot, directly below the ball, and firmly massage the channels between the foot bones, the toes, the arch, and the heel with gentle circular presses.

### ≈ Pedicure ≈

*This luxurious pedicure will take about 1 hour. Enjoy a pot of soothing tea, and as you soak your feet, relax and listen to some beautiful music.*

First, remove any nail polish in a well-ventilated area to avoid fumes from the polish remover. Fill a large basin with warm water and, if you wish, add one of the herbal infusions mentioned in the foot soaks above, or 3 to 4 drops lavender or peppermint essential oil. Soak your feet for 10 to 15 minutes. Towel-dry and gently rub each foot with a pumice stone in gentle circular movements, concentrating on the heels and the balls of the feet where the skin hardens. Replace each foot in the water and massage. Dry your feet with a soft towel and rub cuticle softener into the cuticles around around your toes (see page 28). Using a cotton ball–covered orange stick (wooden cuticle stick), press down the cuticles. Trim your toenails, cutting straight across and smoothing any rough edges with an emery board. Apply lotion to the entire foot and massage it in well.

## Eye Care

Here are three methods to reduce puffiness and soothe tired eyes:

- Place 1 or 2 cucumber slices or raw potato slices over each eye to cover the entire eye area. Drape your eyes with a damp, cool washcloth. Lie back and relax for 5 or 10 minutes.

- Soak 2 sterile cotton balls in whole milk, then squeeze them out so they are quite moist but not runny. Place the cotton balls over your eyes, covering the entire eye area, and rest for 10 minutes.

- Make a strong cup of camomile tea and soak 4 to 6 cotton balls in the liquid. Squeeze the cotton balls so they're still wet, but not dripping. Place them in the refrigerator for 5 minutes, or until chilled. Place the cotton balls over your eyes, then lie back and relax for 5 or 10 minutes.

# Hair Care

Use a gentle shampoo that doesn't strip your hair of its natural oils, and follow with a conditioner and final rinse. Conditioners and rinses will make your hair shinier and give it more body.

## ≈ Olive Oil Pre-Shampoo Conditioner ≈

*A good time to use this conditioner is while you are soaking in a warm bath.*

**1 tablespoon olive oil**
**3 to 4 drops essential oil of choice**

In a bowl, whisk the ingredients together. Pour over your hair and massage into your hair and scalp. Wrap your hair with a towel or cover it with a shower cap and leave on for 15 or 20 minutes. Wash out with a gentle shampoo.

## ≈ Rosemary Rinse for Dark Hair ≈

**1/4 cup (1/2 oz/15 g) chopped fresh rosemary,**
**or 2 tablespoons dried rosemary**
**2 cups (16 fl oz/500 ml) water**

In a small saucepan, combine the ingredients and bring to a boil. Remove from heat, cover, and let cool. Strain and pour the rinse through your hair after shampooing and conditioning. Gently pat dry with a towel.

## ≈ Camomile-Lemon Rinse for Light Hair ≈

**1/3 cup (1/3 oz/10 g) dried camomile flowers**
**2 cups (16 fl oz/500 ml) water**
**Juice of 1 lemon**

In a small saucepan, combine all the ingredients and bring to a boil. Remove from heat, cover, and let cool. Strain and pour the rinse through your hair after shampooing and conditioning. Gently pat dry with a towel.

# Aromatherapy

Aromatherapy is the use of essential oils—essences extracted from flowers, spices, fruits, woods, and leaves—to affect the mind, body, and spirit. Through their aromas and chemical properties, these oils can induce calm moods and peaceful emotional states, awaken deep-seated memories, and simply make you feel wonderful. The most popular way of using essential oils is in the bath. A few drops of pine, lavender, rosemary, or jasmine oil in a tub of warm water can have an energizing, relaxing, or sensuous effect.

Essential oils can also be diffused into the air, applied in a poultice, directly inhaled from the bottle, and massaged onto the skin. When applying essential oils to the skin, dilute 2 or 3 drops with 1 tablespoon of vegetable oil or aloe vera gel to prevent irritation. Never apply an essential oil to the skin straight from the bottle. Pregnant women should always check with their doctor before using essential oils, and those with medical ailments or sensitive skin should also first consult a physician.

Aromatherapy began as a formal science in 1937, when a French chemist, René Maurice Gattefossé, burned his hand while working in a perfumery. To relieve his pain, he plunged it into the nearest container of cold liquid, which happened to be lavender oil. His hand healed quickly, and with so little scarring, that Gattefossé devoted the remainder of his life to the study of the medicinal powers of essential oils.

Today, more and more people are becoming interested in aromatherapy, as they become more conscious of the side effects of drugs used in conventional medicine and simultaneously desire to take more responsibility for their own health and well-being. Aromatherapy is commonly used to cope with minor but annoying conditions such as jet lag, insomnia, indigestion, headaches, hangovers, dry skin, and minor stress. In France, herbal oils are prescribed by doctors, and in Japan peppermint oil is diffused in office buildings to keep workers alert.

Discover essential oils for yourself: Try one or two from the following list in a bath, in a diffuser, or in a massage oil. Note that essential oils are extremely volatile and are usually sold in dark glass bottles, which should be stored in a cool place out of direct sunlight. If stored correctly, their shelf life is many years.

**Camomile** A soothing herb that calms and relaxes. Well-known for its sedative properties, it is anti-inflammatory. Add 6 to 10 camomile oil drops to a warm bath and relax. For an additional effect, you might want to sip a soothing cup of camomile tea at the same time.

**Clary Sage** Relaxes and alleviates insomnia.

**Cypress** Good for soothing shaving cuts.

**Eucalyptus** A decongestent that is invigorating and refreshing. Its leaves have an active ingredient, cineole, whose tingling effect helps to clear the chests of those with colds and flu. Add 2 to 3 drops to some hot water and breathe deeply. To soothe muscular aches and pains, add 2 to 3 drops to a warm bath. Add it to aloe vera and rub it onto the skin to lessen arthritic pain. *Note:* Do not take orally.

**Geranium** Excellent for troubled skin; it is antiseptic and astringent.

**Ginger** Energizes.

**Jasmine** Good for all skin types, jasmine oil is invigorating and uplifts the spirits.

**Lavender** Best known of all the essential oils, lavender eases insomnia, minor stress, fatigue, and headaches. Also an effective antiseptic, it is good for burns, cuts, and insect bites. Lavender essential oil can be used directly on the skin, but do not take it orally. (*Note:* It also makes a good moth repellent in sachets.)

**Lemon** Refreshes and sharpens the senses; antiseptic.

**Lemon Balm** Calms and relaxes; good for relieving minor depression.

**Marjoram:** Relieves stress.

**Neroli** Considered to be a sedative and antidepressant.

**Peppermint** Refreshing and cooling. Add 2 to 3 drops peppermint oil to a warm bath to ease aching muscles. It's also ideal for an invigorating or stimulating foot bath or foot massage (see page 29).

**Pine** Warms and invigorates.

**Rose** Calms, relaxes, uplifts emotionally, and is good for headaches. Rose essential oil is antibacterial and a gentle astringent that helps to reduce redness and irritation. A mixture of milk and rose essential oil or rose petals have been used in baths since the days of Cleopatra.

**Rosemary** A light astringent that stimulates circulation. Mix rosemary oil with vegetable oil and rub on your temples for headache relief. Add 2 to 3 drops to a tub of warm water for an invigorating and stimulating bath.

**Sandalwood** Good for dry skin; alleviates insomnia.

**Tea Tree** Good for acne, sore throats, and yeast infections; an antiseptic.

**Thyme** Antiseptic and astringent; speeds healing. Makes an excellent foot bath.

**Ylang-ylang** Soothing and sensuous.

# Body Care

## All-Over Body Scrubs

Body scrubs are popular in spas around the world. They exfoliate the skin, clean the pores, stimulate cirulation, and leave the skin glowing.

### ≈ Salt Scrub ≈

*Cleansing and invigorating, this scrub removes dry skin without causing dehydration. Do not use on your face or other delicate areas.*

**2 cups (16 oz/500 g) sea salt, kosher salt, or any other coarse-ground salt**
**1 cup (8 oz/250 ml) almond oil, coconut oil, or sunflower oil**
**5 to 7 drops essential oil of choice**

In a bowl, mix the salt and oils together until well blended. Take a warm shower to moisten your skin and do not dry. Coat your entire body with the salt mixture and gently massage, using a washcloth or mitt. Rinse off in a warm shower, followed by a cool shower. Pat dry.

### ≈ Sugar Scrub ≈

*Milder than a salt scrub, this all-over body scrub is suitable for any skin type.*

**2 cups (16 oz/500 g) granulated sugar**
**1/2 cup (4 fl oz/125 ml) canola oil**

In a bowl, mix the ingredients together to form a paste, adding more oil if needed. Take a warm shower to moisten your skin and do not dry. Dip your fingers into the sugar mixture and gently massage it all over your body. Rinse off in a warm, then cool shower. Pat dry.

## Baths

A bath can be a luxurious, sensual experience. Not to be confused with simple washing, bathing has little to do with brisk efficiency and everything to do with relaxing and slowing down life's hectic pace. The ultimate spa therapy, bathing will clean and hydrate your skin, relax tense muscles, and influence your mood with pleasant herbal infusions.

To assure a spalike bathing experience at home, first assure yourself of peace and quiet for at least 45 minutes. While you are drawing yourself a bath, create an environment that will melt away tension by turning off the ringer on the phone, dimming the lights or lighting some candles, and putting on some beautiful music. You can also make yourself a nice cup of tea and bring along a favorite book or magazine. Slip into the soothing tub of warm water and soak for 20 minutes. After bathing, apply a moisturizer, wrap yourself in a warm towel, and lie down for 20 minutes, breathing deeply. As you breathe, gradually release all tension.

Your bath should be between 80°F (27°C) and 100°F (38°C). (Bathing in water over 100°F can cause dehydration, burst capillaries, and strip oils from the skin.) Soak for at least 20 minutes in order for your skin to hydrate and absorb whatever herbs and oils you may have added to the bath. Take a bath whenever you're feeling like you need a break—or make it a weekly or monthly ritual!

## ≈ Herbal Bath Infusions and Aromatherapy Baths ≈

Herbal infusions can soothe the skin, relax tense muscles, and lift the spirit. To make them, steep organic herbs in boiling water until the liquid reaches room temperature, then strain into a warm bath or a container for future use.

To make an aromatherapy bath, add 12 to 15 drops of your favorite essential oil to 2 tablespoons mild vegetable oil, such as canola or almond oil, or a bath gel and pour into a tub of warm water. Alternatively, mix 1 tablespoon essential oil with 1/4 cup (2 fl oz/60 ml) milk or yogurt and pour into a tub of warm water.

## ≈ Relaxing Herbal Bath ≈

**4 cups (32 fl oz/1 l) boiling water**
**1 cup (1 oz/30 g) loose-leaf camomile tea, dried calendula flowers,**
**and/or dried lavender blossoms, tied in a muslin sachet bag**
**or a square of cheesecloth**

Pour the water into a large bowl, add the herbal sachet, and steep for 20 to 30 minutes. Squeeze all liquid from the sachet, and pour the infusion into a warm bath.

### ≈ Moisturizing Milk and Honey Bath ≈

*Milk softens the skin, while honey seals in moisture.*

**4 cups (32 fl oz/1 l) water**
**1 cup (8 oz/250 ml) whole milk**
**1/2 cup (6 oz/185 g) honey**
**7 to 10 drops rose or lavender essential oil**

In a large saucepan, combine the water and milk and heat until almost boiling. Stir in the honey and essential oil. Add the mixture to warm running bath water and soak for 15 to 20 minutes. Rinse off in a warm shower and gently towel-dry.

### ≈ Aromatherapy Bath to Relieve Tension ≈

**1/4 cup (2 fl oz/60 ml) canola or almond oil or bath gel**
**12 to 15 drops lavender essential oil**

Mix the ingredients together and pour into a tub of warm water. Geranium, camomile, rose, jasmine, or ylang-ylang essential oil may be substituted for the lavender. Soak for 20 minutes—relax and enjoy.

### ≈ Salt Bath ≈

*A salt bath eases muscular aches and pains and makes your skin feel wonderful.*

Add 1 to 2 cups (8–16 oz/250–500 g) sea salt or kosher salt to the tub along with fast-running hot water until it dissolves. Add cool water until the temperature is to your liking. Soak in the warm tub for 20 minutes.

### ≈ Reviving Lavender Soda Bath ≈

**2 cups (12 oz/375 g) baking soda**
**1 teaspoon lavender essential oil**

In a medium glass jar, combine the ingredients. Cover and shake well. Set the jar aside for 1 to 2 weeks, shaking from time to time. For each bath, add 1/2 to 1 cup (3–6 oz/90–185 g) of the soda mixture under warm running tap water and soak for 15 to 20 minutes. Makes 2 cups (12 oz/375 g).

# The Spa Experience
# at Home

## A Healthy Lifestyle

A healthy lifestyle includes good nutrition, physical fitness, stress reduction, and medical management for prevention and treatment of health problems. You hold the key to determining the quality of your life, and choosing good nutrition and exercise habits will help your body respond to your needs.

## Fitness

Exercise, which can help to reduce stress, tone the body, beautify the skin, and raise spirits, is essential for cardiovascular health and should be part of everyday life. In 1996, the U.S. Surgeon General concluded that exercise is important for good health and that it has a positive effect on body weight, bone strength, the cardiovascular system, and our sense of well-being. An inactive lifestyle is now considered to be a health hazard!

At a minimum, try to exercise at a moderate intensity for 30 minutes on most days of the week. These 30 minutes need not be consecutive. Walking your dog, house work, gardening, and using the stairs instead of the elevator at work all count toward the 30-minute daily goal. If you have trouble finding time for such exercise, try including it as part of your social life by walking, jogging, or cycling with family and friends. Soon exercising will become a habit, and you will notice an increased sense of well-being and a higher level of energy.

In addition to such daily exercise, the American College of Sports Medicine recommends that most people get some form of aerobic exercise three to five times per week in one block, preferably spacing the workouts every other day. Aerobic exercise is working out at an elevated heart rate for at least 15 minutes. Walking, hiking, running, jogging, bicycling, stationary cycling, cross-country skiing, dancing, rope skipping, rowing, stair climbing, swimming, and skating all improve aerobic fitness. However, almost any exercise has some health benefit, such as burning calories, improving bone density (which may help prevent osteoporosis), improving your cholesterol profile, and reducing your chance of heart attack and stroke. If you aren't a self-motivater when it comes to exercise, join a gym, hire a personal trainer, or get one of your friends to become a regular work-out buddy.

For recommendations about the amount and type of exercise for you, consult a physician or certified exercise professional. Before starting an exercise program, see a doctor if you're over forty, or if you smoke, are overweight, or have heart trouble, high blood pressure, or any serious medical condition.

## Stress Reduction

Stress is the way we react to the physical and emotional challenges in our lives. There will always be stress, so it is important to learn how to cope with it and if possible to reduce it before it becomes overwhelming.

Short-term physical reactions to stress include increased breathing and heart rates, a queasy stomach, headaches, irritability, tense muscles, and a decreased ability to concentrate. Over time, stress can lead to a wide range of directly related ailments—including insomnia, high blood pressure, hair loss, skin breakouts, ulcers, gastritis, muscle twitching, and more—and it can make us more susceptible to disease and more prone to injury.

As a first step to stress reduction, think about the events and situations in your life that may be causing undue stress. Note that seemingly minor things such as speeding tickets or being late to work can be quite stressful, and even happy events like marriage, the purchase of a new home, or a new job are major causes of stress for most people.

At times of great change, be aware of the stress you are under and manage it by not taking on anything extra, cutting down on your responsibilities if possible, and taking periodic stress-relieving breaks every day—for a hike or a walk, a bath, a massage, yoga, meditation, tai chi, or physical exercise. Communication is also beneficial: talk to your friends, family, colleagues at work, and a professional therapist if necessary. If the stressful situations in your life can't be controlled, use acceptance, a positive attitude, and perspective to reduce the stress they cause.

**Acceptance**   An important step in effectively managing stress is to accept when things are beyond your control. When you can't do anything about a situation, try to alleviate your stress with such thoughts as "Someday I'll laugh about this," "It's a learning experience," or "It could be worse."

**Attitude**   Try to focus on the positive side of situations, and you'll find that solutions come more easily and that your stress level is reduced. If conflict is involved, keep in mind that a compromise can *always* be reached, even it it isn't obvious at first.

**Perspective**   We often worry or become upset about things that, in the end, never happen. Try to keep things in perspective by asking yourself, "How important is this situation to my life as a whole?" or "Can I get help?"

## Meditation

Meditation clears the mind through relaxed concentration. Practiced and perfected in India, China, and Japan, meditation is now recognized by Western medicine as an aid to overall health and well-being. Just twenty minutes of quiet contemplation can help you to manage stress, lower your blood pressure and pulse rate, and clear your mind. You can integrate meditation into your daily routine while taking a break during the day, while walking to work, just before falling asleep, or even while eating (at least try to practice mindfulness while chewing your food).

### ≈ A Simple Meditation ≈

Find a quiet place where you won't be interrupted. Sit, lie, or stand quietly in a comfortable position (lean against a wall, if you find this more comfortable) for a couple of minutes, breathing evenly and regularly. Concentrate on your breathing, feeling the air come in through your nostrils in long, slow breaths. Fill your lower lungs first, causing the stomach to expand, and then fill up the top of your lungs. Feel the breath leave your lungs from the bottom upward, contracting your stomach muscles gently as the air runs out evenly through your slightly opened lips. Ideally, try to exhale almost twice as long as you inhale—this will become easier with practice.

Let your focus on the world around you fade. You may completely close your eyes, or leave them fully or three-quarters open. (People new to meditation often find it easier to leave their eyes three-quarters open). By focusing on your breathing, you bring awareness out of your head, away from your worries, and into the present reality and the physical sensations of being in a particular place in a particular moment. After your meditation, return to the world slowly.

## Massage

Therapeutic massage relieves stress, relaxes overly tense muscles, and induces relaxation. An aromatherapy massage combines the effects and advantages of the senses of touch and smell, increasing the benefits of both. Massage oil helps hands glide smoothly over the skin, moisturizes, and provides aromatherapy when scented with essential oils.

### ≈ *Relaxing Massage Oil* ≈

$^1/_3$ cup (3 fl oz/90 ml) canola or almond oil
10 to 15 drops chamomile, rose, or geranium essential oil

In a small bowl, whisk the oils together. Use liberally during massage.

### ≈ *Massage Oil for Sore Muscles* ≈

$^1/_4$ cup (2 oz/60 ml) clear sesame, almond, or canola oil
$^1/_2$ teaspoon lavender or lemon balm essential oil

In a small bowl, whisk the oils together. Use liberally during massage.

### ≈ *Relaxing Scalp Massage* ≈

2 drops geranium essential oil
2 drops rose or lavender essential oil
$^1/_4$ cup (2 oz/60 ml) almond oil or sesame oil

Mix all the ingredients together and gently massage the scalp.

# Spa Talk

**Acupressure**   An ancient Chinese massage technique that is used to open the body's energy flow by stimulating pressure points.

**Aqua aerobics**   Aerobic exercise in a swimming pool; water resistance and body movements are combined in stretch, strength, and stamina workouts.

**Aromatherapy**   Treatments such as massage, facials, hydrobaths, and body wraps with the application of fragrant essential oils. Different oils are used to induce various therapeutic benefits (see page 33).

**Ayurvedic**   Four-thousand-year-old Indian treatments based on teachings from the Vedic scriptures. A variety of techniques—including nutrition, herbal medicine, aromatherapy, massage, and meditation—are used to restore the body's balance.

**Exfoliation**   Sloughing off the upper layer of dead skin cells with a loofah sponge, salt, sugar, or other gentle abrasive to stimulate circulation and leave the skin glowing.

**Fango**   The application to the body of mud, typically with a high mineral content and often combined with oil, that detoxifies, relieves muscular and arthritic pain, opens pores, and stimulates circulation.

**Gommage**   A cleansing and rehydrating treatment that uses creams, which are applied in massage-type movements.

**Herbal wrap**   Linens soaked in a heated herbal solution are wrapped around the body to promote muscle relaxation and eliminate toxins and impurities.

**Hydrotherapy**   Water therapy in the forms of underwater jet massage, showers, jet sprays, and mineral baths.

**Lomi-lomi**   A rhythmical, rocking massage that originated in Hawaii.

**Pilates**   Strength-training exercises developed in Germany by Dr. Joseph Pilates during the 1920s.

**Reflexology**   An ancient Chinese technique using pressure-point massage to the feet, hands, and ears to restore full energy flow to the body.

**Shiatsu**   A Japanese massage technique developed by Tokujiro Namikoshi in which finger pressure is applied to specific points on the body to stimulate and unblock pathways through which energy flows.

**Sports massage**   Deep tissue massage directed at muscles used in athletic activity.

**Swedish massage**   A classic massage technique developed at the University of Stockholm early in the nineteenth century that gently manipulates the muscles with the use of massage oils.

**Tai chi**   An ancient Asian discipline for exercise and meditation with a series of movements intended to unite body and mind.

**Thalassotherapy**   A therapeutic sea-based treatment that includes seaweed, algae, and seawater hydrotherapy.

**Yoga**   A discipline of stretching and toning the body through movements and postures to attain well-being and physical and mental control.

# Music Notes

**Frédéric Chopin (1810–1849)**

*Nocturne, Op. 9, No. 1*

*Nocturne, Op. 9, No. 2*

*Nocturne, Op. 27, No. 2*

Chopin combined an extraordinary gift for melody, an adventurous harmonic sense, an intuitive understanding of formal design, and a brilliant piano technique to create a large body of piano music. He was one of the leading nineteenth-century composers, and his music represents the quintessence of the Romantic piano tradition, fully embodying the expressive and technical characteristics of the instrument. Chopin Nocturnes isolate the right-hand melody, allowing the fullest possible expression in its playing, while the left hand provides the rhythmic and harmonic background in broken-chord accompaniment.

**Claude Debussy (1862–1918)**

*Arabesque I*

*Rêverie*

*La plus que lente*

*Reflets dans l'eau*

Debussy was one of the greatest composers of French music, and almost all later composers were influenced by him. His works were unusually independent of traditional form, harmony, and coloring, and his desire to free himself from tonality led him to the use of church modes and the whole-tone scale and chords. Debussy's compositions brought a new rhythmic fluidity to classical composition, and his scoring was influenced by the Javanese gamelan, which he first heard in 1889 at the World Exhibition in Paris. Debussy idolized the music of Chopin, and he completed a revision of the complete piano works of the Polish genius for A. Durand, a noted Paris publisher.

Debussy's gently florid *Deux Arabesques* are his first published piano compositions (the first *Arabesque* in E major is recorded here). Completed in 1891, the pieces were written in the style of contemporary salon music. *Rêverie* begins with a gentle melody over a repeated accompanimental pattern, which is followed by a central chordal passage of contrasting mood and tonality before the return of the opening material. The slightly mischievous *La plus que lente* ("A Slower Than Slow Waltz"), was composed in 1910 and has been the source of many transcriptions. *Reflets dans l'eau* ("Reflections in the Water") is one of the composer's many water pieces. Debussy envisioned the opening as an image of dropping a pebble into the water and watching the ripples make concentric circles. In a 1903 article for the journal *Musica*, Debussy wrote: "Music is a mysterious mathematical process whose elements share something of the nature of infinity. It is allied to the movement of the waters, to the play of curves described by the changing breezes."

### Erik Satie (1866–1925)

*Gymnopédies, Nos. 2 and 3*

Satie composed sophisticated yet deliberately modest music that influenced later composers such as Debussy, Ravel, Varèse, and Cage. Most of his compositions are for piano, and some have bizarre titles, such as *Trois Morceaux en Forme de Poire* ("Three Pear-Shaped Pieces"). Satie's score for the ballet *Parade*—which uses jazz rhythms and makes use of a typewriter, a steamship whistle, and a siren—was first performed by Diaghilev's celebrated Ballet Russe. Satie composed the *Gymnopédies* in 1888 when he was only twenty. The simple modal melodies are reminiscent of plainsong and reflect his interest in Rosicrucianism. The title refers to ritual dances performed by young athletes in ancient Greece. The first and third *Gymnopédies* were orchestrated by Debussy.

**Maurice Ravel (1875–1937)**

*Pavane pour une infante défunte*

*Prélude*

*Mouvement de menuet*

*La vallée des cloches*

Ravel's fastidiously polished compositions make important additions to the piano repertoire, to the repertoire of French song, and with commissions from Diaghilev, to ballet. He composed *Pavane pour une infante défunte* ("Pavane for a Dead Princess") in 1899 and later orchestrated the euphonistically titled work. With its dance rhythm of sixteenth-century Spain and the poignancy of its melodic line, *Pavane* is among the most evocative of Ravel's compositions. *Prélude* was composed in 1913 as a sight-reading test for women students at the Paris Conservatory. A brief, luminous work, it is based on harmonies later used by American jazz composers. *Mouvement de menuet* is the second movement from Ravel's *Sonatine*. Completed in 1905, the movement shifts subtly in tonality and takes the mood, if not the form, of a classical minuet. Ravel said that his inspiration for the beautiful *La vallée des cloches* ("Valley of the Bells") was the many church bells heard at noon in Paris. The bells are first heard tolling in the distance in this work of subtle beauty.

# MENU

## *BREAKFAST*

*Gratin of Apples and Apricots with Cal-a-Vie Granola*

## *LUNCH*

*Tarragon-Walnut Wild Rice Salad with Chicken*

❖

*Butternut Squash Sorbet*

## *DINNER*

*Grilled Asparagus Salad with Sherry Vinaigrette*

❖

*Boneless Lamb Loins with Port Wine Sauce*

❖

*Almond Ricotta Torte with Cocoa-Kahlúa Sauce*

# Cal-a-Vie

Vista, California

*A glorious indulgence . . . one of the best and most beneficial holidays.*
— Elle *magazine*

### ❖ PROFILE ❖

Nestled in a secluded valley forty miles north of San Diego, informally luxurious Cal-a-Vie combines American-style exercise and diet with European water treatments and aromatherapy. A maximum of twenty-four guests enjoy week-long spa programs at this peaceful retreat, where, as *Time* magazine reports, the byword is elegance: "Fresh flowers are everywhere, and gourmet though low-cal meals are served on china." The ambiance is nurturing and friendly, and the attentive, knowledgeable staff outnumbers guests by more than four to one. Founded in 1986 by Marlene and William Power, Cal-a-Vie was created to be a "sweet refuge from the stresses and strains of modern living." The couple created the spa as a combination of Old and New World programs—the European pleasure principle modified with a dollop of Yankee discipline. After a week in this fitness paradise, guests find they possess a remarkable sense of renewal. Relaxed yet energized, well-fed and well-scrubbed, they go back to the "real world" ready to take on its challenges once again.

### ❖ CUISINE ❖

Culinary excellence at its healthiest is central to the Cal-a-Vie experience (in fact, Oprah lured her famous personal chef—and now bestselling cookbook author— Rosie Daley away from Cal-a-Vie after staying there in 1991). The cuisine is high in nutrients and low in fat and combines international and regional American flavors with classic gourmet traditions. Meals are graciously served in the dining room or outside at tables on an inviting patio. An emphasis on freshness, variety, and exquisite presentation guarantees that each meal is a feast for the senses, and for those who want to learn how to re-create it at home, chef Steve Pernetti's cooking class revolves around the actual preparation of that evening's dinner.

## ✦ SETTING ✦

No expense was spared in creating this serene oasis, and the spa's beautiful, intimate surroundings play a therapeutic role. Guests stay in private cottages with tile roofs, French country interiors, and sundecks that look out on natural expanses of manzanita and chaparral. Patterned after a charming Mediterranean village, the grounds are complete with stone paths, a babbling brook, and lush plantings of roses, jasmine, bougainvillea, citrus, and lavender. The landscaping, exterior details, and interior decorating were designed by Marlene Power and Sherry Thomson, and together they have created a lovely, healing environment.

## ✦ ACTIVITIES, TREATMENTS, AND FACILITIES ✦

The Cal-a-Vie program educates guests about the fundamentals of a healthy lifestyle. After a state-of-the-art computerized fitness evaluation, guests participate in a well-paced exercise and treatment program that changes daily. The day usually begins with a warm-up session followed by a prebreakfast walk around the nearby golf course or a brisk hike into the surrounding hills looking out at fields, vineyards, and mountain ranges covered with wisps of fog. After breakfast, each guest receives a personalized schedule for the day. Classes include aerobic conditioning, body contouring, personalized workouts on state-of-the-art equipment, aqua aerobics, and pool volleyball, as well as less strenuous activities like stretch, yoga, and tai chi. After a morning of workouts comes an afternoon of luxurious pampering: Swedish, shiatsu, and aromatherapy massages; hydrotherapy; thalassotherapy (a seawater and seaweed wrap that takes two hours); reflexology; and skin, hair, hand, and foot treatments to melt away stress and the effects of aging. Informal evening programs cover such topics as fitness, nutrition, and stress management. Facilities include an outdoor tennis court, a heated pool, a recessed Roman whirlpool, an aerobics room, a Jacuzzi, wet and dry saunas, underwater massage tubs, and lounges. Cal-a-Vie packages are available for week-long segments, with an option for the number of treatments and classes. Most of the weeks are coed, and women-only weeks are also offered regularly.

# Gratin of Apples and Apricots
# with Cal-a-Vie Granola

*This nutritious dish is so delicious that it seems like eating dessert for breakfast.*

²/₃ cup (4 oz/125 g) dried insulphured apricots, diced

1 cup (8 fl oz/250 ml) water

4 cups (1 lb/500 g) peeled and sliced tart apples (about 3 apples)

2 tablespoons raisins or dried currants

¹/₂ teaspoon ground cinnamon or allspice

2 teaspoons fresh lemon juice

²/₃ cup (2¹/₂ oz/75 g) Cal-a-Vie Granola (recipe follows)
   or other low-fat or nonfat granola

³/₄ cup (6 oz/185 g) nonfat or low-fat vanilla yogurt

Soak the apricots in the water for 1 hour. Pour the apricots and water into a small saucepan, bring to a boil, reduce heat, and simmer for 15 minutes. Add the apples, raisins or currants, cinnamon or allspice, and lemon juice and simmer, stirring occasionally, for 15 to 20 minutes, or until the apples are tender.

Preheat the oven to 350°F (180°C). Transfer the apple mixture to a 4-cup (1-l) baking dish or six 4-inch-diameter (10-cm) ramekins. Top with the granola and bake for 10 minutes. Serve warm, with a dollop of vanilla yogurt.

*Makes 6 servings*

### PER SERVING

*Calories 160 • Carbohydrates 35 g • Cholesterol 0 mg • Fat 1.5 g • Protein 4 g • Sodium 25 mg*

## Cal-a-Vie Granola

*Puréed banana coats the oats and helps to hold this very low-fat granola together. Delicious served with skim milk or nonfat yogurt and fresh fruit, the granola can also be used as a crumb crust.*

> 4 cups (12 oz/375 g) rolled oats
>
> 1/4 cup (1 oz/30 g) unsalted raw sunflower seeds
>
> 1/4 cup (1 oz/30 g) sliced almonds or unsweetened coconut
>
> 1 ripe banana, chopped
>
> 3 tablespoons pure maple syrup, honey, or liquid Fruit Sweet
>
> 1 1/2 tablespoons almond oil or canola oil
>
> 1 1/2 teaspoons ground cinnamon
>
> 1/4 cup (1/2 oz/15 g) wheat germ or bran
>
> 1/2 cup (3 oz/90 g) raisins

Preheat the oven to 275°F (135°C). In a 9-by-13-inch (23-by-32.5-cm) baking pan, combine the oats, sunflower seeds, and almonds or coconut.

In blender or food processor, combine the banana, maple syrup or honey, almond or canola oil, and cinnamon and purée. Drizzle the purée over the oats and mix until thoroughly coated. Bake for 35 to 40 minutes, stirring several times, until lightly toasted. Stir in the wheat germ or bran and bake for another 8 to 10 minutes.

Remove from the oven and stir in the raisins. Let cool completely. Store in an airtight container.

*Makes about 6 cups (19 oz/590 g)*

PER SERVING (each 1/4 cup or 3/4 oz/20 g)

*Calories 100 • Carbohydrates 16 g • Cholesterol 0 mg • Fat 3 g • Protein 3 g • Sodium 0 mg*

# Tarragon-Walnut Wild Rice Salad with Chicken

*To make this a vegetarian dish, substitute seitan, a high-protein food from Asia made from wheat gluten, for the chicken*

> 4 ounces (125 g) boneless, skinless chicken breast, poached
> and torn into strips, or 4 ounces (125 g) seitan, cut into thin strips
> 2¾ cups (13 oz/410 g) cooked wild rice
> 1½ cups (9 oz/280 g) red or green seedless grapes, sliced in half
> 1 cup (5 oz/155 g) chopped celery
> ¼ cup (⅓ oz/10 g) minced fresh parsley
> ¼ cup (⅓ oz/10 g) chopped fresh chives

## Dressing

> 2 shallots, minced
> 3 garlic cloves, minced
> ¼ cup (2 fl oz/60 ml) dry white wine or white grape juice
> ¼ cup (2 fl oz/60 ml) white wine vinegar or tarragon vinegar
> 1 tablespoon almond oil or safflower oil
> 1 teaspoon low-salt soy sauce
> Freshly cracked pepper to taste
> 2 tablespoons minced fresh tarragon
>
> 2 large heads butter lettuce
> ¼ cup (1 oz/30 g) chopped walnuts, toasted (see Basics)
> 6 tarragon sprigs and 6 nasturtium flowers for garnish (optional)

In a large bowl, combine the chicken or seitan, wild rice, grapes, celery, parsley, and chives and toss until well mixed.

To make the dressing: In a blender or food processor, combine the shallots, garlic, wine or grape juice, and vinegar and purée. With the machine running, slowly pour in the oil until the mixture emulsifies. Stir in the soy sauce, cracked pepper, and minced tarragon.

Separate 12 large leaves from the butter lettuce. Core and shred the remaining lettuce. Add the dressing to the rice mixture and toss until well mixed. Stir in the walnuts. Arrange 2 whole lettuce leaves on each of 6 plates, fill with a mound of shredded lettuce, and top with one-sixth of the rice mixture. If desired, garnish each serving with a tarragon sprig and a nasturtium flower.

*Makes 6 servings*

PER SERVING

*Calories 200 • Carbohydrates 28 g • Cholesterol 10 mg • Fat 7 g • Protein 9 g • Sodium 65 mg*

## Butternut Squash Sorbet

*Garnish the sorbet with a fragrant citrus blossom, either lemon, lime, or orange. Crisp cookies or wafers go perfectly with this ice.*

- 3 cups (2 lb/1 kg) butternut squash or pumpkin purée (see Basics)
- 1 banana
- 3 cups (24 fl oz/750 ml) fresh orange juice
- 1/4 cup (2 fl oz/60 ml) fresh lime juice
- 1 tablespoon orange liqueur (optional)
- 1/3 cup (4 oz/125 g) honey, maple syrup, or liquid Fruit Sweet, or to taste
- 1 tablespoon grated orange zest (see Basics)
- 1/4 teaspoon ground cinnamon

In a blender or food processor, combine all the ingredients, in batches if necessary, and process until smooth. Transfer to an ice cream maker and freeze according to the manufacturer's instructions. Alternatively, pour the purée into a baking pan and freeze until ice crystals form; beat to break up the crystals and then freeze until solid. Or, freeze the sorbet in ice cube trays and process in a blender or food processor.

*Makes 12 servings*

PER SERVING

*Calories 90 • Carbohydrates 23 g • Cholesterol 0 mg • Fat 0 g • Protein 1 g • Sodium 0 mg*

# Grilled Asparagus Salad with Sherry Vinaigrette

42 large fresh asparagus spears
Leaves from 1 head romaine
Leaves from 2 heads radicchio
6 cherry tomatoes, cut into quarters
1 basket clover or alfalfa sprouts

*Sherry Vinaigrette*
1/4 cup (2 fl oz/60 ml) sherry wine vinegar
1 tablespoon fresh lemon juice
1/4 cup (2 fl oz/60 ml) water
1 teaspoon Dijon mustard
1 teaspoon honey
2 tablespoons extra-virgin olive oil
1 teaspoon *each* chopped fresh parsley, tarragon, and chives
Sea salt and freshly ground pepper to taste

Light a fire in a charcoal grill. Using a small, sharp knife or vegetable peeler, peel the butt ends of the asparagus. Place the asparagus in a grilling basket and grill for 3 to 5 minutes, or until crisp-tender. Alternatively, place the asparagus in a steamer basket and steam, covered, over boiling water for 5 minutes, or until crisp-tender. Immediately remove the spears from the pan, run under cold water, and drain.

To make the vinaigrette: In a small bowl, whisk all the ingredients together.

Arrange the lettuce and radicchio leaves on each of 6 plates. Top with the asparagus spears, garnish with cherry tomatoes and sprouts, and drizzle with the sherry vinaigrette.

*Makes 6 servings*

### PER SERVING

*Calories 100 • Carbohydrates 11 g • Cholesterol 0 mg • Fat 5 g • Protein 5 g • Sodium 45 mg*

# Boneless Lamb Loins with Port Wine Sauce

*Lamb is the one red meat that Cal-a-Vie serves on occasion. The organic meat is from animals less than one year old, which are generally more healthy than many older commercially raised animals.*

<sup></sup>

$^1$/4 cup (1$^1$/2 oz/45 g) minced shallots

1 tablespoon minced garlic

1 tablespoon honey

1 tablespoon minced fresh thyme

1 teaspoon black peppercorns

1 cup (8 fl oz/250 ml) port wine

3 cups (24 fl oz/750 ml) lamb stock or vegetable stock (see Basics) or canned low-salt vegetable broth

2 lamb loins

Preheat the oven to 400°F (200°C).

To make the port sauce: In a medium saucepan, combine the shallots, garlic, honey, thyme, peppercorns, and port. Bring to a boil and cook until the liquid is reduced by half. Pour in the stock and cook to reduce the liquid by half.

Coat a stove-top grill pan with vegetable oil spray and heat it over medium-high heat. Grill the lamb loins for 2 minutes on each side. Transfer to the preheated oven and bake for 10 minutes, or to preferred doneness. Cut into 18 slices and arrange 3 slices on each of 6 plates. Drizzle the slices with port sauce and serve immediately.

*Makes 6 servings*

PER SERVING (with 4 oz/125 g cooked lamb loin)

*Calories 290 • Carbohydrates 7 g • Cholesterol 100 mg • Fat 11 g • Protein 32 g • Sodium 95 mg*

# Almond Ricotta Torte with Cocoa-Kahlúa Sauce

$^1/_3$ cup (2 oz/60 g) blanched almonds, toasted (see Basics)

2 honey graham crackers, broken

2 egg yolks

15 ounces (470 g) low-fat ricotta cheese or cottage cheese

3 tablespoons flour

$^1/_3$ cup (2$^1/_2$ oz/75 g) sugar or Fruit Source*

Grated zest of 1 lemon (see Basics)

1 teaspoon vanilla extract

$^1/_4$ teaspoon almond extract

4 egg whites

Cocoa-Kahlúa Sauce (recipe follows) or fresh berry coulis (see Basics)

12 fanned strawberries for garnish (optional)

Preheat the oven to 375°F (190°C). Spray a 4-cup (1-l) soufflé dish with vegetable oil spray. In a blender or food processor, process the almonds until coarsely ground. Add the graham crackers and process until finely ground. Add the egg yolks, ricotta or cottage cheese, flour, sugar or Fruit Source, lemon zest, and vanilla and almond extracts and process to mix thoroughly.

In a large bowl, beat the egg whites until stiff, glossy peaks form. Stir one-fourth of the egg whites into the ricotta mixture, then fold in the remaining whites until blended. Pour the batter into the prepared dish and bake in the preheated oven for 40 minutes, or until puffed and golden. Remove from the oven and let cool for 20 minutes. Unmold the torte (it will sink a bit) and cut into wedges. Serve with a drizzle of cocoa-Kahlúa sauce or berry coulis and, if desired, garnish with a fanned strawberry.

*Makes 12 servings*

PER SERVING (with 1 tablespoon sauce)

*Calories 160 • Carbohydrates 21 g • Cholesterol 45 mg • Fat 6 g • Protein 7 g • Sodium 85 mg*

---

*\*Fruit Source is a granulated sweetener derived from fruit juice concentrates and malted rice. It is available in many natural foods stores.*

## Cocoa-Kahlúa Sauce

*A delicious sauce that satisfies chocolate-lovers' cravings.*

   1/2 cup (4 fl oz/125 ml) 1 percent milk

   1/4 cup (2 oz/60 g) honey, maple syrup, or Fruit Sweet

   1/3 cup (1 oz/30 g) unsweetened cocoa powder

   1 teaspoon arrowroot or cornstarch

   2 tablespoons Kahlúa, or 1 tablespoon vanilla extract

   1 teaspoon grated orange zest (optional; see Basics)

In a small saucepan, combine all the ingredients and cook over medium-low heat, stirring frequently, until the sauce thickens slightly. Remove from heat and let cool slightly before serving.

*Makes 1 cup (8 fl oz/250 ml)*

### PER TABLESPOON

*Calories 30 • Carbohydrates 7 g • Cholesterol 0 mg • Fat 0 g • Protein 1 g • Sodium 5 mg*

# Canyon Ranch

## Tucson, Arizona

*The seduction of Canyon Ranch [is that] the mind thinks it's on vacation, while the body's lured into working out.*

—Spirit *magazine*

### ✤ PROFILE ✤

A pioneer among Southwest fitness destinations, Canyon Ranch was founded in 1979 by Mel and Enid Zuckerman. Located near Tucson, this spa-vacation resort encourages optimum health and creative personal growth. Its beautiful setting on the edge of the Sonoran Desert and sunny year-round weather combine to make a powerful and energizing environment. While at the Ranch, guests enjoy delicious spa cuisine and engage in pursuits to strengthen the body, calm the mind, and nourish the spirit. The support and enthusiasm of other guests is an important part of the Canyon Ranch program, as is the knowledge and care of the experts on staff, who outnumber guests by almost three to one and whose main goal is to help people begin to live their lives with greater vitality, enjoyment, and satisfaction. The resort has been named Best Spa by the readers of *Condé Nast Traveler*.

### ✤ CUISINE ✤

The Canyon Ranch food philosophy goes well beyond counting calories and fat grams. As they put it, "We've vowed never to starve or bore a guest with ho-hum meals. At Canyon Ranch, you'll have the kind of dining experience you expect at any world-class resort—only healthier." Guests learn about "mindful eating," which leads to better appetite awareness, makes dining more pleasurable, and ensures that every meal is a nourishing experience. Classes offer nutrition information, teach home-cooking skills, and outline ways to create a healthy eating plan that can last a lifetime.

## ✤ SETTING ✤

Located on seventy acres in the foothills of the Santa Catalina Mountains, Canyon Ranch is a sprawling ranch with clusters of single-story adobe casitas, suites, health centers, and private condominium cottages. Its tranquil interior grounds are richly landscaped with flowers, cactus gardens, tropical trees, streams, and fountains, and the surrounding acreage consists of natural desert vegetation crisscrossed by walking trails. All of the 140 rooms are decorated with modern Southwestern furnishings, and feature large beds, phones, televisions, and private baths. Golf courses, horseback riding, and mountain biking are all available close by.

## ✤ ACTIVITIES, TREATMENTS, AND FACILITIES ✤

The Ranch offers a wide variety of exercise classes, body treatments, therapies, and educational lectures, all focused on helping you achieve a healthier, more stress-free lifestyle. As a guest, you'll choose among an extensive selection of indoor and outdoor activities for either a four- or a seven-day stay—and find that your schedule, while busy, proves to be invigorating and restorative rather than hectic. Each day begins with a prebreakfast hike in the local mountains, past saguaro cactuses and scenic rocky overhangs. After a healthy and tasty breakfast, guests move on to their chosen treatments, workshops, and hands-on classes, which might range from a body scrub with crushed pearls to weight-training in one of several gyms to music therapy (using sound to enhance relaxation and meditation). In the evening, there are talks by authors, naturalists, psychologists, and other specialists. The selection of spa, sports, and health services encompasses over forty-five fitness activities, plus stress-management techniques, medical evaluations, behavioral counseling, spiritual growth, exercise physiology, massage, facials, seaweed body treatments, aromatherapy, and arts classes. Facilities include an indoor and three outdoor pools; tennis and raquetball courts; a yoga/meditation dome; cardiovascular equipment; saunas, steam baths, and whirlpools; and private sunbathing areas.

# MENU

## *LUNCH*

*Chili Soup with Tortilla Strips*

❖

*Vegetarian Tostadas with Roasted-Corn Salsa*

❖

*Apple Empanadas*

# Chili Soup with Tortilla Strips

1 tablespoon olive oil

$^1/_2$ cup (2 oz/60 g) diced red onion

$^1/_3$ cup (1$^1/_2$ oz/45 g) diced Anaheim chili

$^1/_4$ teaspoon minced jalapeño chili

1 tablespoon minced garlic

$^1/_2$ cup (2$^1/_2$ oz/75 g) diced celery

3 pounds (1.5 kg) tomatoes, peeled, seeded (see Basics), and diced

2 cups (16 fl oz/500 ml) vegetable stock (see Basics)
   or canned low-salt vegetable broth

2 tablespoons chopped fresh chives

1 tablespoon fresh lemon juice

Pinch of salt

3 corn tortillas, sliced into strips, for garnish

2 tablespoons sliced green onion for garnish

In a medium sauté pan or skillet over medium heat, heat the olive oil and sauté the onion, Anaheim chili, jalapeño, garlic, and celery for 8 to 10 minutes, or until softened and lightly browned.

In a blender or food processor, in batches if necessary, combine the tomatoes, stock or broth, chives, lemon juice, and salt. Process until just mixed. Cover and refrigerate for at least 2 hours.

Preheat the broiler. On a nonstick baking sheet or a baking sheet lightly coated with vegetable oil spray, arrange the tortilla strips in a single layer. Place under the preheated broiler for 1 to 2 minutes on each side, or until crisp.

Ladle $^3/_4$ cup (6 fl oz/375 ml) soup into each of 6 bowls and top with chopped green onion and tortilla strips.

*Makes 6 servings*

PER SERVING

*Calories 110 • Carbohydrates 20 g • Cholesterol 0 mg • Fat 3.5 g • Protein 4 g • Sodium 85 mg*

# Vegetarian Tostadas with Roasted-Corn Salsa

2$\frac{1}{2}$ cups (20 fl oz/625 ml) vegetable stock (see Basics),
    canned low-salt vegetable broth, or water

Pinch *each* of ground chili, cayenne pepper, ground cumin, and garlic

1$\frac{1}{4}$ cups (7$\frac{1}{2}$ oz/235 g) bulgur wheat

3 cups (24 oz/750 g) canned vegetarian refried black beans

6 corn tortillas, warmed

1 head iceberg lettuce, cored and shredded

3 cups (18 oz/560 g) Roasted-Corn Salsa (recipe follows)

3 green onions, sliced, for garnish

In a medium saucepan, bring the stock, broth, or water and the chili, cayenne, cumin, and garlic to a boil. Add the bulgur wheat, reduce heat to low, and simmer, covered, for 20 to 25 minutes, or until the bulgur is softened but still slightly crunchy. Remove from heat and set aside.

In a saucepan, cook the beans over medium heat until heated through.

To assemble: Top each of the 6 tortillas with one-sixth of the refried beans, cooked bulgur, shredded lettuce, and salsa. Garnish with green onions and serve immediately.

*Makes 6 servings*

## PER SERVING

*Calories 340 • Carbohydrates 69 g • Cholesterol 0 mg • Fat 2 g • Protein 17 g • Sodium 400 mg*

---

## Roasted-Corn Salsa

3 cups (18 oz/560 g) fresh corn kernels (from 4 ears of corn)
1/2 cup (4 oz/125 g) canned diced green chilies, drained
1/2 cup (4 oz/125 g) canned diced pimientos, drained
1/2 cup (2 1/2 oz/75 g) finely diced red onion
1/2 cup (3 oz/90 g) diced tomato
1/2 cup (4 fl oz/125 ml) fresh lime juice
2 tablespoons chopped fresh cilantro
1/2 teaspoon freshly ground pepper

Preheat the oven to 350°F (180°C). Lightly coat a baking sheet with vegetable oil spray.

Spread the corn kernels evenly on the prepared pan. Bake in the preheated oven for 20 minutes, or until slightly brown. In a large bowl, gently combine the roasted corn with all the remaining ingredients. Cover and refrigerate for at least 1 hour before serving. Stir gently before serving.

*Makes 5 cups (30 oz/940 g)*

PER 1/2 CUP (3 oz/90 g)

*Calories 50 • Carbohydrates 12 g • Cholesterol 0 mg • Fat 0.5 g • Protein 2 g • Sodium 25 mg*

# Apple Empanadas

2 small Granny Smith apples, peeled, cored, and finely chopped

4 dates, pitted and finely chopped

Pinch of ground cloves

$2^1/2$ tablespoons apple juice

1 teaspoon cornstarch

2 tablespoons water

2 tablespoons nonfat ricotta cheese

1 tablespoon nonfat sour cream

$1^1/2$ teaspoons nonfat milk

1 egg white, slightly beaten

2 teaspoons canola oil

$^1/2$ teaspoon vanilla extract

1 cup (5 oz/155 g) all-purpose flour

1 tablespoon fructose* or sugar

$^1/2$ teaspoon baking powder

$^3/4$ teaspoon ground cinnamon, plus more for sprinkling

Preheat the oven to 325°F (165°C). Lightly coat a baking sheet with vegetable oil spray.

In a medium saucepan, combine the apples, dates, cloves, and apple juice. Bring to a boil, reduce heat, and simmer for 15 minutes, or until the fruit is soft.

In a small bowl, mix the cornstarch and water together. Stir into the apple mixture and continue simmering until the fruit begins to thicken. Remove from heat and let cool.

In a medium bowl, combine the ricotta, sour cream, milk, egg white, oil, and vanilla and mix well.

In a small bowl, combine $^1/2$ cup ($2^1/2$ oz/75 g) of the flour, the fructose or sugar, the baking powder, and the $^3/4$ teaspoon cinnamon. Add the flour mixture to the ricotta cheese mixture and mix to form a soft dough.

Using some of the remaining $^{1}/_{2}$ cup ($2^{1}/_{2}$ oz/75 g) flour, heavily flour a work surface and begin kneading the dough. Add flour 1 tablespoon at a time, kneading until the dough is elastic and no longer sticky. Roll out to a $^{1}/_{8}$-inch (3-mm) thickness, sprinkling with flour as necessary to prevent sticking.

Using a 3-inch (7.5-cm) round cookie cutter or glass, cut rounds from the dough. Spoon 1 tablespoon apple filling into the center of each round. Using a pastry brush, brush water around the edge of each round. Fold the dough in half over the filling and crimp the edges.

Place the empanadas on the prepared baking sheet and sprinkle with cinnamon. Bake in the preheated oven for 15 minutes, or until golden. Serve warm.

*Makes 12 empanadas; serves 6*

### PER SERVING

*Calories 130 • Carbohydrates 26 g • Cholesterol 0 mg • Fat 2 g • Protein 3 g • Sodium 30 mg*

---

*\*Fructose is a refined sugar derived mainly from corn. It is available in natural foods stores.*

# Canyon Ranch
# in the Berkshires

### Lenox, Massachusetts

*Sitting by a roaring fireplace at Canyon Ranch and stirring a cup of herbal tea with a cinnamon stick after a hard workout and a foot massage can do wonders for a case of those winter blues.*

—**Boston Herald**

## ❖ PROFILE ❖

A resort dedicated to healthy living, Canyon Ranch in the Berkshires is imbued with quintessential New England charm and surrounded by vistas of forested mountains. Sister spa to the original Canyon Ranch in Tucson, Arizona, it offers a full health-and-fitness vacation on the grounds of a spectacular old mansion. The Canyon Ranch philosophy—from the workout classes to the nutrition notes on the menu—is not "We do it all for you," it's "We show you how to do it for yourself, so you can take it home with you!" Guests report a new awareness and vitality after their stay here, and many return year after year to reduce overall stress, pamper themselves, and jump-start home fitness programs. The staff at Canyon Ranch in the Berkshires is both professional and warm, and there's a nearly three-to-one staff-to-guest ratio, ensuring that all questions are answered and all needs graciously met.

## ❖ CUISINE ❖

*HomeStyle Magazine* says, "Canyon Ranch has made a science out of proving that fat-free need not be flavor-free," and the menu at the Ranch offers a wealth of delicious selections prepared with flair. At around 6 p.m., "mocktails" (fruit or vegetable juices) and crudités are served after the evening massage and before a light gourmet dinner. In the demonstration kitchen, chefs show guests how to prepare Canyon Ranch–style dishes at home. Staff nutritionists explain how to shop for the right foods, dine out healthfully, deal with cravings, and develop a nutritious meal plan that's easy to live with on a daily basis.

## ❖ SETTING ❖

High in the green rolling hills of the Berkshires, sloping lawns and a reflecting pool lead to the guest entrance of the historic mansion of Bellefontaine, designed in 1897 and reminiscent of the Petit Trianon in Versailles. Glass-enclosed walkways connect the mansion, an ultramodern spa complex, and a 120-room New England–style inn, so guests can wander and explore protected from the weather. The Ranch's grounds contain lush gardens and a fifty-foot heated outdoor pool, and the local natural landscape provides for such activities as cross-country skiing in the winter and boating and biking in the summer. The comfortable rooms are decorated in soft pastels and jewel tones.

## ❖ ACTIVITIES, TREATMENTS, AND FACILITIES ❖

The extensive range of services at Canyon Ranch in the Berkshires encompasses fitness, weight loss, stress reduction, and beauty and body care. Also provided is a health-and-fitness assessment and brief medical evaluation. One of the most popular treatments here is deep nourishment for the skin, in which organic "mud"—actually an herbal mixture—is first gently painted on the body. You are then wrapped in blankets and left to enjoy the earthy smell of the herbs and let your mind float as you listen to relaxing music for twenty minutes. The next step is to stand under a Swiss jet shower, and then finish with a rubdown of lavender and rosemary oils, soothing for both the skin and nervous system.

One of the top indoor fitness centers in the Northeast, Canyon Ranch offers cardiovascular and weight-training equipment, racquetball, squash, tennis courts, an inside running track, and a seventy-five-foot pool. There are upwards of forty exercise classes, an extensive indoor and outdoor sports program including hiking, kayaking, and tai chi, and breathing classes for improved health and stress relief. After a day of exercising, guests enjoy saunas, steam baths, hydrotherapies, and massages. The services included with a Canyon Ranch program are based on the length of stay, and additional treatments can be booked à la carte.

# MENU

*Butternut Squash and Cider Soup*

❖

*Turkey Burgers with Cranberry Ketchup*
*or*
*Chicken and Barley "Risotto"*

❖

*Blackberry-Orange Cobbler*

# Butternut Squash and Cider Soup

*Buy a butternut squash that is firm and heavy, with no cracks or soft spots. Squash with the stub of a stem will keep longer. If stored in a cool, well-ventilated, dry spot, the squash should keep at room temperature for about a month.*

1 shallot, minced

1 garlic clove, minced

3 cups (1 lb/500 g) cubed butternut squash

1/2 cup (4 fl oz/125 ml) chicken stock (see Basics)
or canned low-salt chicken broth

3/4 cup (6 fl oz/185 ml) apple cider

1/4 cup (2 fl oz/60 ml) low-fat sour cream

1/2 unpeeled red Rome or Golden Delicious apple, cored and finely diced

Cracked black pepper to taste

In a medium saucepan, sauté the shallot and garlic in a little water over low heat, being careful not to burn them. Add the squash and stock or broth, bring to a boil, reduce heat to low, cover, and simmer for 30 minutes, or until the squash is tender.

Transfer the soup to a blender or food processor and purée, in batches if necessary. Add the apple cider and sour cream and process until thoroughly blended.

Return to the saucepan and reheat briefly. Ladle the soup into 4 shallow bowls and garnish each bowl with a little diced apple and cracked pepper.

*Makes 4 servings*

### PER SERVING

*Calories 120 • Carbohydrates 18 g • Cholesterol 10 mg • Fat 3 g • Protein 2 g • Sodium 20 mg*

# Turkey Burgers with Cranberry Ketchup

*Make sure the ground turkey you purchase is ground skinless turkey breast. You can also ask your butcher to grind skinless turkey breast for you, or grind it at home in your food processor.*

> **12 ounces (375 g) ground skinless turkey breast**
>
> **4 whole-grain buns**
>
> **8 teaspoons Cranberry Ketchup (recipe follows)**
>
> **4 romaine lettuce leaves**
>
> **4 thin onion slices**
>
> **4 thin tomato slices**

Light a fire in a charcoal grill (coat the cooking rack with vegetable oil spray away from the fire) or preheat a gas grill or a broiler.

Form the ground turkey into 4 patties. Grill or broil the turkey burgers for 2 to 3 minutes on each side. Toast the cut sides of the buns on the grill or under the broiler until lightly browned.

Spread each bun with 2 teaspoons cranberry ketchup. Place the turkey burgers on the bottom halves of the buns and top with lettuce, onion, and tomato. Cover with the top halves of the buns and serve immediately.

*Makes 4 servings*

### PER SERVING

*Calories 240 • Carbohydrates 25 g • Cholesterol 60 mg • Fat 3.5 g • Protein 27 g • Sodium 260 mg*

## Cranberry Ketchup

*Buy extra bags of fresh cranberries when they are available in the late fall. Freeze them right in the plastic bags for use throughout the year.*

1 cup (4 oz/125 g) fresh cranberries

¼ cup (1½ oz/45 g) finely chopped onion

¼ cup (2 fl oz/60 ml) water

3 tablespoons thawed apple juice concentrate

¼ cup (2 fl oz/60 ml) distilled white vinegar

¼ teaspoon *each* ground cloves, cinnamon, and allspice

¼ teaspoon salt

¼ teaspoon ground white pepper

Rinse and pick over the cranberries and remove any stems or spoiled berries. In a small saucepan, combine the cranberries, onion, and water and bring to a boil. Reduce heat to low and simmer for 5 minutes, stirring occasionally.

Remove from heat and let cool. Transfer to a blender or food processor and blend until smooth.

Return the cranberries to the saucepan and add all the remaining ingredients. Cook over medium heat until slightly thickened. Remove from heat and let cool. Cover and refrigerate for at least 2 hours or up to 1 week.

*Makes 1 cup (8 fl oz/250 ml)*

PER TABLESPOON

*Calories 10 • Carbohydrates 3 g • Cholesterol 0 mg • Fat 0 g • Protein 0 g • Sodium 40 mg*

# Chicken and Barley "Risotto"

$^2/_3$ cup (4 oz/125 g) pearl barley

3 cups (24 fl oz/750 ml) water

1$^1/_2$ tablespoons finely chopped onion

$^3/_4$ cup (4 oz/125 g) peeled and diced carrots

$^3/_4$ cup (4 oz/125 g) diced celery

$^3/_4$ cup (3 oz/90 g) diced leek (white part only)

$^1/_2$ cup (4 fl oz/125 ml) chicken stock (see Basics)
   or canned low-salt chicken broth

2 skinless, boneless chicken breast halves (about $^3/_4$ lb/375 g)

6 tablespoons (1$^1/_2$ oz/45 g) grated Parmesan cheese

$^1/_2$ cup ($^3/_4$ oz/20 g) chopped fresh parsley

In a medium saucepan, bring the barley and water to a boil. Reduce heat to low, cover, and simmer for 45 minutes, or until the barley is tender. Drain and set aside.

Light a fire in a charcoal grill or preheat a gas grill or a broiler. Lightly coat a nonstick frying pan or a sauté pan with vegetable oil spray and heat over medium heat. Sauté the onion, carrots, celery, and leek for 10 minutes. Using a slotted spoon, remove half the vegetables and reserve them. Pour the stock or broth into the pan, bring to a rapid boil, and cook until reduced by half.

Meanwhile, grill or broil the chicken for 3 to 5 minutes on each side, or until the juices run clear. Remove from heat and let cool. With a sharp knife, cut the chicken into long, thin strips.

In a large bowl, gently combine the chicken, cooked barley, all the vegetables, Parmesan cheese, and parsley. Serve warm.

*Makes 4 servings*

### PER SERVING

*Calories 280 • Carbohydrates 33 g • Cholesterol 55 mg • Fat 5 g • Protein 26 g • Sodium 260 mg*

# Blackberry-Orange Cobbler

3 cups (12 oz/375 g) blackberries
1/2 teaspoon grated orange zest (see Basics)
4 tablespoons fructose* or sugar
1 egg
3 tablespoons nonfat milk
1 tablespoon butter, melted
2 tablespoons nonfat sour cream
1/2 cup (2 1/2 oz/75 g) unbleached all-purpose flour
1/2 teaspoon baking powder
Pinch of salt

Preheat the oven to 350°F (180°C). In a medium bowl, gently mix the blackberries, zest, and 2 tablespoons of the fructose or sugar. Spoon the berries into 6 ovenproof 1/2-cup (4-fl oz/125-ml) ramekins.

In a small bowl, beat the egg lightly with a fork. Discard half the beaten egg. Stir in the milk, butter, sour cream, and the remaining 2 tablespoons fructose or sugar. Set aside.

In another small bowl, combine the flour, baking powder, and salt. Add the flour mixture to the egg mixture and mix until just blended; do not overmix.

Spoon 1 1/2 tablespoons of the batter into each ramekin. Place the ramekins on a baking sheet and bake in the preheated oven for 15 to 20 minutes, or until the tops are golden brown.

*Makes 6 servings*

### PER SERVING

*Calories 140 • Carbohydrates 27 g • Cholesterol 40 mg • Fat 3 g • Protein 3 g • Sodium 80 mg*

*\*Fructose is a refined sugar derived mainly from corn. It is available in natural foods stores. Substitute granulated sugar if necessary.*

# Château Élan

*A quiet, warm, and friendly atmosphere prevails. . . . [and] don't expect lots*
*of exercise equipment and group programs. In this vision of Southern comfort,*
*there's no place for regimentation.*

—**Fodor's Healthy Escapes**

## ❖ PROFILE ❖

Just thirty minutes from the bustle of Atlanta, the spa at Château Élan offers guests the ultimate getaway: a restful retreat on a private lake within a 3,100-acre gated resort community. You can fill your days with activities or simply lounge in the warm Southern sunshine, pampered from head to toe and enjoying Georgia-style graciousness. The château itself—an actual working winery—is built in the style of a French sixteenth-century manor house and is surrounded by vineyards and woodlands. In addition to the fourteen-room spa, the resort also comprises a large inn, three golf courses, an equestrian show center, a Stan Smith–designed tennis center, several restaurants, an art gallery, and a concert pavilion. Spa treatments and fitness classes can be alternated with winery tours and tastings, hikes and bike rides on the nature trails running through the estate (gourmet picnic boxes are available), and croquet and volleyball on the lawn.

## ❖ CUISINE ❖

Chef Yves Samake oversees Fleur-de-lis, the spa dining room at Château Élan, where he has designed gourmet menus specifically for the health-conscious diner. As described in the *New York Times*: "The food, served in a lovely, sunny room that can seat thirty-two overlooking the pond, is fabulous, the kind of light, healthy, appetizing fare you always say you'll cook for yourself . . . it's low in calories but entirely satisfying." Afternoon tea is served in the library every day, and you can also explore the other restaurants in the complex, which include the Clubhouse Grille, the Versailles Room, Café Élan, and the elegant Le Clos, located in the winery.

## ❖ SETTING ❖

On acres of softly rolling land, the spa at Château Élan has fourteen uniquely decorated rooms aimed to lift your spirits and suit your whims. Each room and bath—many with Jacuzzi tubs—is appointed with flair: the Vintage Room features a Philco radio, an iron queen-size bed, an oversized tub, and other antiques, while the all-white Gatsby Room is designed in 1920s style with a romantic view. Also available are a Greek Room, Hi-Tech Room, Victorian Room, Lodge Loft, and more. If you choose, you can stay in the Mobil four-star Inn at the Château, with 275 rooms and suites in French-country style, or in one of eight golf villas.

## ❖ ACTIVITIES, TREATMENTS, AND FACILITIES ❖

The full-service European-style spa at Château Élan offers an escape from the stress of everyday life with extensive beauty treatments, preventive health care, and body maintenance, complete with one-on-one consultations on nutrition, fitness, wellness, and smoking cessation. Facilities include a sauna, a steam room, four pools, a sundeck, a whirlpool, and twenty treatment rooms, where the variety of offerings include classic facials, hair and nail care, Swedish massage, hydrotherapy massage, salt glow with Vichy shower, mineral baths, herbal wraps, mango treatment for the neck and around the eyes, thalassotherapy, foot reflexology, and aromatherapy baths. There is a selection of fitness classes as well: regular and low-impact aerobics, yoga, step, aqua aerobics, and body sculpting. A variety of spa packages and stays are available, from à la carte to day spas to six-day retreats. Sign up for a program or create a unique spa experience for yourself, making your schedule as full or as free as you like.

# MENU

*Shrimp Salad with Japanese Rice Rolls*

❖

*Chicken Breasts with English Peas, French Style*

❖

*Pineapple Parfait*

# Shrimp Salad with Japanese Rice Rolls

*The marinade can also be used for fish steaks.*

1 cup (7 oz/220 g) uncooked short-grain rice

1¼ cups (10 fl oz/310 ml) water

⅔ cup (5 fl oz/160 ml) rice vinegar

2 teaspoons sugar

1 teaspoon salt

2 nori sheets, each 7 by 8 inches (18 by 20 cm), toasted*

3 tablespoons *each* finely julienned celery, carrot, cucumber, and green onion

## Marinade

2 teaspoons Asian (toasted) sesame oil

1 tablespoon minced shallot

1 teaspoon minced garlic

1 teaspoon packed brown sugar

2 tablespoons low-salt soy sauce

2 cups (16 fl oz/500 ml) water

2 teaspoons minced fresh ginger

1 teaspoon cornstarch, mixed with 1 tablespoon water

30 medium shrimp, shelled and deveined

Leaves from 1 head butter lettuce

Rinse the rice until the water runs clear; drain. In a medium saucepan, bring the 1¼ cups (10 fl oz/310 ml) water to a boil. Add the rice, cover, reduce heat to low, and cook for 15 minutes. Remove from heat and let sit for 20 minutes, or until the rice absorbs all the water.

In a small saucepan, combine the vinegar, sugar, and salt and bring to a boil; remove from heat and set aside until cool. Sprinkle the vinegar mixture over the rice until lightly coated.

Lay a nori sheet, shiny side down, on a sushi mat or bamboo place mat. Spread half the rice over the nori. On one long edge of the sheet, layer a strip of half the celery, carrot, cucumber, and green onion. Using the sushi mat to help, roll up the nori. Repeat with the remaining nori sheet, rice, and vegetables. Using a wet, sharp knife, cut each rice roll crosswise into eight 1-inch-thick (2.5-cm) sections.

To make the marinade: In a medium sauté pan or skillet over medium-low heat, heat the sesame oil and sauté the shallot and garlic for 2 minutes. Add the brown sugar and cook until melted. Stir in the soy sauce and water, then stir in the ginger and cornstarch mixture until blended and thickened. Remove from heat and let cool.

Lightly coat a medium sauté pan or skillet with vegetable oil spray. Place the pan over medium heat and sauté the shrimp until they are pink, about 4 minutes. Remove the shrimp from the pan. Add the marinade, bring to a boil, and cook until reduced by half.

Arrange 3 slices of the rice roll on each of 6 plates. Make a bed of lettuce leaves on each plate and place 5 shrimp on each. Pour a little of the reduced marinade over the shrimp and serve immediately.

*Makes 6 servings*

### PER SERVING

*Calories 190 • Carbohydrates 32 g • Cholesterol 45 mg • Fat 2.5 g • Protein 9 g • Sodium 620 mg*

---

*\*Nori are dark-colored sheets of dried seaweed. They are available in natural foods stores and Asian markets. To toast nori, pass the shiny side of the seaweed over an open gas flame several times until it crisps slightly and becomes fragrant.*

# Chicken Breasts with English Peas, French Style

Four 5-ounce (155-g) skinless, boneless chicken breasts

Pinch of dried thyme

1 tablespoon olive oil

2 slices Canadian bacon or turkey bacon, chopped

2 shallots, minced

2 garlic cloves, minced

2 tablespoons dry white wine

2 cups (16 fl oz/500 ml) chicken stock (see Basics)
   or canned low-salt chicken broth

4 ounces (125 g) pearl onions, peeled (about 20 onions)

1 small carrot, thinly sliced

2 pounds (2 kg) English peas, shelled (2 cups)

1 teaspoon butter

8 butter lettuce leaves

Pinch of sugar

Sprinkle the chicken with thyme. In a large sauté pan over medium heat, heat the olive oil and sauté the breasts until golden brown on both sides. Reduce heat to low and cook for a total of 10 minutes, turning once, or until the meat is springy to the touch; remove the breasts from the pan and set them aside.

In the same pan over medium heat, add the bacon, shallots, and garlic and cook for 5 minutes, or until the shallots are translucent. Stir in the wine and cook, stirring to scrape up any browned bits. Add the stock or broth and onions and bring to a boil. Reduce heat and simmer for 20 minutes, or until the onions are tender and the liquid is reduced by half. Add the carrot, peas, butter, lettuce, and sugar and cook for 10 minutes, or until the vegetables are crisp-tender. Arrange the chicken breasts on each of 4 plates. Top with the vegetables and sauce and serve.

*Makes 4 servings*

PER SERVING

*Calories 320 • Carbohydrates 19 g • Cholesterol 90 mg • Fat 9 g • Protein 37 g • Sodium 310 mg*

# Pineapple Parfait

¹/₄ cup (2 oz/60 g) sugar
1 tablespoon water
1 egg, separated
³/₄ cup (6 fl oz/180 ml) heavy cream
¹/₄ cup (2 oz/60 g) nonfat plain yogurt
³/₄ cup (4 oz/125 g) diced pineapple
¹/₂ teaspoon ground cinnamon

In a small, heavy saucepan, cook the sugar and water over medium heat, stirring occasionally, to the soft ball stage (when a small amount of syrup is dropped into cold water it will form a soft ball that flattens when picked up with the fingers). Remove from heat and set aside.

In an electric mixer, beat the egg yolk until pale. With the motor running, slowly pour in the sugar syrup in a thin stream. Continue beating until the egg yolk mixture forms a slowly dissolving ribbon when the beaters are lifted.

In an electric mixer, beat the egg white until stiff, glossy peaks form. With the motor running, pour the egg yolk mixture into the egg white and beat until a slowly dissolving ribbon forms when the beater is lifted. In a deep bowl, beat the cream until stiff peaks form. Fold the whipped cream, yogurt, pineapple, and cinnamon gently into the egg mixture until blended. Pour into 6 individual molds and refrigerate the parfaits for at least 2 hours.

*Makes 6 servings*

PER SERVING

*Calories 200 • Carbohydrates 21 g • Cholesterol 75 mg • Fat 12 g • Protein 2 g • Sodium 30 mg*

# MENU

*Shrimp in Kataifi with Artichoke Hearts and Ginger Vinaigrette*

❖

*Grilled-Vegetable Lasagnas*

❖

*Roasted Pear Elegante*

# Givenchy Hotel & Spa

### Palm Springs, California

*The Spa is a testament to the benefits of taking time out for a little unapologetic self-indulgence while luxuriating in an atmosphere of well-ordered tranquility.*

—Gourmet

## ❖ PROFILE ❖

A temple of aesthetics and a haven of serenity, this garden oasis in the desert community of Palm Springs offers the French beauty treatments, body care, personalized service, and superb cuisine of the original Givenchy Spa in Versailles. Its restorative programs emphasize mind and body harmony and can be personalized for any length of stay, even for day visitors. As *Condé Nast Traveler* puts it, "Forget calorie-counting and a strict regimen of strenuous activity. At Givenchy . . . the focus is on indulgence, not denial." On arrival, each guest is greeted personally by proprietor Rose Narva, whose contribution in restoring four historic hotels in Washington, D.C., has been recognized by the American Hotel Association and the AIA with a Certificate of Excellence. Givenchy Hotel & Spa was voted one of the 25 Coolest Places to Stay Now by *Condé Nast Traveler* in 1997.

## ❖ CUISINE ❖

*Gourmet* magazine found that at Givenchy, the "philosophy of pampering extends to one's taste buds as well." The food consists of calorie-conscious spa recipes *(cuisine légère),* plus Mediterranean-California indulgences with a light touch. Based on recipes created by chef Gerard Vie at the Michelin two-starred Trianon Palace Hotel at the original Givenchy Spa, these dishes are intended to refresh palates overwhelmed by too much rich, heavy, or unhealthy food. A cheerful cafe serves calorie- and fat-reduced breakfasts, lunches, and snacks, and a healthy menu is available from room service throughout the day. The evening meal, which is treated as a special event, is graciously served in the softly lighted, comfortable main dining room.

## ✤ SETTING ✤

A lushly landscaped hotel of French Renaissance design, Givenchy Hotel & Spa is set against the majestic backdrop of the San Jacinto Mountains and enjoys a desert climate. Its ninety-eight accommodations are individually decorated and designed for maximum peace, comfort, and privacy. Fine linens, marble bathrooms, and estate antiques add to the tone of European refinement, while a collection of vintage photographs recalls the hotel's beginnings as the "Autry," when it was owned by Gene Autry and frequented by the Hollywood stars of yesteryear. Givenchy's fourteen immaculately groomed acres contain formal gardens, rose and herb gardens, citrus groves, four swimming pools, a gazebo, and walking paths throughout. In the Main Pavilion, guests will find a large library stocked with books and games, and arrangements can be made for nearby hiking, horseback riding, canyon sightseeing, hot-air ballooning, and shopping excursions.

## ✤ ACTIVITIES, TREATMENTS, AND FACILITIES ✤

Whether for a weekend, a week or two, or just a day, programs at Givenchy are designed to soothe the spirit, rejuvenate the skin, and revitalize the body. The care treatments are classically European and feature Swisscare pour Givenchy beauty products. The state-of-the-art spa also offers a variety of therapeutic baths and massages, reflexology, facials, mud wraps, hydrating body wraps, seaweed "body masks," aromatherapy, aerobic and weight equipment, tai chi, yoga, six championship tennis courts, cycling, and an eighteen-hole golf course. The sleek spa building, with a pale stone and marble interior, houses private women's and men's facilities, each with its own sauna, steam room, whirlpool, and lap pool.

# Shrimp in Kataifi with Artichoke Hearts and Ginger Vinaigrette

1 cup (8 fl oz/250 ml) low-fat milk

2 eggs

8 large shrimp, peeled and deveined

2 cups (1½ oz/45 g) Kataifi*

Leaves from 1 head frisée lettuce (curly endive)

4 artichoke hearts, sliced

2 tomatoes, thinly sliced

Ginger Vinaigrette (recipe follows)

Preheat the oven to 375°F (190°C). Lightly coat a baking sheet with vegetable oil spray.

Pour the milk into a small bowl. In another small bowl, whisk the eggs together. Dip the shrimp in the milk and then in the beaten eggs.

Roll the shrimp in the kataifi until they are coated. Arrange the shrimp on the prepared pan and bake in the preheated oven for 10 minutes, or until golden brown.

Arrange the frisée on 4 plates and top each with 2 shrimp. Garnish with an artichoke heart and tomato slices and drizzle with 2 tablespoons ginger vinaigrette.

*Makes 4 servings*

PER SERVING (with 2 tablespoons vinaigrette)

*Calories 300 • Carbohydrates 35 g • Cholesterol 115 mg • Fat 13 g • Protein 12 g • Sodium 550 mg*

---

*\*Kataifi is shredded phyllo dough. It has no cholesterol or saturated fat and is available at specialty foods stores.*

## Ginger Vinaigrette

2 tablespoons minced, peeled fresh ginger

1 tablespoon fresh lemon juice

$1/2$ tablespoon Dijon mustard

1 tablespoon Asian (toasted) sesame oil

1 tablespoon grapeseed oil

1 tablespoon low-salt soy sauce

1 tablespoon honey

In a blender or food processor, combine the ginger and lemon juice and purée. Push through a fine-meshed sieve with the back of a large spoon.

In a small bowl, whisk the ginger purée, mustard, sesame oil, grapeseed oil, soy sauce, and honey together.

*Makes about $1/2$ cup (4 fl oz/125 ml)*

### PER TABLESPOON

*Calories 40 • Carbohydrates 3 g • Cholesterol 0 mg • Fat 3.5 g • Protein 0 g • Sodium 90 mg*

# Grilled-Vegetable Lasagnas

*These triangular individual lasagnas make a dramatic presentation.*

### Tomato Coulis

    2 tablespoons olive oil

    6 shallots, minced

    2 cups (16 fl oz/500 ml) chicken stock (see Basics)
      or canned low-salt chicken broth

    Leaves from 1/2 bunch fresh thyme, minced

    3 yellow tomatoes, seeded and chopped

    3 red tomatoes, seeded and chopped

    Salt and freshly ground pepper to taste

### Concassée

    2 tablespoons olive oil

    1 cup (5 oz/155 g) finely chopped onion

    3 garlic cloves, minced

    1 teaspoon tomato paste

    2 large tomatoes, peeled, seeded (see Basics), and finely diced

    Leaves from 1/2 small bunch *each* fresh thyme, basil,
      and tarragon, minced (reserve some sprigs for garnish)

    4 green zucchini

    4 yellow zucchini

    4 Japanese eggplants

    2 sheets fresh pasta

    1 cup (4 oz/125 g) shredded Gruyère cheese

To make the coulis: In a large sauté pan or skillet over medium heat, heat the olive oil and sauté the shallots for 3 minutes, or until translucent. Divide the shallots, stock or broth, and thyme between 2 medium saucepans. Add the yellow tomatoes to one saucepan and the red tomatoes to the other and simmer for 5 to 7 minutes. Remove from heat and season with salt and pepper, if desired. Strain through a fine-meshed sieve; set aside and keep warm.

To make the concassée: In a sauté pan or skillet over medium heat, heat the olive oil and sauté the onion for 5 minutes, or until soft; add the garlic and sauté for 1 minute. Stir in the tomato paste and diced tomatoes and simmer for 10 minutes. Stir in the minced herbs, salt, and pepper, and simmer for 5 minutes. Set aside to cool.

Light a fire in a charcoal grill, preheat a gas grill, or heat a grill pan over medium-high heat. Cut the zucchini and eggplants lengthwise into six $1/8$-inch-thick (3-mm) slices, brush or spray with olive oil, and season with salt and pepper. Grill for about 1 minute on each side, or until just tender. Remove from heat and let cool.

Preheat the oven to 350°F (180°C). Lightly coat a baking sheet with vegetable oil spray.

Cut the sheets of pasta into triangles, about 3 inches (7.5 cm) on each side. You will need 18 triangles. Cook the pasta in a large pot of salted boiling water until al dente; drain. Lay 6 pasta triangles on the prepared baking sheet and spoon $1/2$ tablespoon concassée in the center of each. Fold or cut 6 pieces of eggplant in two and place on top of each triangle. Lay a pasta triangle on top of the eggplant slices and spoon more concassée on top. Arrange a slice of green and yellow zucchini on top of this and place one more pasta triangle on top. Press the individual lasagnas down and sprinkle with Gruyère cheese. Bake in the preheated oven for 10 minutes, or until the cheese melts.

To serve, ladle the yellow tomato coulis onto one side of 6 plates and the red tomato coulis onto the other sides. Place the lasagna triangles in the center of each plate and garnish with fresh herb sprigs.

*Makes 6 servings*

PER SERVING

*Calories 340 • Carbohydrates 38 g • Cholesterol 40 mg • Fat 17 g • Protein 14 g • Sodium 115 mg*

# Roasted Pear Elegante

**4 Bosc pears**
**1 cup (7 oz/220 g) packed brown sugar**
**1 unpeeled Granny Smith apple, cored**
**1/2 cup (2 oz/60 g) powdered sugar**
**1/2 cup (4 oz/125 g) plus 1 teaspoon granulated sugar**
**2 ripe bananas, mashed**
**1 cup (8 fl oz/250 ml) pastry cream (see Basics)**
**2 cups (8 oz/250 g) fresh or thawed frozen raspberries**
**1/4 cup (1 oz/30 g) pistachios, chopped, for garnish (optional)**

Preheat the oven to 350°F (180°C). Lightly coat a baking sheet with vegetable oil spray. Peel the pears and coat them lightly with vegetable oil spray. Lightly roll each pear in the brown sugar and arrange them on a baking sheet. Bake in the preheated oven for 40 minutes. Let cool, then refrigerate for at least 2 hours. Core the pears and cut a thin slice from the bottom of each to allow them to stand upright.

Preheat the oven to 210°F (99°C). Slice the apple paper-thin. Lay the slices on a baking sheet and sprinkle with the powdered sugar. Bake in the preheated oven for 1 hour, or until crisp.

In a heavy, medium saucepan, cook the 1/2 cup (4 oz/125 g) granulated sugar over medium heat until the sugar turns a light caramel brown. Remove from heat and stir in the banana. Let cool and blend in the pastry cream. In a blender or food processor, purée the raspberries and 1 teaspoon sugar.

To assemble: With a pastry bag, fill the cored pears with the banana mousse. Set a pear in the center of each of 4 dessert plates and pipe rosettes of banana mousse at 10, 2, and 6 o'clock. Decorate with dried apple slices standing upright in the mousse and pour some raspberry coulis around the pears.

*Makes 4 servings*

PER SERVING

*Calories 400 • Carbohydrates 89 g • Cholesterol 35 mg • Fat 6 g • Protein 4 g • Sodium 25 mg*

# MENU

*BREAKFAST*

**Butternut Squash–Cranberry Bread with Yogurt Cheese**

*LUNCH*

**Grilled Portobello Mushrooms with Couscous,
Two-Pepper Coulis, and Grilled Asparagus**

*DINNER*

**Watermelon Gazpacho with Cucumber**

❖

**Grilled Swordfish with Papaya-Kiwi Salsa**

❖

**Quinoa with Parsley**

❖

**Oatmeal Cookies and Mango-Banana Sorbet**

# Golden Door

*You arrive at the Golden Door on Sunday night weary and overstressed.*
*You emerge on the following Sunday as though from a chrysalis:*
*leaner, fitter, ready to conquer the world.*

—**Tatler**

## ❖ PROFILE ❖

For four decades, the Golden Door has delighted guests with its legendary service, beautiful grounds, perfect year-round climate, and an approach to fitness that still sets standards worldwide. Founded by Deborah Szekely (who with her husband, Edmond Szekely, launched the North American fitness spa movement at Mexico's Rancho La Puerta in 1940—see pages 202 to 216), the Golden Door emphasizes wellness, nature, exercise, and spirituality. Its week-long program shapes the body, soothes the mind, and replenishes the soul. The serenity and intimacy of the place—there is a maximum of thirty-nine guests—results in a strong sense of camaraderie that brings people back again and again, yet there's peace and privacy for those who wish it. At this highly rated spa, all needs are anticipated, and the knowledgeable staff outnumbers guests by four to one.

## ❖ CUISINE ❖

An early trendsetter in light gourmet cuisine, the Golden Door serves superb meals, artistically presented: a blend of nouvelle California and Asian foods that feature freshly picked organic fruits and vegetables and free-range chicken. Lunch is served poolside. Before dinner, a seventeenth-century Buddhist bell chimes, and guests gather in the lounge for light hors d'oeuvres and non-alcoholic cocktails. Michel Stroot, the Golden Door's chef since 1974, also teaches Conscious Cooking: nutrition basics and healthy preparation techniques. At the conclusion of class, students savor oatmeal cookies hot from the oven (recipe on page 99).

## ❖ SETTING ❖

Located in a coastal valley thirty miles north of San Diego, the Golden Door is built in the style of an ancient Japanese country inn. Its jeweled entry—literally, a golden door—opens onto the spa's serene grounds, a series of courtyards connected by walkways and filled with waterfalls, streams, rustic wooden bridges, koi ponds, contemplative sand gardens, and Japanese statuary. Within the tile-roofed buildings, thirty-nine luxurious private rooms (a room for each person—even those traveling as a couple) feature shoji screens, decks, and private Japanese gardens. The entire setting is imbued with a calm atmosphere that encourages meditation and introspection—instead of a television in your bedroom, you'll find books, flowers, artwork, and antiques—and the 377-acre property is planted with citrus orchards and live oaks.

## ❖ ACTIVITIES, TREATMENTS, AND FACILITIES ❖

The week-long Golden Door program begins even before you get to the spa: expected guests are sent a cassette of daily stretches so they can start immediately! Once you arrive, a personal exercise specialist will be assigned to help you create a custom schedule, chart your progress, make sure your goals and wishes are met, and put together a take-home fitness program. Because the Golden Door equates good health with the great outdoors, a part of each day is spent in the fresh air. Early morning hikes wind upward through mountain lavender and avocado groves to breathtaking views, and are rewarded by breakfast in bed. Afterward, you will alternate vigorous activity with utter relaxation, following fitness classes (rollerblading, country line dancing, aqua aerobics, tai chi, Pilates exercises, yoga) with the Golden Door's legendary pampering. Guests enjoy daily massages, botanical body scrubs, herbal mud wraps, mineral masks, aromatherapy, and classes on nutrition, stress management, and self-development. The facilities include five gyms, Cybex weights, two pools, two tennis courts, a labyrinth, and a bath house with whirlpool baths, a steam room, and a sauna. The programs are Sunday to Sunday and are for women only, with occasional weeks for men only or coed attendance.

# Butternut Squash–Cranberry Bread with Yogurt Cheese

*This moist, sweet bread also makes a delicious dessert.*

1$\frac{1}{2}$ cups (7$\frac{1}{2}$ oz/235 g) unbleached all-purpose flour

1 cup (5 oz/155 g) whole-wheat flour

1 teaspoon baking powder

$\frac{1}{2}$ teaspoon baking soda

$\frac{1}{2}$ teaspoon salt

2 teaspoons ground cinnamon

1 cup (8 oz/250 g) butternut squash or pumpkin purée (see Basics)

$\frac{1}{2}$ cup (3$\frac{1}{2}$ oz/105 g) packed light brown sugar

$\frac{1}{2}$ cup (4 oz/125 g) plain nonfat yogurt or buttermilk

$\frac{1}{4}$ cup (2 fl oz/60 ml) frozen orange juice concentrate, thawed

1 egg, lightly beaten

1 tablespoon grated orange zest (see Basics)

1 tablespoon canola oil

$\frac{3}{4}$ cup (3 oz/90 g) dried cranberries

1 cup (8 oz/250 g) Yogurt Cheese (recipe follows)

Lightly coat an 8$\frac{1}{2}$-by-4$\frac{1}{2}$-inch (21.5-by-10-cm) loaf pan with vegetable oil spray. In a large bowl, mix together the flours, baking powder, baking soda, salt, and cinnamon. In a blender or food processor, combine the squash or pumpkin purée, brown sugar, yogurt or buttermilk, orange juice concentrate, egg, orange zest, and canola oil and process until smooth.

Make a well in the center of the flour mixture and add the squash or pumpkin mixture. Stir just until blended; do not overmix. Stir in the cranberries and scrape the batter into the prepared loaf pan. Bake in the preheated oven for 50 minutes, or until a toothpick inserted in the center comes out clean. Let cool in the pan for about 5 minutes; turn out onto a wire rack and let cool completely. Cut into thin slices to serve. Accompany with yogurt cheese.

*Makes 1 loaf; about 16 slices*

PER SLICE (without yogurt cheese)

*Calories 140 • Carbohydrates 28 g • Cholesterol 15 mg • Fat 1.5 g • Protein 3 g • Sodium 140 mg*

## Yogurt Cheese

*An easy-to-make nonfat replacement for cream cheese to spread on bread or bagels. To use yogurt cheese as a replacement for sour cream in spreads or as a topping for baked potatoes, simply omit the powdered sugar and vanilla. Make the night before if you will be serving it for breakfast.*

> **4 cups (32 oz/1 l) plain nonfat natural yogurt\***
> **4 tablespoons powdered sugar, sifted**
> **2 teaspoons vanilla extract**

In a large bowl, whisk together all the ingredients.

Line a colander or strainer with a double thickness of cheesecloth or a large coffee filter and set the colander over a bowl. Spoon the yogurt mixture into the colander and refrigerate for at least 8 hours, or overnight, so that the yogurt drains.

Spoon the yogurt cheese into a bowl, cover, and refrigerate until ready to use.

*Makes about 1 cup (8 oz/250 g)*

### PER TABLESPOON

*Calories 40 • Carbohydrates 6 g • Cholesterol 0 mg • Fat 0 g • Protein 4 g • Sodium 45 mg*

---

*\*Don't use yogurt that has been thickened with gelatins or gums.*

# Grilled Portobello Mushrooms with Couscous, Two-Pepper Coulis, and Grilled Asparagus

*Golden Door chef Michel Stroot makes the most of fresh mushrooms because they lend flavor and body without fat or a lot of calories. Instead of couscous, you may substitute basmati rice, pasta, or another grain of your choice.*

2 tablespoons olive oil

2 teaspoons fresh lemon juice

4 large portobello mushrooms, stemmed

$^1/_2$ teaspoon freshly ground pepper

4 teaspoons balsamic vinegar

$^3/_4$ cup (6 fl oz/185 ml) vegetable stock (see Basics),
    canned low-salt vegetable broth, or water, plus more as needed

$^1/_2$ cup ($3^1/_2$ oz/105 g) couscous

1 tablespoon minced fresh flat-leaf parsley

1 tablespoon chopped fresh basil or green onion

Sixteen 2-inch (5-cm) asparagus tips, blanched

2 cups (16 fl oz/500 ml) Two-Pepper Coulis (recipe follows)

Prepare a fire in a charcoal grill (coat the cooking rack with vegetable oil spray away from the fire) or heat a stove-top grill pan that has been coated with vegetable oil spray. Preheat the oven to 300°F (150°C).

In a small bowl, whisk together the olive oil and lemon juice to make a vinaigrette. Brush the vinaigrette over the tops of the mushroom caps. Grill, smooth side down, for 3 to 4 minutes, or until the mushrooms are limp and begin to release their juices; turn halfway through to make square or diamond grill marks. Sprinkle the pepper over the insides of the mushroom caps and transfer them, smooth side down, to a shallow baking pan.

Drizzle the balsamic vinegar over the inside of each mushroom cap. Add $^1/_4$ cup (2 fl oz/60 ml) of the stock, broth, or water to the baking pan and cover it with aluminum foil. Keep warm in the preheated oven for up to 10 minutes.

Meanwhile, in a medium saucepan, bring the remaining $^1/_2$ cup (4 fl oz/125 ml) stock, broth, or water to a boil. Add the couscous to a medium bowl and pour the hot liquid over it. Cover and let stand for 5 minutes. Fluff with a fork and fold in the parsley and basil or green onion. Add more liquid if the couscous seems too dry.

Place the asparagus tips in a grill basket and grill, or cook in the hot grill pan, just until lightly browned.

Place a grilled mushroom cap, smooth side down, on each of 4 warmed plates. Mound the couscous on top of the mushrooms. Ladle the pepper coulis around the mushrooms and arrange the asparagus on top of the coulis.

*Makes 4 servings*

PER SERVING

*Calories 240 • Carbohydrates 34 g • Cholesterol 0 mg • Fat 10 g • Protein 8 g • Sodium 15 mg*

## Two-Pepper Coulis

*A delicious way to add color, moisture, texture, and flavor to a number of dishes.*

> 2 red bell peppers, roasted (see Basics), peeled, seeded, and chopped
>
> 2 teaspoons olive oil
>
> 2 pinches of cayenne pepper
>
> 2 tablespoons water, plus more as needed
>
> 2 yellow bell peppers, roasted (see Basics), peeled, seeded, and chopped

In a blender or food processor, combine the red peppers, 1 teaspoon of the olive oil, 1 pinch of cayenne, and 1 tablespoon of the water. Process until smooth. If necessary, add more water to make a smooth consistency. Transfer to a small bowl and set aside.

Rinse the blender or food processor thoroughly. In the clean blender or food processor, combine the yellow peppers with the remaining olive oil, cayenne, and 1 tablespoon water. Process until smooth. If necessary, add more water to make a smooth consistency. Transfer to a small bowl.

Serve the red and yellow pepper coulis separately, or side by side.

*Makes about 2 cups (16 fl oz/500 ml)*

PER $^{1}/_{2}$ CUP (4 fl oz/125 ml)

*Calories 60 • Carbohydrates 10 g • Cholesterol 0 mg • Fat 2.5 g • Protein 1 g • Sodium 0 mg*

# Watermelon Gazpacho with Cucumber

*Watermelon makes an interesting variation on traditional tomato-based gazpacho. Prepare this soup at least 2 hours before serving.*

1 cup (2¹/₂ oz/75 g) thinly sliced peeled and seeded cucumbers

¹/₄ teaspoon salt

6 cups (4 oz/125 g) seeded cubed watermelon
(from about 2¹/₂ lb/1.25 kg melon)

¹/₂ cup (4 fl oz/125 ml) cranberry juice cocktail

1 red bell pepper, seeded, deribbed, and finely chopped

1 red onion, finely chopped

1 celery stalk, finely diced

¹/₄ cup (¹/₃ oz/10 g) minced fresh flat-leaf parsley

2 to 3 tablespoons fresh lime juice

1 tablespoon sherry vinegar

8 fresh mint leaves for garnish

In a small bowl, toss the cucumbers and salt together. Set aside.

In a blender or food processor, combine the watermelon and cranberry juice and process briefly, just until blended. (Overprocessing will make the juice frothy and pale.) Pour through a fine-meshed sieve set over a bowl, and press the pulp with the back of a large spoon to extract all the juice; discard the pulp.

Stir the bell pepper, red onion, celery, parsley, lime juice, and vinegar into the watermelon juice. Cover and refrigerate for at least 2 hours.

Rinse the cucumbers and pat dry with a paper towel.

Ladle the soup into 8 chilled bowls and garnish with the cucumber slices and mint leaves.

*Makes 8 servings*

### PER SERVING

*Calories 60 • Carbohydrates 14 g • Cholesterol 0 mg • Fat 0.5 g • Protein 1 g • Sodium 45 mg*

# Grilled Swordfish with Papaya-Kiwi Salsa

*Make the salsa at least an hour before cooking the fish.*

*Papaya-Kiwi Salsa*
>1 cup (8 oz/250 g) diced papaya
>
>1 kiwi, peeled and diced
>
>2 tablespoons minced green onion
>
>1/4 cup (2 fl oz/60 ml) fresh orange juice
>
>1 tablespoon fresh lime juice
>
>2 tablespoons chopped fresh cilantro
>
>2 to 3 drops hot pepper sauce
>
>Four 4-ounce (125-g) swordfish steaks or other firm white fish,
>    cut 1/2 inch (12 mm) thick

To make the salsa: In a medium bowl, mix all the ingredients together. Cover and refrigerate for at least 1 hour.

Meanwhile, light a fire in a charcoal grill or preheat the broiler. Coat the cooking rack with vegetable oil spray away from the flame and grill or broil the swordfish for about 3 minutes on each side, or until opaque throughout, turning to make diamond or square grill marks.

Serve the fish with the papaya-kiwi salsa on the side.

*Makes 4 servings*

PER SERVING

*Calories 170 • Carbohydrates 8 g • Cholesterol 45 mg • Fat 4.5 g • Protein 23 g • Sodium 105 mg*

# Quinoa with Parsley

*Quinoa (pronounced* keen-wah*) is a mild-tasting alternative to rice and other grains. It is a good source of protein, calcium, and the amino acid lysine.*

1<sup>1</sup>/2 cups (12 fl oz/375 ml) vegetable stock (see Basics),
   canned low-salt vegetable broth, or water

<sup>1</sup>/2 teaspoon salt (optional)

<sup>3</sup>/4 cup (4<sup>3</sup>/4 oz/135 g) quinoa, rinsed and drained

1 bay leaf

<sup>1</sup>/3 cup (1 oz/30 g) minced fresh flat-leaf parsley

In a medium saucepan, bring the stock, broth, or water to a boil. Add the salt, if using, quinoa, and bay leaf. Reduce heat to low, cover, and simmer for 20 minutes. Remove from heat and let stand for 10 minutes. Remove the bay leaf. Add the parsley and fluff the quinoa with a fork. Serve warm.

*Makes 4 servings*

## PER SERVING

*Calories 130 • Carbohydrates 22 g • Cholesterol 0 mg • Fat 2 g • Protein 5 g • Sodium 20 mg*

# Oatmeal Cookies

*These cookies are very popular with Golden Door guests. For best results, be sure the eggs are at room temperature.*

2 eggs at room temperature

3 egg whites at room temperature

1 teaspoon vanilla extract

1 teaspoon ground cinammon

$^1/_2$ teaspoon salt

1 teaspoon baking powder

$^1/_2$ cup (4 oz/125 g) granulated sugar

$^1/_4$ cup (2 oz/60 g) packed light brown sugar

$2^3/_4$ cups (8 oz/250 g) old-fashioned rolled oats

$^1/_3$ cup (2 oz/60 g) whole-wheat flour

Preheat the oven to 350°F (180°C). Lightly coat 2 baking sheets with vegetable oil spray.

In a large bowl, beat the eggs, egg whites, vanilla, cinnamon, salt, baking powder, granulated sugar, and brown sugar together. Continue beating at high speed until the mixture doubles in volume and forms a slowly dissolving ribbon on its surface when the beaters are raised. Fold in the oats and flour.

Drop tablespoon-size mounds of dough onto the prepared pans, leaving about 1 inch (2.5 cm) between each. Bake in the preheated oven for 15 to 20 minutes, or until lightly browned. Immediately transfer the cookies to wire racks to cool slightly. Serve warm.

*Makes 36 cookies*

### PER COOKIE

*Calories 50 • Carbohydrates 9 g • Cholesterol 10 mg • Fat 0.5 g • Protein 2 g • Sodium 50 mg*

# Mango-Banana Sorbet

*Mango and banana blend together to make a sweet, rich sorbet. Before serving, let the sorbet sit at room temperature until slightly soft. You can substitute 2 peeled and pitted peaches for the mango.*

- 1 mango, peeled, cut from the pit, and chopped
- 1 banana, sliced
- 2½ cups (20 fl oz/625 ml) fresh orange juice (5 to 7 oranges)
- 1 tablespoon fresh lime juice
- 2 to 3 tablespoons honey

In a blender or food processor, combine all the ingredients and process until smooth. Transfer to an ice cream maker and freeze according to the manufacturer's directions. To serve, spoon the sorbet into chilled bowls.

*Makes 8 servings*

### PER SERVING

*Calories 80 • Carbohydrates 20 g • Cholesterol 0 mg • Fat 0 g • Protein 1 g • Sodium 0 mg*

# Grand Wailea Resort
## Spa Grande
### Maui, Hawaii

*It is our desire that our guests will immerse themselves in our "detached world"
body and soul, and return home having had the experience of their lives.*
— *Grand Wailea management*

### ❖ PROFILE ❖

Located on the southwest shore of Maui, Spa Grande at Grand Wailea Resort is Hawaii's largest spa, a beautifully appointed 50,000-square-foot complex with separate women's and men's facilities. The spa combines traditional Hawaiian healing and beauty techniques with the finest European, Indian, American, and Asian therapies for rejuvenation. With an emphasis more on relaxation than strict weight-loss regimens, its mission is to ensure that each guest attains an optimum feeling of fitness, a sense of well-being, and a renewed enthusiasm for life. To this end, Spa Grande brings together lush surroundings, state-of-the-art exercise equipment, a friendly and professional staff, and an inspirational beachfront location. A special day camp for children is also provided—with its own restaurant, theater, crafts, and games room—so parents can enjoy the spa worry-free.

### ❖ CUISINE ❖

Spa Grande offers private consultations on nutrition and diet, and the resort itself features many dining options, from delicious low-cal to vacation-time indulgence. The spa breakfast buffet typically consists of an egg-white omelet, tropical fruits, and variety of cereals. At lunch, Cafe Kula specializes in spa nouvelle cuisine, made with fresh organic produce delivered daily from local farmers. These menus are high in nutrients and low in fat, with an emphasis on presentation. For dinner, there are six restaurants to choose from, including Japanese, Polynesian, and country-style Italian.

## ❖ SETTING ❖

Grand Wailea stands on forty magnificent acres sloping gently toward beautiful Wailea Beach. Noted for its masses of bougainvillea, enormous bronze nudes by sculptor Fernando Botero, and spectacular sunsets, the resort contains fifty-three suites and 735 extra-large guest rooms with ocean and garden views. Many of its tapestries, mosaics, sculptures, and other artworks were created by island artists to reflect Hawaiian culture and are displayed side by side with works by Picasso, Léger, and Warhol. Making full use of its location, the resort offers scuba lessons, tennis courts, and three 18-hole golf courses, and has a sixty-foot catamaran in which guests can take a picnic/snorkeling sail, a romantic sunset cruise, or a whale-watching cruise. The grounds of the resort are filled with flowers, pools, and waterfalls.

## ❖ ACTIVITIES, TREATMENTS, AND FACILITIES ❖

All Spa Grande visitors begin with the Termé Wailea Hydrotherapy Circuit, consisting of a steam, sauna, cool plunge, loofah scrub, waterfall shower, and specialty bath (choose among moor mud, seaweed, enzyme, and aromatherapy). Once you've experienced this ultimate exercise in relaxation, you can go on to whatever fitness class or beauty treatment awaits you at this full-service spa. *Town & Country* recommends the Canyon Water Exercise Challenge in the recreation pool, which has rope swings and water slides. Or perhaps you would benefit from one of the unique island beauty treatments, such as a Royal Hawaiian Facial, ti leaf body wrap, or nourishing scalp treatment with kelp, kuki nut, and other native plants. Many of the guests at Spa Grande are day-users enjoying a few treatments and fitness classes, but there are also specially tailored four- and seven-day programs for destination spa-goers.

# MENU

*BREAKFAST*

**Tofu-and-Vegetable Hash**

*LUNCH*

**Spicy Black Bean Salad in Papayas**

*DINNER*

**Ahi Tuna Napoleon with Sake-Lime Vinaigrette**

❖

**Chicken and Feta Roulades with Red Lentil Ragout**

❖

**Apple Crisp**

# Tofu-and-Vegetable Hash

1 pound (500 g) low-fat firm tofu, cut into ³/₄-inch (2-cm) cubes

³/₄ cup (6 fl oz/185 ml) low-salt soy sauce

2 small new potatoes, peeled and cut into ³/₄-inch (2-cm) cubes

¹/₄ cup (2 fl oz/60 ml) canola oil

1 *each* red and green bell pepper, seeded, deribbed,
  and cut into ³/₄-inch (2-cm) cubes

1 small white onion, cut into ³/₄-inch (2-cm) cubes

1 cup julienned celery (4 oz/125 g)

8 button mushrooms, quartered

¹/₂ tablespoon *each* minced fresh thyme, rosemary, and basil

4 cups (4 oz/125 g) packed fresh spinach leaves

Salt and freshly ground pepper to taste

4 poached eggs (optional)

Diced tomato and minced fresh parsley for garnish

Preheat the oven to 325°F (165°C). In a small bowl, gently combine the tofu and soy sauce; set aside for 5 minutes. Using a slotted spoon, remove the tofu cubes and drain them on paper towels. Place the tofu on a baking pan and bake in the preheated oven for 15 minutes. (This removes the excess liquid and firms up the tofu.) Set aside at room temperature until needed.

In a saucepan of boiling water, cook the potato cubes for 5 minutes. Using a slotted spoon, remove the potato and dry on paper towels. In a large sauté pan or skillet over medium-high heat, heat the canola oil and sauté all the vegetables and herbs, except the spinach, until the vegetables are crisp-tender and the edges are starting to brown. Add the tofu and spinach and gently sauté without breaking up the tofu cubes. When the mixture is hot, remove from heat and divide among 4 plates. Season with salt and pepper and top with a poached egg, if desired. Garnish with diced tomato and parsley and serve immediately.

*Makes 4 servings*

PER SERVING

*Calories 350 • Carbohydrates 18 g • Cholesterol 0 mg • Fat 24 g • Protein 21 g • Sodium 600 mg*

# Spicy Black Bean Salad in Papayas

4 cups (28 oz/875 g) cooked black beans

2 large red tomatoes, diced

2 large yellow tomatoes, diced

2 bunches cilantro, stemmed and coarsely chopped

2 tablespoons Vietnamese chili paste or minced jalapeño chili

1/4 cup (2 fl oz/60 ml) balsamic vinegar

2 tablespoons olive oil

4 ripe papayas

In a large bowl, combine the black beans, red and yellow tomatoes, cilantro, chili paste or jalapeño, balsamic vinegar, and olive oil.

Cut the papayas in half and scoop out the seeds. Scoop mounds of the bean salad into each papaya half and serve.

*Makes 4 servings*

### PER SERVING

*Calories 460 • Carbohydrates 82 g • Cholesterol 0 mg • Fat 9 g • Protein 19 g • Sodium 250 mg*

# Ahi Tuna Napoleon with Sake-Lime Vinaigrette

2 nori sheets (dried seaweed), each 7 by 8 inches (18 by 20 cm)

Four 2-ounce (60-g) ahi tuna steaks, each about 3 by 5 inches (7.5 by 12.5 cm)

Pineapple Risotto (recipe follows)

12 leaves Belgian endive

4 handfuls mixed salad greens

12 lime wedges

2 teaspoons grated lime zest (see Basics)

1/4 cup (2 fl oz/60 ml) Sake-Lime Vinaigrette (recipe on page 108)

Cut the nori into four 3-by-5-inch (7.5-by-12.5-cm) strips. Cut the remaining nori into four 2-by-8-inch (5-by-20-cm) strips. Cut each piece of ahi into 4 horizontal slices about 1/8 inch (3 mm) thick. On a work surface, place 4 slices of ahi tuna down and press 1/4 cup (1 1/2 oz/45 g) pineapple risotto evenly over each slice. Top the risotto with a 3-by-5-inch (7.5-by-12.5-cm) nori sheet. Place a second slice of ahi over each piece of nori. Evenly press another 1/4 cup (1 1/2 oz/45 g) risotto over the top and add another 3-by-5-inch (7.5-by-12.5-cm) nori sheet. Place the third slice of ahi over the nori and spread evenly with the remaining risotto. Top with the fourth slice of ahi.

Wrap the four 2-by-8-inch (5-by-20-cm) nori strips around the outer rim of napoleon and moisten the edges with water; press to seal. Using a wet, sharp knife, cut each napoleon in half. Wet the knife once more and cut each piece in half diagonally. To serve: Fan out the endive on 2 plates. Place a mound of baby greens in the center of each plate over the endive. Arrange 4 slices of each napoleon and 3 lime wedges on each plate. Sprinkle with lime zest and drizzle with the vinaigrette.

*Makes 4 servings*

PER SERVING

*Calories 310 • Carbohydrates 51 g • Cholesterol 25 mg • Fat 3 g • Protein 19 g • Sodium 55 mg*

## Pineapple Risotto

1 teaspoon olive oil

2 tablespoons finely diced onion

1 cup (7 oz/220 g) Arborio rice

2 cups (16 fl oz/500 ml) chicken stock (see Basics)
   or canned low-salt chicken broth, heated

Four ¼-inch-thick (6-mm) slices fresh pineapple

In a saucepan over medium-low heat, heat the olive oil and sauté the onion for 5 to 7 minutes, or until golden. Add the rice and stir for about 1 minute, or until opaque. Pour in the hot stock or broth and bring to a boil. Reduce heat and simmer, stirring constantly, for about 15 minutes, or until the rice is al dente.

Meanwhile, heat a nonstick sauté pan over high heat. Cook the pineapple slices for 3 to 5 minutes on each side, or until lightly browned. Remove from heat, let cool slightly, and dice the pineapple.

Add the pineapple and any drippings to the risotto and cook over medium-low heat for 2 minutes, stirring constantly. Serve immediately.

*Makes 4 servings*

PER SERVING

*Calories 220 • Carbohydrates 44 g • Cholesterol 0 mg • Fat 2 g • Protein 5 g • Sodium 20 mg*

## Sake-Lime Vinaigrette

One 1-inch (2.5-cm) piece of fresh ginger, peeled

2 tablespoons sake

1 tablespoon rice wine vinegar

2 tablespoons sugar

2 tablespoons fresh lime juice

2 tablespoons Thai chili sauce*

1 tablespoon mirin (sweet rice wine) or dry sherry

2 teaspoons canola oil

Grate the ginger into a piece of cheesecloth and twist to squeeze out 2 teaspoons juice.

In a small bowl, whisk the ginger juice and all the remaining ingredients together until blended. Store in an airtight container in the refrigerator for up to 3 days.

*Makes about 1 cup (8 fl oz/250 ml)*

### PER TABLESPOON

*Calories 20 • Carbohydrates 3 g • Cholesterol 0 mg • Fat 0.5 g • Protein 0 g • Sodium 0 mg*

*\*Thai chili sauce can be found in specialty foods stores, Asian markets, and some grocery stores.*

# Chicken and Feta Roulades with Red Lentil Ragout

## Red Lentil Ragout

6 cups (48 fl oz/1.5 l) chicken stock (see Basics)
  or canned low-salt chicken broth

1 cup dried red lentils, preferably Red Chief brand,
  rinsed and drained

1 tablespoon canola oil

$1/2$ cup ($2^1/2$ oz/75 g) julienned red bell pepper

2 ounces (60 g) shiitake mushrooms, stemmed and sliced

$1/4$ cup ($1^1/2$ oz/45 g) finely diced onion

$1/4$ cup ($1^1/2$ oz/45 g) finely diced carrot

1 tablespoon minced garlic

16 pohole fern tops (fiddlehead ferns), chopped (optional)

1 teaspoon minced fresh tarragon

$1/4$ cup (2 fl oz/60 ml) dry white wine

Salt and freshly ground pepper to taste

## Chicken and Feta Roulades

16 fresh spinach leaves

4 ounces (30 g) feta cheese, cut into four 5-by-$1/2$-inch
  (12.5-cm-by-12-mm) rectangles

4 skinless, boneless chicken breast halves, 6 ounces (180 g) each,
  pounded very thin

1 tablespoon olive oil

To make the ragout: In a medium saucepan, heat 3 cups (24 fl oz/750 ml) of the chicken stock or broth. Add the lentils to the hot stock or broth and bring to a boil. Reduce heat to low and simmer for 15 minutes, or until the lentils are just tender. Drain and set aside.

In a large sauté pan or skillet over medium heat, heat the canola oil and sauté the bell pepper, mushrooms, onion, carrot, garlic, and pohole ferns, if using, for 5 minutes. Stir in the tarragon, wine, salt, and pepper and cook for 10 minutes. Raise heat to high, add the lentils and the remaining stock or broth. Bring to a boil and reduce the liquid by half. Set aside and keep warm.

To make the roulades: Preheat the oven to 350°F (180°C). Wrap the spinach leaves around each piece of feta. Place a wrapped feta piece on the short end of each piece of pounded chicken, fold the sides over, and roll tightly. Using pieces of cotton string, tie the roulades tight. In a large sauté pan or skillet over high heat, heat the olive oil and cook the chicken until browned on all sides; remove from heat and set aside. Bake the chicken and feta roulades in the preheated oven for 10 minutes. Cut each roulade in half, then cut in half again on the bias.

To serve: Divide the lentil ragout evenly among 4 shallow soup bowls. Place 4 bias-cut chicken and feta roulades in the center of each bowl.

*Makes 4 servings*

PER SERVING

*Calories 500 • Carbohydrates 36 g • Cholesterol 100 mg • Fat 17 g • Protein 47 g • Sodium 490 mg*

# Apple Crisp

3 Granny Smith apples, peeled, cored, and sliced into $1/8$-inch (3-mm) slices
$1^1/_2$ cups ($14^1/_2$ oz/445 g) applesauce
1 tablespoon vanilla extract
1 tablespoon Calvados
1 teaspoon ground cinnamon
$1/_2$ teaspoon ground nutmeg
3 tablespoons dried currants plumped in apple juice to cover for 15 minutes
4 tablespoons low-fat or nonfat granola for topping
4 scoops low-fat vanilla ice cream for topping

Preheat the oven to 350°F (180°C).

In a medium saucepan, combine the apples, applesauce, vanilla, Calvados, cinnamon, nutmeg, and currants. Spoon the apple mixture into four 1-cup (8-oz/250-ml) ramekins or bowls. Bake in the preheated oven for about 20 minutes, or until the apples are tender. Sprinkle each with 1 tablespoon granola and top with a scoop of low-fat vanilla ice cream.

*Makes 4 servings*

### PER SERVING
*Calories 230 • Carbohydrates 50 g • Cholesterol 5 mg • Fat 2 g • Protein 3 g • Sodium 40 mg*

# MENU

## BREAKFAST

*Fluffy Spinach and Sweet Pepper Omelette*

*Apple-Carrot Muffins*

## LUNCH

*Chicken Tandoori with Stir-Fried Vegetables*

*Strawberry-Tofu Sherbet*

## DINNER

*Hearts of Lettuce with Sherry Dressing and Jicama Slaw*

*Poached Sea Bass with Salmon Mousseline*

*Pear-Polenta Soufflés*

# The Greenhouse

Arlington, Texas

*The women here, under expert care,*
*bloom like hothouse flowers.*

—Harper's Bazaar

## ❖ PROFILE ❖

*Travel & Leisure* calls The Greenhouse "the ultimate in gracious Southern ladies' spas," and *Town & Country* says that it is "the epitome of Southern charm." Set in a Texas mansion, the spa is an intimate oasis of tranquility that is run with every efficiency and courtesy. The Greenhouse provides a luxurious and serene environment exclusively for women, with the motivating idea that these givers and nurterers need some stress-free time off to be nurtured themselves. Listed in the Reader's Choice Top 10 Spas by *Condé Nast Traveler*, the spa limits its guest list to just thirty-nine women a week (Sunday to Sunday), in order to offer them the ultimate in personal attention, privacy, and individual care.

## ❖ CUISINE ❖

The superb spa cuisine at The Greenhouse is overseen by chef Leopoldo Gonzalez. Called "haute wholesome" by *Condé Nast Traveler*, the food is repeatedly rated Best Spa Cuisine by the magazine's readers. As a guest, you will select your menu on arrival and enjoy beautifully presented, healthy meals the rest of the week. Breakfast is brought to your room early each morning on a tray set with china, fresh flowers, and snowy white linen. Lunch is served poolside. Formal candlelit dinners are preceded by hors d'oeuvres and served by white-gloved attendants. Wednesday is "dinner in bed" night, followed by a movie and low-fat popcorn in the living room (wear your bathrobe), and later a fifteen-minute tuck-in massage—the ultimate in pampering and relaxation! Delicious fruit frappés are served as a break at 4 o'clock.

## ❖ SETTING ❖

Just fifteen minutes from Dallas, The Greenhouse is a serene hideaway on a hilly compound. Airy, bright, and exquisitely furnished, it surrounds guests with an atmosphere of luxury in which every detail is attended to. At the center of the house is a white-latticed glass atrium enclosing a swimming pool and lush plants, capped by a magnificent domed skylight. The guest rooms are on two floors surrounding the atrium and feature large marble bathtubs; feminine decor in pinks, mauves, and chintzes; and beds with white hand-embroidered coverlets and an abundance of pillows.

## ❖ ACTIVITIES, TREATMENTS, AND FACILITIES ❖

The Greenhouse is serious about helping women stay healthy, and to that end offers first-rate instructors and the latest methods for physical and emotional rejuvenation. As program director Cynthia Lefferts puts it, "The words [today are] *moderation* and *balance*, and every guest is carefully assessed to be sure her program matches her level of fitness. In the well-paced daily schedules, mornings are reserved for fitness classes, afternoons for pampering and relaxation. Activities include tai chi, power walks, Pilates exercises, strength training, aqua aerobics, jazz dance, stretch, the popular yoga aerobics, outdoor circuit classes, and interval training. There are also nutritional consultations available and classes on mind-body connection. After lunch, you will undergo total pampering: massages, facials, and hair and makeup lessons with the beauty team—manicurist, masseuse, facialist, and hair stylist—that has been assigned to you for the week. (A staff of 125 serves 39 guests.) While Greenhouse programs are usually for a full week, shorter three-day stays are offered during the winter holiday season.

# Fluffy Spinach and Sweet Pepper Omelette

*Egg whites and egg substitute make a nice yellow, low-cholesterol omelette.*

1 teaspoon olive oil
1/4 cup (1 oz/30 g) finely chopped onion
1 cup (5 oz/155 g) julienned red bell pepper
8 ounces (250 g) fresh spinach, washed and stemmed
1/2 cup (4 fl oz/125 ml) chicken velouté (see Basics)
Salt and ground white pepper to taste
1/2 cup (4 fl oz/125 ml) liquid egg substitute
1/4 cup (1/3 oz/10 g) chopped fresh chives
4 egg whites
1/2 cup (2 oz/60 g) shredded low-fat Cheddar cheese

Preheat the oven to 375°F (190°C). In a nonstick sauté pan or skillet over medium heat, heat the olive oil and sauté the onion and pepper for 3 minutes, or until soft. Add the spinach and sauté for 5 minutes. Pour in the chicken velouté and season with salt and white pepper.

In a medium bowl, whisk together the egg substitute, chives, salt, and white pepper. In a large bowl, beat the egg whites until soft peaks form. Fold the egg whites into the egg substitute mixture.

Coat an ovenproof nonstick pan or 8-inch (20-cm) ovenproof skillet with vegetable oil spray and heat over medium heat. Pour the egg mixture into the pan and cook for 1 minute, or until lightly browned on the bottom. Transfer the pan to the preheated oven and bake for 3 to 4 minutes, or until the omelette is nicely puffed.

Preheat the broiler. Spread the omelette with the spinach mixture and fold it in half. Sprinkle with the Cheddar cheese and place under the broiler until the cheese melts. Transfer the omelette to a warmed serving plate and serve immediately, while the omelette is still fluffy.

*Makes 1 omelette; serves 4*

PER SERVING

*Calories 130 • Carbohydrates 7 g • Cholesterol 10 mg • Fat 6 g • Protein 19 g • Sodium 470 mg*

---

# Apple-Carrot Muffins

1 teaspoon baking powder

1/8 teaspoon ground allspice

1/8 teaspoon ground nutmeg

1/2 teaspoon ground cinnamon

1/4 cup (2 oz/60 g) sugar

1/4 cup (1 1/2 oz/45 g) whole-wheat flour

3/4 cup (4 oz/125 g) unbleached all-purpose flour

1 tablespoon canola oil

4 egg whites

3/4 cup (6 fl oz/185 ml) low-fat milk

1 teaspoon vanilla extract

1/2 cup (2 oz/60 g) grated carrot

1/2 cup (2 oz/60 g) grated unpeeled apple

Preheat the oven to 400°F (200°C). Lightly coat 6 muffin cups with vegetable oil spray.

In a medium bowl, combine the baking powder, allspice, nutmeg, cinnamon, sugar, whole-wheat flour, and all-purpose flour and stir until mixed.

In a large bowl, whisk the canola oil, egg whites, milk, and vanilla together. Add the flour mixture and stir until just mixed. Fold in the grated carrot and apple. Spoon the batter into the prepared muffin cups, filling each half full. Bake in the preheated oven for 20 to 25 minutes, or until lightly browned.

*Makes 6 muffins*

PER MUFFIN

*Calories 160 • Carbohydrates 27 g • Cholesterol 0 mg • Fat 3 g • Protein 6 g • Sodium 95 mg*

# Chicken Tandoori with Stir-Fried Vegetables

*Marinate the chicken for at least 3 hours before you plan to cook it.*

### Marinade

 $^{1}/_{2}$ cup (4 fl oz/125 ml) nonfat plain yogurt

 3 tablespoons fresh lemon juice

 1 tablespoon grated fresh ginger

 1 teaspoon minced garlic

 $^{1}/_{8}$ teaspoon cayenne pepper

 $^{1}/_{2}$ teaspoon ground cumin

 1 tablespoon chopped fresh cilantro

 $^{1}/_{2}$ teaspoon salt

 Four 4-ounce (125-g) skinless, boneless chicken breast halves

 Stir-Fried Vegetables (recipe follows)

In a medium bowl, combine all the marinade ingredients and stir until well mixed. Spread the marinade thickly on the chicken breasts. Cover and refrigerate for at least 3 hours.

Remove the chicken from the refrigerator 30 minutes before cooking. Light a fire in a charcoal grill or preheat the broiler. Grill the chicken over hot coals or under the broiler until opaque throughout, about 5 minutes on each side. Set aside.

To serve, divide the stir-fried vegetables among 4 plates and arrange a chicken breast on top of each.

### Makes 4 servings

### PER SERVING

*Calories 290 • Carbohydrates 22 g • Cholesterol 65 mg • Fat 10 g • Protein 31 g • Sodium 580 mg*

## Stir-Fried Vegetables

1 teaspoon peanut oil

1 cup (4 oz/125 g) thinly sliced carrots

1 cup (4 oz/125 g) thinly sliced celery

1 cup (2 oz/60 g) broccoli florets

1 cup (3 oz/90 g) snow peas

1 cup (3 oz/90 g) bean sprouts

3/4 cup (3 oz/90 g) sliced water chestnuts

3/4 cup (3 oz/90 g) thinly sliced zucchini

1/4 cup (1 1/2 oz/45 g) peanuts

1 cup (8 fl oz/250 ml) chicken or vegetable stock (see Basics)
  or canned low-salt chicken or vegetable broth

2 tablespoons low-salt soy sauce or teriyaki sauce

1 1/2 tablespoons cornstarch

Freshly ground pepper to taste

1 tablespoon chopped fresh cilantro

In a wok or a large, heavy skillet over medium-high heat, heat the peanut oil
and stir-fry the carrots, celery, and broccoli for 3 minutes. Stir in the snow
peas, bean sprouts, water chestnuts, zucchini, and peanuts and stir-fry for
2 more minutes. Stir in the stock or broth.

In a small bowl, whisk the soy or teriyaki sauce and cornstarch together. Pour
the mixture into the vegetables, stirring constantly until thickened. Season
with pepper. Serve immediately, sprinkled with cilantro.

*Makes 4 servings*

### PER SERVING

*Calories 150 • Carbohydrates 19 g • Cholesterol 0 mg • Fat 7 g • Protein 6 g • Sodium 320 mg*

# Strawberry-Tofu Sherbet

4 cups (1 lb/500 g) fresh strawberries, hulled
12 ounces (375 g) silken tofu
¹/₂ cup (6 oz/185 g) honey
¹/₂ cup (4 fl oz/125 ml) water
2 tablespoons fresh lemon juice

In a blender or food processor, purée the strawberries and tofu, in batches if necessary. Add the honey, water, and lemon juice and blend until well mixed.

Transfer the tofu mixture to an ice cream maker and freeze according to the manufacturer's instructions. Serve at once, or store in the freezer for up to 3 weeks.

*Makes 8 servings*

### PER SERVING

*Calories 110 • Carbohydrates 24 g • Cholesterol 0 mg • Fat 1.5 g • Protein 3 g • Sodium 15 mg*

## Hearts of Lettuce with Sherry Dressing and Jicama Slaw

**2 heads butterhead lettuce**
**$^1/_2$ cup (4 fl oz/125 ml) Sherry Dressing (recipe follows)**
**Jicama Slaw (recipe follows)**
**$^1/_2$ cup (1 oz/30 g) alfalfa sprouts or spicy sprouts***

Core the lettuce without disturbing the inner leaves. Carefully rinse the lettuce heads and place them upside down on a wire rack or on paper towels to dry. Cut each head in half.

Place a lettuce half on each of 4 plates and carefully open the leaves until they resemble a blossom. Drizzle 2 tablespoons sherry dressing over each salad and top with one-fourth of the jicama slaw and alfalfa or spicy sprouts.

*Makes 4 servings*

### PER SERVING

*Calories 60 • Carbohydrates 11 g • Cholesterol 0 mg • Fat 1.5 g • Protein 2 g • Sodium 420 mg*

*\*Spicy sprouts are a mixture of various sprouts, including radish sprouts, which have a spicy flavor.*

## Sherry Dressing

- 2 tablespoons dry sherry
- 2 tablespoons white wine vinegar
- ¹/₂ garlic clove
- 3 tablespoons water
- ¹/₂ cup (4 oz/125 g) fat-free mayonnaise
- ¹/₂ tablespoon canola oil

In a blender, combine all the ingredients and process for 1 minute. Scrape down the sides and process for 30 seconds. The dressing can be stored in an airtight container in the refrigerator for up to 1 week.

*Makes about ³/₄ cup (6 fl oz/180 ml)*

PER TABLESPOON

*Calories 13 • Carbohydrates 1 g • Cholesterol 0 mg • Fat 0.5 g • Protein 0 g • Sodium 60 mg*

## Jicama Slaw

*Jicama is a large, bulbous root vegetable with a sweet, nutty flavor. Be sure to prepare the slaw at least an hour before serving.*

- ¹/₂ cup (2¹/₂ oz/45 g) julienned jicama
- ¹/₂ cup (2¹/₂ oz/45 g) julienned carrots
- ¹/₂ cup (2¹/₂ oz/45 g) julienned cucumber
- 1 tablespoon chopped fresh cilantro
- 2 tablespoons orange juice
- 2 tablespoons fresh lime juice
- ¹/₂ tablespoon rice vinegar
- ¹/₂ teaspoon *each* salt and ground white pepper

In a medium bowl, toss all the ingredients together. Cover and refrigerate for at least 1 hour before serving.

*Makes 1¹/₂ cups (5¹/₂ oz/170 g)*

PER SERVING

*Calories 30 • Carbohydrates 7 g • Cholesterol 0 mg • Fat 0 g • Protein 1 g • Sodium 300 mg*

# Poached Sea Bass with Salmon Mousseline

*Serve with steamed vegetables of your choice.*

*Salmon Mousseline*

> 4 ounces (125 g) salmon fillet, boned, skinned, and diced
>
> 2 tablespoons egg white
>
> 2 tablespoons low-fat plain yogurt
>
> 1/4 teaspoon chopped fresh basil
>
> 1/4 teaspoon chopped fresh dill
>
> 1/4 teaspoon *each* salt and ground white pepper

> Four 3-ounce (90-g) sea bass fillets
>
> 1 small zucchini, thinly sliced
>
> 1 small yellow squash, thinly sliced
>
> 1 tablespoon minced shallot
>
> 3 tablespoons dry white wine
>
> 1/3 cup (3 fl oz/80 ml) fish or chicken stock (see Basics),
>   or canned low-salt chicken broth
>
> 3/4 cup (6 fl oz/180 ml) fish or chicken velouté (see Basics)
>
> 1/4 cup (1/3 oz/10 g) chopped fresh chives
>
> 1/2 teaspoon salt
>
> 1/8 teaspoon ground white pepper
>
> Steamed vegetables for serving

To make the mousseline: In a blender or food processor, combine the salmon, egg white, and yogurt and purée. Transfer the salmon mixture to a medium bowl and stir in the basil, dill, salt, and pepper.

Preheat the oven to 325°F (165°C). Top each sea bass fillet with 2 tablespoons salmon mousseline, then with alternating layers of zucchini and yellow squash to completely cover the fish.

Scatter the shallots in an ovenproof skillet, place the fish on top, and pour in the wine and stock or broth. Place the pan over medium heat and bring the liquid to a bare simmer; remove the pan from heat.

Cover the fish loosely with parchment paper and bake in the preheated oven for 6 minutes, or until the fish is opaque and the mousseline just set. Carefully remove the fish from the pan and keep warm.

Place the pan over high heat and boil the poaching liquid to reduce by half. Stir in the velouté, chives, salt, and pepper and bring to a simmer. Serve the fish with the sauce.

*Makes 4 servings*

PER SERVING

*Calories 160 • Carbohydrates 7 g • Cholesterol 50 mg • Fat 3 g • Protein 25 g • Sodium 620 mg*

# Pear-Polenta Soufflés

1 cup (8 fl oz/250 ml) low-fat milk

1 teaspoon grated orange zest (see Basics)

1/2 large ripe pear, cored and peeled

3 tablespoons sugar

2 tablespoons cornmeal

2 egg whites

Powdered sugar for dusting

In a small, heavy saucepan, bring the milk and orange zest to a boil. Remove from heat and let steep for about 25 minutes. Discard the orange zest. Meanwhile, in a blender, purée the pear until smooth. You should have 1/4 cup (2 fl oz/60 ml) purée.

Bring the orange-flavored milk back up to a simmer. Add 2 tablespoons of the sugar and the cornmeal, stirring constantly. Add the pear purée and continue cooking and stirring for 15 minutes, or until the mixture pulls away from the sides of the pan. Pour the cornmeal mixture into a medium bowl, cover with plastic wrap or parchment paper, and let cool.

Preheat the oven to 400°F (200°C). In a large bowl, beat the egg whites until soft peaks form. Add the remaining 1 tablespoon sugar and continue beating until stiff, glossy peaks form. Gently fold the egg whites into the cornmeal mixture and pour into four 3-inch (7.5-cm) ramekins. Set the ramekins in a baking dish and add hot water to the dish to come halfway up the sides of the ramekins. Bake in the preheated oven for 10 minutes, or until the soufflés are golden brown, but still creamy in the center. Dust with powdered sugar and serve immediately.

*Makes 4 servings*

### PER SERVING

*Calories 100 • Carbohydrates 20 g • Cholesterol 5 mg • Fat 1 g • Protein 4 g • Sodium 60 mg*

# The Hills Health Ranch

British Columbia

*Saddle up for a Western-style ranch workout . . . Facials, skin treatments, herbal wraps, and massages mix with hay rides and trail rides or, in winter, cross-country skiing, bringing together fun and fitness.*

**—Fodor's Healthy Escapes**

## ❖ PROFILE ❖

The Hills Health Ranch opened in 1985 as one of Canada's premier year-round health and fitness vacation resorts. The informal spa specializes in packaged "wellness vacations" that integrate gourmet spa cuisine with daily fitness workouts, educational workshops, and body and beauty treatments. It has the charm of an authentic Western ranch and is a great way to combine a winter ski holiday or summer horse-riding adventure with spa pampering and wellness activities. A true refuge from urban—and suburban—stress, the Ranch is located in unspoiled Canadian wilderness with unpolluted air, clear lakes, a dry climate, and the quiet sounds of the country. People say they begin to feel better the minute they arrive at The Hills Health Ranch, and they return home feeling fit and relaxed, with renewed vigor and enthusiasm for life.

## ❖ CUISINE ❖

The country-style Trail's End Dining Room offers both a seasonal international menu and an outstanding spa menu featuring appetizing, low-fat, and low-calorie meals. The chef and nutritionist have collaborated to ensure that The Hills' spa cuisine provides optimum energy, and all dishes are prepared with flair. A source of health in itself, the water at The Hills is pure, clear, and cold, coming from the Ranch's own deep underground source. In addition to enjoying the nutritious spa meals, guests can take seminars on healthy shopping, cooking, and eating.

## ❖ SETTING ❖

The Hills Health Ranch represents the best of the Canadian West in both natural scenery and outdoor activities. Its deluxe accommodations—twenty-six rooms and twenty Swiss-style chalets—are located on twenty thousand acres in the Cariboo region of British Columbia. In the summer, guests can take hour- or day-long nature treks on horseback, fish or canoe on one of the many lakes, hike to a waterfall, or observe birds and wildlife. In the winter, cross-country skiers make good use of the two hundred kilometers of trails, with terrain ranging from gently rolling countryside to challenging descents. There is also a downhill ski and snowboard park that is lit at night, dog-sled tours, toboggan runs, and a skating rink. True to its ranch atmosphere, The Hills offers hay-ride sing-along parties and line-dance lessons to get everyone into the spirit of things.

## ❖ ACTIVITIES, TREATMENTS, AND FACILITIES ❖

A place for physical, emotional, and spiritual renewal, the Canadian Wellness Center at The Hills Health Ranch combines education and physical activity with pampering skin and body treatments. The Center encourages health through medically supported lifestyle changes and has formed partnerships with Canadian universities to pursue research on long-term health. Here, guests can choose their focus and level of activity, perhaps starting each day with a guided wilderness walk, alternating spa workouts with outdoor activities, and finishing with a luxurious facial, manicure, herbal wrap, massage, reflexology session, or soothing ice-paraffin treatment for sore muscles. Facilities include an indoor pool, saunas, hot tubs, and exercise and weight equipment, and are staffed by highly qualified fitness instructors, a kinesiologist, and personal ski trainers. Classes include toning, strengthening, stretching, step, and aqua aerobics, and there are wellness workshops on stress reduction, fitness, holistic health, and weight loss. A wide variety of spa packages are available to suit the services and length of stay desired.

# MENU

*Black Bean Soup with Fresh Tomato Salsa*

❖

*Poached Chicken with Cheese, Spinach, and Red Pepper Coulis*

❖

*Wild Rice with Lemon*

❖

*Apple Strudels with Cinnamon Sauce*

127

THE HILLS HEALTH RANCH

# Black Bean Soup with Fresh Tomato Salsa

*Start this dish the day before you plan to serve it.*

1¹/₂ cups (11 oz/345 g) dried black beans

5 cups (40 fl oz/1.25 l) chicken stock (see Basics)
   or canned low-salt chicken broth

1 tablespoon ground cumin

1 teaspoon salt

1 teaspoon chili powder

1 teaspoon *each* dried thyme and ground coriander

1 garlic clove, minced

¹/₃ cup (2 oz/60 g) diced onion

2 teaspoons red wine vinegar

¹/₄ cup (2 fl oz/60 ml) Fresh Tomato Salsa (recipe follows)

4 teaspoons nonfat sour cream

Rinse and pick over the beans. Soak overnight in cold water to cover by 2 inches (5 cm); drain. Alternatively, place the beans in a large saucepan with cold water to cover by 2 inches (5 cm). Bring to a boil, cook for 2 minutes, then turn off heat and let soak for 1 hour; drain.

In a soup pot, combine the beans, stock or broth, cumin, salt, chili powder, thyme, and coriander and bring to a boil. Reduce heat to low, cover, and simmer for 1 hour. Add the garlic, onion, and vinegar and simmer for 1 hour, or until the beans are tender.

Transfer two-thirds of the bean mixture to a blender or food processor and purée. Pour the purée back into the pot and stir to blend. Heat through over medium heat. Ladle the soup into 4 shallow soup bowls and top with a little salsa and sour cream.

*Makes 4 servings*

PER SERVING

*Calories 280 • Carbohydrates 47 g • Cholesterol 0 mg • Fat 2.5 g • Protein 20 g • Sodium 660 mg*

## Fresh Tomato Salsa

2 large tomatoes, peeled, seeded (see Basics), and diced
2 green onions, thinly sliced
2 tablespoons minced fresh cilantro
1 small jalapeño chili, minced
Dash of salt
1 teaspoon balsamic vinegar

In a medium bowl, combine all of the ingredients. Cover and refrigerate for at least 1 hour. Stir gently before serving. Store, covered, in the refrigerator for up to 3 days.

*Makes about 1¹/₂ cups (12 fl oz/375 ml)*

### PER TABLESPOON

*Calories 5 • Carbohydrates 1 g • Cholesterol 0 mg • Fat 0 g • Protein 0 g • Sodium 15 mg*

# Poached Chicken with Cheese, Spinach, and Red Pepper Coulis

*Serve with Wild Rice with Lemon (page 132) and steamed fresh seasonal vegetables.*

**Four 4-ounce (125-g) boneless, skinless chicken breast halves, preferably free-range**

**12 spinach leaves**

**4 tablespoons quark,\* or Yogurt Cheese (recipe on page 92)**

**12 strips roasted red bell pepper (see Basics)**

**Mrs. Dash (any flavor) or other salt-free seasoning to taste**

**Red Pepper Coulis (recipe follows)**

Lay 1 chicken breast between 2 sheets of plastic wrap. Using the smooth side of a meat mallet, a rolling pin, or the side of a heavy bottle, pound the breast firmly until it is an even ¼ inch (6 mm) all over. Repeat with the remaining breasts. Top each breast with 3 spinach leaves, 1 tablespoon cheese, and 3 strips roasted red pepper. Lightly sprinkle with salt-free seasoning and roll up.

Tightly wrap each breast in plastic wrap and poach in simmering water for 7 to 10 minutes, or until done. Unwrap and serve with 2 tablespoons red pepper coulis.

*Makes 4 servings*

## PER SERVING

*Calories 220 • Carbohydrates 19 g • Cholesterol 65 mg • Fat 3 g • Protein 28 g • Sodium 310 mg*

---

*\*Quark is a soft, fresh, nonfat cheese with the texture and flavor of sour cream.*

## Red Pepper Coulis

    1 large red bell pepper, roasted and seeded (see Basics)
    1 tablespoon honey
    1/2 teaspoon minced garlic
    2 tablespoons dry white wine

In a blender or food processor, purée the roasted pepper. Transfer the purée to a small saucepan. Add the remaining ingredients and simmer for 5 minutes, stirring occasionally.

*Makes about 1/2 cup (4 fl oz/125 ml)*

### PER TABLESPOON

*Calories 15 • Carbohydrates 4 g • Cholesterol 0 mg • Fat 0 g • Protein 0 g • Sodium 0 mg*

# Wild Rice with Lemon

1¹/₂ cups (12 fl oz/375 ml) chicken stock (see Basics)
    or canned low-salt chicken broth

1 tablespoon fresh lemon juice

1 bay leaf

¹/₂ cup (3 oz/90 g) wild rice, well rinsed

1 green onion, sliced

¹/₂ teaspoon grated lemon zest (see Basics)

1 tablespoon minced fresh parsley

Freshly ground pepper to taste

In a medium saucepan, combine the stock or broth, lemon juice, and bay leaf and bring to a boil. Add the wild rice, reduce heat to low, cover, and simmer for 40 minutes, or until the rice is tender and has absorbed the liquid. Remove from heat and let stand, covered, for 5 minutes.

Lightly coat a nonstick sauté pan or skillet with olive oil spray and heat over medium heat. Sauté the green onion for 2 minutes. Add the lemon zest and sauté for 2 minutes, or until the green onion is soft. Set aside.

Remove the bay leaf from the rice and stir in the green onion mixture, parsley, and pepper.

*Makes 2 servings*

### PER SERVING

*Calories 170 • Carbohydrates 32 g • Cholesterol 0 mg • Fat 1 g • Protein 8 g • Sodium 35 mg*

# Apple Strudels with Cinnamon Sauce

1 green apple, peeled and sliced

2 teaspoons dried cranberries

Dash of ground cinnamon

4 sheets frozen phyllo dough, thawed

*Cinnamon Sauce*

$^1/_2$ cup (4 fl oz/125 ml) unsweetened apple juice

1 teaspoon ground cinnamon

1 tablespoon cornstarch

$^1/_2$ cup (4 fl oz/125 ml) fresh orange juice

4 teaspoons Fruit Source* or sugar

Preheat the oven to 350°F (180°C). In a medium bowl, mix the apple, cranberries, and cinnamon together.

Lay 1 sheet of phyllo dough on a flat work surface. Keep the remaining phyllo covered with a damp cloth. Coat the sheet lightly with vegetable oil spray. Fold the sheet in half and top with one-fourth of the apple mixture. Fold the sheet into a large triangle. Coat lightly with vegetable oil spray and press the edges together to seal. Repeat the process with the remaining sheets of phyllo to make 4 triangles. Place the triangles on a nonstick baking sheet and bake in the preheated oven for 8 to 10 minutes, or until golden brown.

Meanwhile, make the cinnamon sauce: In a small saucepan, combine all the ingredients and bring to a boil over medium heat, stirring constantly. Cook for 1 to 2 minutes, or until the sauce thickens. Arrange a warm triangle on each of 4 plates and serve with the cinnamon sauce.

*Makes 4 servings*

### PER SERVING

*Calories 140 • Carbohydrates 31 g • Cholesterol 0 mg • Fat 1.5 g • Protein 2 g • Sodium 110 mg*

---

*\*Fruit Source is a granulated sweetener derived from fruit juice concentrates and malted rice. It is available in many natural foods stores.*

# MENU

## BREAKFAST

*French Toast with Blueberry Syrup*

## LUNCH

*Wild Rice and Chicken Chowder*

*Salade Niçoise*

## DINNER

*Baked Salmon in a Garlic Crust with Cucumber Relish*

*Orange Rice*

*German Pear Strudel*

# Hilton Head Health Institute

Hilton Head Island, South Carolina

*You come to this all-inclusive spa to change what's wrong in your life
alongside spectacular Atlantic beachfront.*

—**Condé Nast Traveler**

## ✤ PROFILE ✤

Founded in 1976 by nutrition expert Dr. Peter Miller, the Hilton Head Health Institute is one of the premier lifestyle-management programs in the United States and has an international reputation in the fields of weight loss, stress reduction, smoking cessation, and overall health enhancement. Located on semitropical Hilton Head Island, the Institute provides a secluded resort environment where guests (up to forty maximum) can put the world on hold and focus exclusively on themselves and their fitness goals, whether they are to get in shape, increase energy and stamina, or lower blood pressure. Although the emphasis is more on health and fitness than luxury pampering, Hilton Head nevertheless creates a wonderful, relaxing retreat from the stresses of everyday life. It has been named one of the top five health resorts in the country by *Condé Nast Traveler* and a Pick of the Best by *Shape Magazine*.

## ✤ CUISINE ✤

The Institute's kitchen and menu plans are overseen by executive chef Erich Striegel, who makes sure that his dishes are as tasty as they are balanced and nutritious. Programs include three meals and a daily fruit snack; vegetarian options are always available, and special dishes can be created for those with food allergies or other health conditions. In addition to preparing meals and researching recipes, chef Striegel speaks on good nutrition and conducts demonstrations so that guests will be able to emulate his healthy cooking style once they return home.

## ❖ SETTING ❖

Hilton Head Island—a forty-two-square-mile barrier sea island off the coast of South Carolina—is one of the world's most acclaimed resort destinations. Located in the Shipyard Plantation community, the Hilton Head Health Institute takes advantage of the island's tranquility and natural beauty. Guests find themselves rejuvenated while they enjoy its miles of white sand beaches, walking and biking trails, nature preserves, and moderate year-round temperatures. The health resort's accommodations consist of semiprivate two- and three-bedroom apartments: Guests have their own room and bath and share a living room, fully equipped kitchen, and laundry facilities. The rooms are characterized by fine fabrics, traditional furniture, private porches, and a casual, unpretentious ambience.

## ❖ ACTIVITIES, TREATMENTS, AND FACILITIES ❖

Guests at the Hilton Head Institute are serious about fitness, nutrition, weight management, and healthy living, and a highly trained, caring staff provides a friendly environment in which to make important lifestyle changes. Everyone's individual needs are assessed in advance (including a blood profile), and guests are monitored to make sure they proceed at their own manageable pace. Facilities are outfitted with treadmills, bikes, weight machines, and other fitness equipment, and classes include low-impact aerobics, step, tai chi, evening yoga, stretching, resistance and flexibility, aqua aerobics, basic conditioning, cycling, and country line dancing. Outdoor activities include golf, tennis, swimming, beach walking, and sea kayaking. In addition to physical exercise, the daily curriculum features educational seminars—either in a group or one-on-one with a staff member—designed to help break old habits, increase long-term motivation, and meet health goals. Other spa services include early morning walks, massage, and some beauty treatments. Hilton Head health programs are for a week or longer, beginning on Sunday (the average length of stay is two weeks), and couples are encouraged to attend together.

# French Toast with Blueberry Syrup

*Blueberry Syrup*

    **2 tablespoons maple syrup**
    **$1/4$ cup fresh or frozen blueberries**
    **$1/2$ teaspoon finely grated orange zest (see Basics)**
    **Pinch of ground cinnamon**

    **1 cup (8 fl oz/250 ml) liquid egg substitute, or 6 egg whites**
    **$1/4$ cup (2 fl oz/60 ml) low-fat milk**
    **2 teaspoons ground cinnamon**
    **1 teaspoon vanilla extract**
    **6 slices whole-wheat bread**

To make the blueberry syrup: In a small saucepan, combine the maple syrup, blueberries, orange zest, and cinnamon. Bring to a simmer and cook until the syrup thickens. Set aside and keep warm.

In a medium bowl, whisk together the egg substitute or egg whites, milk, cinnamon, and vanilla.

Lightly coat a large nonstick pan or skillet with vegetable oil spray and heat it over medium heat.

Dip the bread slices into the egg mixture and fry them in batches until lightly browned on both sides. Serve immediately, with the warm blueberry syrup.

*Makes 2 servings*

### PER SERVING

*Calories 410 • Carbohydrates 62 g • Cholesterol 5 mg • Fat 8 g • Protein 26 g • Sodium 680 mg*

# Wild Rice and Chicken Chowder

¹/4 cup (2 oz/60 g) finely chopped onion

2 tablespoons minced shallot

1 cup (7 oz/220 g) mixed brown and wild rice

¹/4 cup (2 oz/60 g) shredded carrot

8 cups (2 qt/2 l) chicken stock (see Basics) or
canned low-salt chicken broth, plus more as needed

1 tablespoon *each* minced fresh parsley and chives

2 bay leaves

Pinch *each* of dried thyme and freshly ground pepper

One 4-ounce (125-g) boneless, skinless chicken breast half,
poached (see Basics) and shredded

¹/2 cup (4 oz/125 g) fresh corn kernels

¹/4 cup (2 oz/60 g) *each* diced green and red bell pepper

1 cup (8 fl oz/250 ml) low-fat milk

1 tablespoon cornstarch

¹/4 cup (2 oz/60 g) shredded Cheddar cheese

Pinch of ground turmeric for color

Cayenne pepper to taste

Lightly coat a 4-quart (4-l) pot with vegetable oil spray and heat over medium heat. Sauté the onion and shallot for 2 minutes, or until soft. Add the rice and carrot and sauté for 2 minutes. Add the stock or broth, parsley, chives, bay leaves, thyme, and pepper. Increase heat to high and bring to a boil. Reduce heat to low, cover, and simmer for 45 minutes. Stir in the shredded chicken, corn, and bell pepper. In a small bowl, mix the milk and cornstarch together. Stir the milk mixture, Cheddar cheese, and turmeric into the chowder and simmer for 10 minutes. Season with cayenne pepper.

*Makes 10 servings*

PER SERVING

*Calories 130 • Carbohydrates 18 g • Cholesterol 10 mg • Fat 2.5 g • Protein 8 g • Sodium 70 mg*

# Salade Niçoise

*Dressing*

 1 tablespoon capers, rinsed and drained

 1 tablespoon Dijon mustard

 2 tablespoons fresh lemon juice

 3 tablespoons extra-virgin olive oil

 1 tablespoon red wine vinegar

 2 tablespoons minced fresh herbs (parsley, basil, and/or dill)

 2 small new potatoes, halved

 1 cup (3 oz/90 g) fresh green beans, trimmed

 2 ounces (60 g) water-packed light tuna, drained and flaked (about ⅓ cup)

 1 tomato, cut into thin wedges

 1 tablespoon sliced pitted black olives

 1 head romaine or butterhead lettuce, cored and chopped

 ½ red onion, thinly sliced and rings separated

To make the dressing: In a small bowl, whisk together all the ingredients.

Cook the potatoes in salted boiling water for 7 to 8 minutes, or until tender. Drain and dice. Cook the green beans in salted boiling water for 2 minutes, or until crisp-tender. Drain, rinse under cold running water, and pat dry.

In a large serving bowl, toss the potatoes, green beans, and all the remaining ingredients together with the dressing.

*Makes 4 servings*

### PER SERVING

*Calories 160 • Carbohydrates 11 g • Cholesterol 5 mg • Fat 11 g • Protein 6 g • Sodium 250 mg*

## Baked Salmon in a Garlic Crust with Cucumber Relish

½ cup (2 oz/60 g) crushed bran flake cereal or dried bread crumbs

2 teaspoons paprika

1 teaspoon minced fresh dill

Two 4-ounce (125-g) salmon fillets, boned and skinned

2 teaspoons minced garlic

Cucumber Relish (recipe follows)

Preheat the oven to 350°F (180°C). Lightly coat a baking pan with vegetable oil spray.

In a pie plate, stir together the crushed bran cereal or bread crumbs, paprika, and dill. Spray the mixture lightly with vegetable oil spray to adhere the spices to the crumbs.

Rub all sides of the salmon with the minced garlic. Firmly press the salmon into the crumbs to coat all sides. Place the salmon in the prepared pan and bake in the preheated oven for 15 to 20 minutes, or until the salmon is opaque. Serve immediately, with cucumber relish.

*Makes 2 servings*

PER SERVING (with ¼ cup or 1¼ oz/37 g relish)

*Calories 250 • Carbohydrates 28 g • Cholesterol 60 mg • Fat 5 g • Protein 27 g • Sodium 340 mg*

## Cucumber Relish

*Serve with baked, poached, or grilled fish.*

> $^1/_4$ cup ($1^1/_2$ oz/45 g) diced onion
> $^1/_2$ red bell pepper, seeded, deribbed, and diced
> $^1/_4$ cup (2 fl oz/60 ml) cider vinegar
> 1 shallot, minced
> 1 garlic clove, minced
> $^1/_2$ teaspoon grated fresh ginger
> $^1/_2$ teaspoon grated orange zest (see Basics)
> $^1/_4$ teaspoon low-salt soy sauce
> Pinch of freshly ground pepper
> $^1/_2$ teaspoon chopped fresh dill
> 1 cucumber, peeled and finely sliced

In a medium saucepan, combine all the ingredients except the cucumber and bring to a boil. Remove from heat, stir in the cucumber, and let sit for at least 15 minutes before serving. The relish can be stored, covered, in the refrigerator for 2 or 3 days.

*Makes about 2 cups (10 oz/315 g)*

PER $^1/_4$ CUP ($1^1/_4$ oz/37 g)

*Calories 10 • Carbohydrates 3 g • Cholesterol 0 mg • Fat 0 g • Protein 0 g • Sodium 5 mg*

# Orange Rice

*Delicious served alongside fish, poultry, or pork, or as a stuffing.*

$^1/_4$ cup ($1^1/_2$ oz/45 g) chopped onion

1 cup (5 oz/155 g) chopped celery, with leaves

1 cup (7 oz/220 g) brown rice

$1^1/_2$ cups (12 fl oz/375 ml) water, chicken stock (see Basics),
    or canned low-salt chicken broth

1 teaspoon grated orange zest (see Basics)

$^1/_2$ cup (4 fl oz/125 ml) fresh orange juice

1 tablespoon fresh lemon juice

$^1/_4$ cup (1 oz/30 g) slivered blanched almonds, toasted (see Basics)

$^1/_4$ cup (2 oz/60 g) pimientos, drained and diced

Lightly coat a large saucepan with vegetable oil spray and heat over medium heat. Sauté the onion for 5 minutes, then add the celery and sauté for 3 minutes. Add the rice and sauté for 2 minutes. Add the water, stock, or broth, zest, orange juice, lemon juice, almonds, and pimientos. Cover and reduce heat to low. Cook the rice for 15 to 20 minutes, or until all of the liquid has evaporated.

*Makes 8 servings*

### PER SERVING

*Calories 120 • Carbohydrates 22 g • Cholesterol 0 mg • Fat 2.5 g • Protein 3 g • Sodium 20 mg*

# German Pear Strudel

*If you wish, apples can be substituted for the pears.*

$^1\!/_2$ cup (2 oz/60 g) low-fat granola

$2^1\!/_2$ cups (15 oz/470 g) diced pears (3 or 4 pears)

$^1\!/_2$ cup (2 oz/60 g) dried cranberries

$^1\!/_4$ cup ($1^1\!/_2$ oz/45 g) chopped dried apricots

$^1\!/_2$ cup (4 fl oz/125 ml) maple syrup

1 tablespoon ground cinnamon

$^1\!/_4$ teaspoon ground nutmeg

6 sheets frozen phyllo dough, thawed

Preheat the oven to 350°F (180°C). In a medium bowl, combine all the ingredients except the phyllo dough and mix well.

Lay 1 sheet of phyllo dough on a sheet of parchment paper. Keep the remaining dough covered with a damp cloth. Lightly coat the sheet with vegetable oil spray and top with a second phyllo sheet; spray again. Continue layering until all 6 sheets are stacked.

To assemble the strudel, work quickly, as the phyllo will begin to dry and crack. Spread the pear filling along a wide edge of the phyllo stack, leaving a 1-inch (2.5-cm) border. Fold over the sides and roll up the strudel, lifting the paper to help roll.

Place on a baking sheet, seam side down, and bake in the preheated oven for 30 to 35 minutes, or until golden brown. Cut into 8 crosswise pieces and serve warm.

*Makes 8 servings*

PER SERVING

*Calories 200 • Carbohydrates 45 g • Cholesterol 0 mg • Fat 1.5 g • Protein 2 g • Sodium 95 mg*

# MENU

## *DINNER*

*Gazpacho with Poached Scallops*

❖

*Seared Ahi Tuna with Couscous Salad*

❖

*Mango Yogurt Flan with Almond Crisps and Tropical Fruit*

# Ihilani Resort & Spa

O a h u ,  H a w a i i

*Staying at the Ihilani is like being a guest at the beach
with a nurturing, ever-indulgent, invisible host.*

**—Town & Country**

## ❖ PROFILE ❖

Ihilani is a full-service spa contained within a luxury hotel on the sunny western shore of Oahu's 640-acre Ko'Olina Resort. (*Ihilani* is the Hawaiian word for "heavenly splendor," while *Ko'Olina* means "fulfillment of joy," and—according to guests and travel critics alike—they more than live up to their names!) The exceptional one-on-one attention benefits all spa-goers, and children are entertained at the Keiki Beachcomber Club, so parents have time to truly relax. Personal touches abound: as *Bazaar* magazine notes, "Instead of unspalike chocolates, treatment products such as a juniper foot-scrub lotion are left nightly with the bed turndown." Ihilani was chosen as one of the Top 10 Spa Resorts by readers of *Condé Nast Traveler* in 1997.

## ❖ CUISINE ❖

Executive chef Mark Adair says, "There are endless opportunities for creativity with the fresh seafood, exotic fruit, seaweeds, and farm-fresh vegetables that surround me in Hawaii." Currently using his talents to create delicious island-inspired spa cuisine, this award-winning chef has worked for several prominent hotels in the United States and Europe, and was guest chef for Prince Andrew's thirty-first birthday at Balmoral Castle. Guests enjoy fruit smoothies and herbal granitas between meals, and in the locker rooms sip complimentary "tea" made from passionfruit juice, cranberry juice, honey, and water.

## ✦ SETTING ✦

Sitting on a secluded lagoon and awash with the scent of plumeria blossoms, Ihilani has been called the "quintessential tropical playground." The hotel is set among thousands of coconut palms, banyans, monkeypods, and silver buttonwood trees, as well as flowering bougainvillea and firecracker plants. In addition to the spa, the resort offers a PGA-tournament golf course, six Kramer-surfaced tennis courts, and five restaurants. There are 387 rooms, including 42 suites, showcasing ocean vistas and featuring marble bathrooms with deep-soaking European tubs, state-of-the-art electronics, and private lanais with custom teak furnishings. On leaving the luxurious comfort of their rooms, guests will find the unspoiled white-sand beaches of four tranquil lagoons, and warm shore waters full of active marine life (complimentary snorkeling equipment is available).

## ✦ ACTIVITIES, TREATMENTS, AND FACILITIES ✦

Taking their cue from early Hawaiians, Ihilani therapists use herbs, ti leaves, and uhaloa leaves in body wraps, and offer traditional Hawaiian lomi lomi and Polynesian massage among their selection of body treatments. Ihilani also provides authentic thalassotherapy, an underwater massage utilizing warmed seawater that results in an almost euphoric sense of well-being. Emphasizing the ocean setting, activities include a morning beach power walk, seawater workouts in the hotel's pristine private lagoon, and invigorating "grand jet" and "needle shower" hydrotherapies. The ultramodern fitness facility contains the latest cardiovascular and strength-training equipment, a swimming pool, and a whirlpool bath. The full range of spa services includes facials with marine algae, stretching, yoga, tai chi, and "hulaerobics." There are four-day, seven-day, and single-day spa packages, each of which can be tailored to guests' needs, whether for weight-loss, energy-boosting, or simply relaxation and pampering.

# Gazpacho with Poached Scallops

*Start the gazpacho 24 hours before you plan to serve it, and the scallops at least 3 hours before.*

*Gazpacho*

¹/₂ ounce (15 g) guajillo chilies, stemmed and seeded,
   or 3 drops hot pepper sauce

³/₄ cup (6 fl oz/185 ml) chicken stock (see Basics)
   or canned low-salt chicken broth

4 large Roma (plum) tomatoes

1 small yellow onion, sliced

1 garlic clove

1 teaspoon extra-virgin olive oil

3 tablespoons fresh lime juice

2¹/₂ tablespoons chopped fresh cilantro

Salt and ground white pepper to taste


2 cups (16 fl oz/500 ml) dry white wine

2 teaspoons extra-virgin olive oil

2 garlic cloves, crushed

1 shallot, minced

12 sea scallops

¹/₃ cup (¹/₂ oz/15 g) *each* minced fresh flat-leaf parsley and cilantro

4 tablespoons pumpkin seeds, toasted (see Basics)

4 fresh cilantro sprigs

To make the gazpacho: Preheat the oven to 425°F (220°C). Arrange the chilies, if using, on a baking sheet and bake in the preheated oven for 2 minutes, being careful not to scorch them. Remove from the oven (leave the oven on).

In a saucepan, heat the stock or broth over medium heat. Add the roasted chilies or hot pepper sauce and simmer for 5 minutes. Remove from heat and set aside to cool.

Lightly coat the tomatoes, onion, and garlic clove with the olive oil. Place them in a baking ban and bake in the preheated oven for 35 to 45 minutes, or until the onion begins to brown, stirring occasionally. (If the onion begins to stick, add a few tablespoons of water). Remove from the oven and set aside to cool.

In a blender or food processor, combine the roasted vegetables, lime juice, cilantro, chilies, and stock or broth and purée. Strain through a fine-meshed sieve. Cover and refrigerate for 24 hours.

Just before serving, season the gazpacho with salt and white pepper. In a saucepan, bring the wine, olive oil, garlic, and shallot to a simmer. Add the scallops and simmer for 4 minutes. Remove from heat and stir in the minced herbs. Cover and refrigerate for 3 hours. Using a slotted spoon, remove the scallops from the broth and slice them thinly.

To serve: Arrange the scallop slices in an overlapping circle in the center of each of 4 chilled shallow soup bowls. Garnish each with 1 tablespoon pumpkin seeds and a cilantro sprig. Present the soup bowls and then ladle in the gazpacho.

*Makes 4 servings*

PER SERVING

*Calories 140 • Carbohydrates 9 g • Cholesterol 5 mg • Fat 8 g • Protein 9 g • Sodium 50 mg*

# Seared Ahi Tuna with Couscous Salad

## Tuna

    12 ounces (375 g) ahi tuna

    2 tablespoons togaroshi pepper* or other pepper seasoning

    1/4 teaspoon olive oil

## Marinated Beans

    4 ounces (125 g) shelled, blanched, and peeled fava beans

    12 red pear or cherry tomatoes, halved

    12 yellow pear or cherry tomatoes, halved

    1 teaspoon fresh opal or sweet basil, cut into julienne

    2 teaspoons balsamic vinegar

    1 teaspoon extra-virgin olive oil

    Salt and ground white pepper to taste

## Couscous

    1 cup (8 fl oz/250 ml) chicken stock (see Basics),
        canned low-salt chicken broth, or water

    3/4 cup (6 1/2 oz/200 g) couscous

    2 tablespoons ogo (fresh seaweed), chopped (optional)

    2 tablespoons peeled, seeded (see Basics), and chopped tomato

    2 tablespoons sliced green onion

    1 teaspoon Asian (toasted) sesame oil

    1/2 teaspoon cayenne pepper

    1/2 teaspoon salt

Have your fishmonger cut the ahi tuna into rectangular 2-by-3-inch (5-by-7.5-cm) sashimi blocks. Dust the tuna with pepper seasoning. Heat a sauté pan or skillet over high heat and film with the olive oil. Sear the ahi tuna for 6 seconds on each side. Remove from the pan and set aside to cool.

In a pot of lightly salted boiling water, cook the fava beans for 3 minutes. Drain in a colander and run under cold water to stop the cooking process; drain again.

In a medium bowl, toss the fava beans with the tomatoes, basil, vinegar, and olive oil. Season lightly with salt and pepper. Set aside.

In a medium saucepan, bring the stock, broth, or water just to a boil. Stir in the couscous and cover the pan. Remove from heat and let stand for 5 minutes. Lightly fluff the couscous with a fork.

In a medium bowl, combine the couscous, ogo, tomato, green onion, sesame oil, cayenne, and salt. Mix well and set aside for 1 hour.

Mound the couscous salad attractively in the center of each of 4 plates. (The Ihilani Resort & Spa uses a seashell to mold the couscous salad.) Spread the marinated beans around the couscous. Slice the tuna very thinly and arrange it over the bean salad.

*Makes 4 servings*

### PER SERVING

*Calories 290 • Carbohydrates 35 g • Cholesterol 40 mg • Fat 4.5 g • Protein 27 g • Sodium 360 mg*

---

*\*Togaroshi pepper blend can be found in Japanese markets. If you cannot find it, substitute another pepper seasoning, such as a Cajun spice blend.*

# Mango Yogurt Flan with Almond Crisps and Tropical Fruit

*The flan must be refrigerated for 4 hours before serving.*

*Flan*

> ¼ cup (2 fl oz/60 ml) low-fat milk
> ¼ cup (2 fl oz/60 ml) mango purée (see Basics)
> ½ cup (6 oz/185 g) honey
> 1 envelope (1 tablespoon) plain gelatin
> ¼ cup (2 fl oz/60 ml) cold water
> 2 cups (16 oz/500 g) plain low-fat yogurt

*Almond Crisps*

> ⅓ cup (2 oz/60 g) plus 3 tablespoons all-purpose flour
> ¼ teaspoon baking soda
> ½ cup (4 oz/125 g) sugar
> ½ cup (2½ oz/45 g) almonds, toasted (see Basics) and ground
> 1 egg white

> 3 cups (12 oz/375 g) sliced fresh tropical fruit (papaya, mango, guava, or banana) and/or fresh berries
> 6 fresh mint sprigs for garnish

Lightly coat six 3-ounce (90-ml) ramekins with vegetable oil spray.

In a medium saucepan, combine the milk, mango purée, and honey and simmer for 10 minutes, stirring occasionally.

In a small bowl, soak the gelatin in the cold water for 5 minutes. Stir into the hot mango mixture. Remove the saucepan from heat and stir the mixture until the gelatin is completely dissolved. Set aside to cool to room temperature. Fold in the yogurt and divide the mixture evenly among the ramekins. Refrigerate for 4 hours, or until set.

To make the almond crisps: Preheat the oven to 375°F (190°C). Line 2 baking sheets with parchment paper.

In a medium bowl, combine the flour, baking soda, sugar, and ground almonds. In a second bowl, beat the egg white until stiff, glossy peaks form. Fold the egg white into the almond mixture to form a smooth, sticky dough.

Fill a pastry bag fitted with a ¼-inch (6-mm) plain tip and pipe 2-inch (5-cm) lengths of dough onto the parchment paper, spacing the cookies 2 inches (5 cm) apart. Bake in the preheated oven for 7 to 8 minutes, or until golden brown. Remove the crisps and transfer them from the pan to a wire rack. If the crisps are made ahead, they can be stored in an airtight container.

To serve, unmold the flans onto 6 chilled plates and arrange the tropical fruit and/or berries around the flan. Scatter the crisps around each plate and garnish with a mint sprig.

*Makes 6 servings*

PER SERVING

*Calories 360 • Carbohydrates 66 g • Cholesterol 5 mg • Fat 8 g • Protein 10 g • Sodium 130 mg*

# The Inn at Manitou

McKELLAR, ONTARIO

*An uncommonly satisfying, outrageously calming resort complex, exactly
where the rest of the world might least expect it.*

—Gourmet

### ✦ PROFILE ✦

This intimate spa and tennis resort is located on the pristine shores of Lake
Manitouwabing, on five hundred spectacular acres just north of Toronto.
The creation of Ben and Sheila Wise, The Inn at Manitou is a country retreat
with European amenities, combining a world-class tennis club and health spa
with luxurious lodgings, gourmet cuisine, and a recently added golf academy.
As reported in the *Globe and Mail*, this is "one of the finest inns on the continent . . . remarkable for its comfortable ambience and sophisticated elegance,"
and it is a member of the prestigious Relais & Chateaux. Open from May to
late October, The Inn makes the most of the season's clement weather and the
area's natural beauty. Guests enjoy the innkeepers' passion for detail, style, and
warm personalized service, as well as such special events as chamber-music
concerts, cooking classes by guest chefs, and jazz performances by top
Canadian musicians. Families will be especially interested in the adjacent camp
for kids—Manitou Sports & Arts Centre—located just down the lake.

### ✦ CUISINE ✦

Great meals are part of the experience at The Inn at Manitou, whether you prefer low-fat spa food, bistro fare, or remarkable French contemporary cuisine.
Breakfasts are full American or English in style; light, healthful lunches are
served on the terrace; and the candlelit dining room features nightly piano
music for romantic evenings. Truly a food-lover's destination, The Inn boasts a
kitchen of twelve French chefs who have won international accolades.

## ❖ SETTING ❖

The Inn at Manitou's gracious accommodations are clustered near the tennis courts and on a knoll with lake views. The thirty-three deluxe rooms, suites, and lakeshore "country houses" have natural-cedar cathedral ceilings, log-burning fireplaces, marble washrooms, private sundecks, and comfortably luxurious interiors. Also on the grounds are an outdoor heated swimming pool with a dry sauna and Jacuzzi, a billiards room, a tea room, and several comfortable spots for reading and relaxing. The Manitou Golf Academy offers clinics for players at all levels, plus special programs for juniors, and the tennis center features thirteen courts and fourteen pros for lessons and games. Other recreational pursuits include swimming, horseback riding, windsurfing, sailing, kayaking, fishing, and mountain biking.

## ❖ ACTIVITIES, TREATMENTS, AND FACILITIES ❖

Treatments at Manitou's health and beauty spa include Swedish, sports, and shiatsu massages; reflexology, aromatherapy, and hydrotherapy; algae wraps, toning leg wraps, and mud wraps; facial treatments; and fitness consultations. Fitness activities include a variety of aerobics and body-toning classes, plus workouts with the latest exercise/weight equipment and early morning walks around the property. Containing a large aerobics studio, spacious treatment rooms, and a state-of-the-art gym, the 13,000-square-foot spa facility is decorated in restful hues of beige, cream, and white and is bathed in natural light. In the lounge, guests can select from an array of herbal teas and fresh juices while they relax or wait for a treatment. Spa at Manitou services are available à la carte or as part of three-, four-, or seven-day spa packages.

# MENU

*Roast Tomatoes Filled with Pine Nuts, Couscous, and Chanterelles*

❖

*Salmon with Potatoes and Cabbage Cream Sauce*

❖

*Baked Apples with Raisins and Cinnamon-Vanilla Ice Cream*

# Roast Tomatoes Filled with Pine Nuts, Couscous, and Chanterelles

8 tomatoes, peeled (see Basics)

4 teaspoons rosemary olive oil* or extra-virgin olive oil

8 garlic cloves

8 *each* fresh thyme sprigs, tarragon sprigs, and basil leaves

8 bay leaves

3/4 cup (6 fl oz/180 ml) vegetable stock (see Basics),
  canned low-salt vegetable broth, or water

1/2 cup (31/4 oz/95 g) couscous

3 ounces (90 g) chanterelle mushrooms, diced and sautéed

2 tablespoons finely chopped cucumber

2 tablespoons pine nuts, toasted (see Basics)

2 tablespoons corn kernels, sautéed

1 teaspoon olive oil

1 teaspoon *each* minced fresh mint, tarragon, and chives

2 teaspoons tomato purée

Salt and freshly ground pepper

24 chives, each 3 inches (7.5 cm) long, for garnish

Preheat the oven to 300°F (150°C). Slice off the bottom and top of each tomato; reserve the tops to use later as lids. Using a melon-ball cutter or a small spoon, scoop out the center pulp of the tomato shells and remove the seeds; reserve the tomato pulp.

Rub the inside of each tomato with the olive oil. Place a garlic clove, thyme sprig, tarragon sprig, bay leaf, and basil leaf inside each tomato shell. Place the lids back on and bake the tomatoes in the preheated oven for 15 minutes, or until they are softened but not losing their shape. Remove the herbs and garlic and discard.

In a medium saucepan, bring the stock, broth, or water just to a boil. Stir in the couscous and cover the pan. Remove from heat and let stand for 5 minutes. Lightly fluff the couscous with a fork. Gently stir in the mushrooms, reserved tomato pulp, cucumber, pine nuts, and corn. Add the 1 teaspoon olive oil, minced herbs, tomato purée, salt, and pepper and stir until thoroughly combined.

Spoon the couscous mixture into the still-warm tomatoes and replace the lids. Rub a little olive oil on the outside of the tomatoes and transfer them to a baking sheet. Bake in the preheated oven for 5 to 7 minutes.

Place 2 tomatoes on each of 4 plates and garnish with 3 chives. For a more dramatic presentation, spill some of the couscous out of the tomatoes onto the plate.

*Makes 8 stuffed tomatoes; serves 4*

## PER SERVING

*Calories 300 • Carbohydrates 45 g • Cholesterol 0 mg • Fat 11 g • Protein 11 g • Sodium 55 mg*

---

*Rosemary olive oil can be found in specialty foods stores and some grocery stores.*

THE INN AT MANITOU

# Salmon with Potatoes and Cabbage Cream Sauce

2 cups (16 fl oz/500 ml) chicken stock (see Basics)
  or canned low-salt chicken broth

3 ounces (90 g) smoked pork

4 large Savoy cabbage leaves

1 pound (500 g) potatoes, sliced

$^{1}/_{2}$ cup (4 fl oz/125 ml) half and half

1 tablespoon truffle oil

Salt and freshly ground pepper to taste

2 tablespoons extra-virgin olive oil

Four 5-ounce (155-g) salmon fillets, boned

4 handfuls mixed salad greens

16 fresh chervil sprigs

In a medium saucepan, combine the stock or broth and smoked pork and bring to a boil. Remove from heat and let sit until cool. Remove and discard the pork.

In a large pot of salted boiling water, cook the cabbage leaves for 2 minutes, or until completely soft. Drain and run under cold water to stop the cooking process. Drain again and transfer the leaves to a blender or food processor and purée.

Meanwhile, in a pot of salted boiling water, cook the potatoes for 15 minutes, or until tender when pierced with a fork.

In a small saucepan, bring the infused stock or broth to a boil and cook until reduced by about one-third. Pour in the half and half and stir until the sauce thickens enough to coat the back of a spoon. Stir in the cabbage purée, truffle oil, salt, and pepper and remove from heat.

In a large skillet over medium heat, heat the olive oil and cook the salmon, skin side down, for 4 minutes. Turn and cook for 1 minute on the second side, or until the salmon is opaque on the outside but still translucent in the very center.

Arrange the potato slices on each of 4 plates and top with a salmon fillet. Arrange some of the baby salad greens on top of the salmon and scatter 4 chervil sprigs over. Pour some of the cabbage cream sauce around the potatoes. Serve immediately.

*Makes 4 servings*

PER SERVING

*Calories 450 • Carbohydrates 26 g • Cholesterol 95 mg • Fat 21 g • Protein 38 g • Sodium 670 mg*

# Baked Apples with Raisins and Cinnamon-Vanilla Ice Cream

*Both the tulip baskets and the ice cream in this recipe can be prepared 2 or 3 days ahead of serving.*

> **4 large green apples, peeled and cored**
> **³/4 cup (7 oz/220 g) mincemeat**
> **¹/4 cup (2 fl oz/60 ml) water**
> **²/3 cup (5 oz/155 g) sugar**

*Cinnamon-Vanilla Ice Cream*

> **2 cinnamon sticks, broken**
> **³/4 cup (4 oz/125 g) low-fat vanilla ice cream, slightly softened**

*Tulip Baskets*

> **¹/2 cup (4 oz/125 g) unsalted butter, at room temperature**
> **¹/2 cup (4 oz/125 g) sugar**
> **4 egg whites**
> **³/4 cup (4 oz/125 g) unbleached all-purpose flour**

> **Chocolate shavings for garnish (optional)**

Preheat the oven to 350°F (180°C). Place the apples on a baking sheet and fill the cores with mincemeat.

In a small, heavy saucepan, combine the water and sugar and cook over medium heat until caramelized to a light golden-brown color.

Coat each apple with caramel. Bake in the preheated oven for 25 minutes, or until the apples are tender but not losing their shape. Remove the apples, but leave the oven on.

Meanwhile, make the cinnamon-vanilla ice cream: In a spice grinder, grind the cinnamon sticks to a fine powder. In a small bowl, stir the ice cream and cinnamon together until well blended. Scoop the ice cream into 4 balls and refreeze.

To make the tulip baskets: Lightly coat a baking sheet with vegetable oil spray. In a medium bowl, cream the butter and sugar together until light and fluffy. Stir in the egg whites, one at a time. Fold in the flour until blended.

Spoon tablespoonfuls of the batter onto the prepared pan and spread out to make 8 thin circles; do not let the circles touch. Bake in the preheated oven for 7 to 8 minutes, or until golden brown around the edges. Using a metal spatula, remove from the oven and quickly place each tuile over an individual ramekin or small glass. Let the cookies cool over the molds. The tulip baskets may be stored in airtight containers for 2 to 3 days.

To serve, spoon a little caramel on each of 4 plates and top with a warm apple. Place a tulip basket next to the apple and fill it with a ball of cinnamon-vanilla ice cream. If desired, decorate the ice cream with chocolate shavings. Serve immediately.

***Makes 4 servings***

PER SERVING

*Calories 590 • Carbohydrates 116 g • Cholesterol 35 mg • Fat 15 g • Protein 5 g • Sodium 55 mg*

# MENU

---

*BREAKFAST*

---

**Energizer Cereal with Apple Butter**

---

*LUNCH*

---

**Southwestern Taco Salad**

---

*DINNER*

---

**Spa California Rolls**

**Artichoke, Mushroom, and Sun-Dried Tomato Phyllo Pouches**

**Fruit Tabbouleh with Mango and Raspberry Coulis**

# La Costa Resort & Spa

Carlsbad, California

*The war against flabby thighs doesn't detract from the spa's basic philosophy of divine excess and indulgence: smiling women in white will draw you a milk bath before an aromatherapy massage, and there is a choice of fruit-scented gels in the showers.*

—Town & Country

## ❖ PROFILE ❖

Located thirty miles north of San Diego on the California coast, La Costa Resort and Spa is a luxury resort featuring an award-winning health spa, two 18-hole golf courses, and a racquet club. Rated one of the Top Ten Spas by *Condé Nast Traveler* and named the Best Spa Worldwide by *The Robb Report* five years in a row, it is a wonderful place for relaxation and rejuvenation, pampering skin- and body-care treatments, and—if desired—tennis and golf clinics on championship facilities. This is a great hideaway for couples and families, accommodating those who want an action-packed, sports-filled vacation as well as those who just need a leisurely getaway. For kids, Camp La Costa provides day-long supervised activities, and the San Diego Zoo and Sea World are close by.

## ❖ CUISINE ❖

Guests at La Costa enjoy food from five different restaurants, three of which—Brasserie La Costa, Ristorante Figaro, and Pisces—serve spa cuisine alongside their regular menus. Everything is overseen by Josef Lageder, the prize-winning executive chef noted for his inspired blending of French and California cuisines and artistic food presentations. In addition, you may wish to attend low-fat cooking demonstrations, where you will learn to adapt favorite recipes, prepare spa specialties, and stock your home kitchen. A personal nutrition consultation will help you improve eating habits and adjust any deficiencies in your diet.

## ✦ SETTING ✦

La Costa offers 478 accommodations, from deluxe rooms to suites to multi-bedroom residences (you can request rooms adjacent to the spa if that is your main destination). The luxurious lodgings are decorated in relaxing shades of salmon, peach, and terra-cotta, and feature hand-carved mahogany furniture and original artwork. Situated on 450 rolling acres between the Pacific Ocean and nearby foothills, the resort enjoys a temperate climate year-round and is beautifully landscaped and maintained. In addition to the championship golf courses, there are twenty-one tennis courts with tournament-play surfaces, swimming pools, and jogging/walking trails throughout the grounds.

## ✦ ACTIVITIES, TREATMENTS, AND FACILITIES ✦

The spa program at La Costa offers a variety of classes, each aimed at revitalizing the vacationer while providing the foundation for a long-term healthy lifestyle. Spa amenities include separate women's and men's centers, complete with sundecks, saunas, whirlpools, steam rooms, and Swiss showers. Women can enjoy skinny-dipping in the women-only pool, and there is a water complex with a koi-filled lagoon and cascading waterfall. Classes include step, stretch, yoga, circuit training, visualization, and "aquathinics," while the comprehensive selection of spa services includes personal consultations; a variety of massages, aromatherapy, and skin treatments (there's a facial specifically for sun damage); a spirulina wrap, a Turkish scrub, and herbal baths for different skin types. "The true luxury of La Costa is the personal attention guests receive... Locker-room attendants remember your name and slipper size and hand out fresh towels and robes without being asked," says *Fodor's Healthy Escapes*, and lemon water is served everywhere for rehydration after exercising and treatments. Whether you want luxurious pampering or a structured fitness schedule, you may choose à la carte sampling, day-spa indulgence, or a two- to seven-day program.

# Energizer Cereal with Apple Butter

*This hearty breakfast cereal can be kept in the refrigerator for up to 5 days. Simply reheat it in the microwave for a delicious hot breakfast.*

> 3 cups (24 fl oz/750 ml) water
> 1/2 cup (8 oz/250 g) uncooked Kashi Breakfast Pilaf*
> 1 cup (3 oz/90 g) quick-cooking rolled oats
> 4 tablespoons (2 fl oz/60 ml) Apple Butter (recipe follows) or puréed fruit
> 4 tablespoons (1 1/2 oz/45 g) raisins
> 4 tablespoons (1/2 oz/15 g) oat bran

In a small saucepan, bring 1 cup (8 fl oz/250 ml) of the water to a boil. Add the Kashi, cover, and reduce the heat to low. Cook for 40 minutes, or until all the liquid has been absorbed and the Kashi is soft.

Meanwhile, in a medium saucepan, combine the oats and the remaining 2 cups (16 fl oz/500 ml) water. Bring to a boil, reduce heat, and simmer, stirring constantly, until thickened, 3 to 5 minutes.

In a medium bowl, combine the Kashi and oatmeal and blend thoroughly. Serve immediately, or cover and refrigerate until ready to serve. Just before serving, reheat in the microwave.

To serve, spoon into bowls and top with 1 tablespoon each of apple butter or puréed fruit, raisins, and oat bran.

*Makes 4 servings*

### PER SERVING

*Calories 160 • Carbohydrates 33 g • Cholesterol 0 mg • Fat 2 g • Protein 5 g • Sodium 10 mg*

---

*Kashi Breakfast Pilaf is a grain mixture that is sold in many natural foods stores and some supermarkets. Do not confuse it with Kashi Puffed Grain Cereal.*

## Apple Butter

**2 large Granny Smith apples, cored and thinly sliced**
**³/4 cup (6 fl oz/185 ml) unsweetened apple juice**
**¹/2 tablespoon ground cinnamon**
**¹/2 tablespoon fresh lemon juice**
**Dash of ground cloves**

In a medium saucepan, bring the apples, apple juice, cinnamon, and lemon juice to a boil. Reduce heat to a simmer, cover, and cook for 1 hour. Transfer to a blender or food processor, add the cloves, and blend until smooth. Refrigerate until ready to serve.

*Makes 1¹/2 cups (12 fl oz/375 ml)*

### PER TABLESPOON

*Calories 15 • Carbohydrates 4 g • Cholesterol 0 mg • Fat 0 g • Protein 0 g • Sodium 0 mg*

## Southwestern Taco Salad

1 large head romaine lettuce, cored and finely chopped

3 Roma (plum) tomatoes, chopped

$1/2$ cup (4 oz/125 g) nonfat plain yogurt

4 ounces (125 g) skinless chicken breast, grilled or poached and chopped

1 cup (4 oz/125 g) shredded low-fat Cheddar cheese

1 avocado, pitted, peeled, and cut into 16 paper-thin slices

24 Spa Corn Chips (recipe follows)

1 cup (8 fl oz/250 ml) Fresh Tomato Salsa (see page 129)

In a large bowl, mix together the lettuce, tomatoes, and yogurt. Divide the lettuce mixture evenly among 4 plates, piling the mixture into the center and trying to make it stand up as much as possible. Sprinkle one-fourth of the chicken and one-fourth of the cheese onto the top of each salad. Top each with 4 slices of avocado and decorate with 6 spa corn chips. Serve with salsa.

*Makes 4 servings*

### PER SERVING

*Calories 280 • Carbohydrates 27 g • Cholesterol 20 mg • Fat 12 g • Protein 20 g • Sodium 320 mg*

## Spa Corn Chips

*Try sprinkling on salt-free seasonings for added flavor.*

4 corn tortillas

Preheat the oven to 300°F (150°C). Lightly coat a baking sheet with vegetable oil spray. Slice each tortilla into 6 even wedges. Arrange the tortilla pieces on the baking sheet and bake in the preheated oven for 7 minutes. Turn the chips over and bake for 7 minutes more, or until crisp. Watch carefully, as the chips can burn very quickly.

*Makes 24 chips; 4 servings*

### PER SERVING

*Calories 60 • Carbohydrates 12 g • Cholesterol 0 mg • Fat 0.5 g • Protein 2 g • Sodium 40 mg*

# Spa California Rolls

3 tablespoons rice vinegar

2 cups (10 oz/315 g) cooked brown rice

4 sheets (2 oz/60 g) nori*

1/2 avocado, peeled, pitted, and cut into thin slices

1 carrot, peeled, cut into matchsticks, and blanched

1/2 cup (2 oz/60 g) finely chopped celery

1/4 cup (3/4 oz/20 g) green onion, thinly sliced

10 ounces (315 g) cooked medium shrimp, peeled, deveined, and halved horizontally

Low-salt soy sauce (optional)

Wasabi** (optional)

In a medium bowl, sprinkle the rice vinegar over the rice and toss.

Lay a nori sheet on a sushi mat or a bamboo place mat. Spread 1/2 cup (3 oz/90 g) of the brown rice over the nori. On a long edge of the sheet, layer one-fourth of the avocado, carrot, celery, green onion, and shrimp. Using the sushi mat to help, roll up the nori. Repeat with the remaining nori sheets, rice, vegetables, and shrimp.

Cut each sushi roll into 6 slices. Serve with soy sauce and wasabi, if desired.

*Makes 6 servings, 4 rolls each*

### PER SERVING

*Calories 230 • Carbohydrates 31 g • Cholesterol 110 mg • Fat 5 g • Protein 17 g • Sodium 160 mg*

*Nori are dark-colored sheets of dried seaweed. They are available in natural foods stores and Asian markets.*

**Wasabi is hot green Japanese horseradish that is sold as a paste or a powder. The powder is mixed with an equal amount of water to make a paste. Wasabi is available in specialty foods stores and Asian markets.*

# Artichoke, Mushroom, and Sun-Dried Tomato Phyllo Pouches

- 5 ounces (155 g) mixed mushrooms, such as shiitakes, cremini, and/or white mushrooms, sliced
- 1 red onion, thinly sliced
- 2 tablespoons minced garlic
- 18 frozen artichoke hearts, thawed and drained
- 1/2 cup (1 1/2 oz/45 g) sun-dried tomatoes, soaked in water, drained, and sliced
- 2 tablespoons low-salt soy sauce
- 1/2 teaspoon ground white pepper
- 2 eggs, beaten
- 2 cups (16 oz/500 g) nonfat cottage cheese, drained
- 1/4 cup (1 oz/30 g) grated Parmesan cheese
- 3 tablespoons minced fresh herbs, such as oregano, basil, and dill
- 6 sheets frozen phyllo dough, thawed

Preheat the oven to 300°F (150°C). Lightly coat a large sauté pan with vegetable oil spray and heat over medium heat. Sauté the onion for 4 minutes. Add the garlic and sauté for 1 minute. Add the artichoke hearts, sun-dried tomatoes, sliced mushrooms, soy sauce, and pepper. Sauté for 10 minutes, or until the mushrooms are soft. In a large bowl, mix together the eggs, cottage cheese, Parmesan cheese, and herbs. Stir in the artichoke mixture and mix until well blended.

Lay 1 phyllo sheet on a flat work surface. Cover the remaining phyllo with a damp cloth. Fold the phyllo sheet in half and lightly coat the edges with vegetable oil spray. Place 3/4 cup (12 oz/375 g) of the artichoke mixture in the center of the sheet. Gather all the corners into the center and push together to close. Spray the outside of the pouch with vegetable oil spray. Repeat with the remaining phyllo. Place the 6 pouches on the prepared pan and bake in the preheated oven for 12 to 15 minutes, or until golden brown.

*Makes 6 servings*

### PER SERVING

*Calories 200 • Carbohydrates 23 g • Cholesterol 80 mg • Fat 4.5 g • Protein 18 g • Sodium 740 mg*

# Fruit Tabbouleh with Mango and Raspberry Coulis

### Tabbouleh

$^3/_4$ cup (6$^1/_2$ oz/200 g) couscous

1 cup (8 fl oz/250 ml) fresh orange juice, at room temperature

$^1/_2$ cup (4 fl oz/125 ml) pineapple juice, at room temperature

2 tablespoons fructose* or sugar

### Mango and Raspberry Coulis

1 ripe mango, peeled, cut away from the pit, and chopped

3 tablespoons fructose* or sugar

2 tablespoons plus 1 teaspoon fresh lemon juice

$^1/_2$ cup (2 oz/60 g) fresh raspberries

### Fresh-Fruit Ratatouille

1 small kiwifruit, peeled and finely diced

1 cup (6 oz/185 g) finely diced cantaloupe

1 cup (4 oz/125 g) finely diced strawberries

1 cup (6 oz/185 g) finely diced pineapple

To make the tabbouleh: In a medium bowl, stir the couscous, $^1/_2$ cup (4 fl oz/125 ml) of the orange juice, the pineapple juice, and fructose or sugar together. Cover and set aside for about 2 hours, or until all the juice has been absorbed by the couscous. Stir in the remaining $^1/_2$ cup (4 fl oz/125 ml) orange juice and let stand until absorbed, about 20 minutes longer.

Meanwhile, make the coulis: In a blender or food processor, purée the mango, 1$^1/_2$ tablespoons of the fructose or sugar, and the 2 tablespoons lemon juice. Strain the purée through a fine-meshed sieve.

Clean the processor bowl. Add the raspberries, the remaining 1$^1/_2$ tablespoons fructose or sugar, and the 1 teaspoon lemon juice, and purée. Strain the sauce through a fine-meshed sieve. Reserve the two coulis separately.

Set twelve 2-inch-deep (5-cm), 3$^1/_2$-inch-diameter (9-cm) ring molds on a baking sheet. Divide the couscous among the molds and lightly fluff up the couscous in each mold at an angle so there is a higher side, and a very low side about $^1/_4$ inch (6 mm) high.

To make the fruit ratatouille: In a medium bowl, toss the diced fruits together. Spoon the ratatouille on top of the couscous in each mold, pressing to form an even layer.

Use a wide spatula to transfer each ring mold to a dessert plate. Carefully lift off the rings so that the ratatouille-topped couscous is free-standing. Spoon the mango coulis around the base of the couscous on each plate. Dot the mango coulis with raspberry coulis and serve.

*Makes 12 servings*

PER SERVING

*Calories 110 • Carbohydrates 25 g • Cholesterol 0 mg • Fat 0 g • Protein 2 g • Sodium 0 mg*

---

*Fructose is a refined sugar derived mainly from corn. It is available in natural foods stores.*

# MENU

*Salmon Mousse with Orange and Chervil*

*Seared Duck Breasts with Green Peppercorns and Mâche*

*Glazed Turnips*

*Chocolate Cake*

# The Lodge at Skylonda

### Woodside, California

*Embrace[s] both the great outdoors and the New Age mind-body connection . . . No mere spa, this "fitness getaway" is equal parts relaxation and rigor. . . . Meals are miraculous.*

**—Condé Nast Traveler**

## ❖ PROFILE ❖

Nestled in the majestic redwood forests of Northern California, on the ridge that separates Silicon Valley from the Pacific Ocean, the Lodge at Skylonda (named for the nineteenth-century logging mill that once occupied the site) offers privacy, quiet relaxation, body work, meditation, and fitness. Recently renovated, this small, rustic spa reopened in 1997 under new ownership (its previous name was Skylonda Retreat) and is a sister property to California's renowned Post Ranch Inn and Jean-Michel Cousteau's famed Fiji Island Resort. Balancing nature with nurture, Skylonda is not so much about beauty treatments as about getting outside and taking pleasure in the sights, sounds, and fragrances of long hikes through coastal forests. It was voted one of the 25 Coolest Places to Stay Now by *Condé Nast Traveler* in 1997.

## ❖ CUISINE ❖

Skylonda's healthy gourmet cuisine features fresh seasonal fare from local sources for all meals (picnic lunches are available for hikers). Meals average 1,500 calories a day and contain less than 15 percent fat. Every evening at sundown, guests gather for appetizers before a delicious dinner, described by *Fitness* magazine as "deceptively low-calorie, high-flavor dishes—like those you might expect to find in one of nearby San Francisco's chic restaurants." In addition to the wonderful meals, the kitchen of executive chef Sue Chapman offers cooking demonstrations that teach people how to make healthy dishes for themselves at home.

## ❖ SETTING ❖

Snug above the fog line at an elevation of two thousand feet in the Santa Cruz Mountains, the Lodge at Skylonda is a three-story log-and-stone building with rooms for seventeen guests and an environment of rustic elegance. The newly redesigned, larger guest rooms feature decks, patios, and spacious bathrooms with oversized soaking tubs. (Televisions and radios are not provided; telephones are available on request.) Serving as a gathering place for everyone, the Great Room has a vaulted ceiling and is made cozy by a crackling fire, a library of books, board games, magazines and newspapers, and a baby grand piano. The comfortable beds, harmonious interiors, soundproofing, and careful lighting combine to create a restful, peaceful experience, and guests report that it is calming just to be at Skylonda, surrounded by the giant redwoods.

## ❖ ACTIVITIES, TREATMENTS, AND FACILITIES ❖

The spa makes good use of fifty different hiking trails—some of them ancient—below towering redwoods, pines, and oaks. During a typical stay, guests go on a three-to nine-mile hike each day, winding through forests and lush meadows. The Skylonda fitness plan also includes circuit training, Cybex weight training, stretching, tai chi, and aquatics in a glass-enclosed, chemical-free pool. But it's not all rigorous: In a yoga pavilion built beneath the trees, yoga, deep breathing, and meditation treat mind and body, and awareness classes teach people how to slow down and become more in tune with themselves. In an outdoor massage area, guests are given daily massages to soothe and relax tight muscles and to promote circulation and flexibility—especially after all that hiking! Also offered are a "silent spirit quest," acupressure, foot reflexology, a bevy of personal-training selections, facials, pedicures, and other body treatments.

# Salmon Mousse with Orange and Chervil

*This delicate-flavored appetizer also makes a delicious light lunch when served with steamed asparagus or a tossed green salad.*

1 pound (500 g) salmon fillets, skinned, boned, and chopped

1 teaspoon minced garlic

4 egg whites

¼ cup (2 fl oz/60 ml) low-fat sour cream

2 teaspoons grated orange zest (see Basics)

1 to 2 tablespoons Grand Marnier or Triple Sec

¼ cup (½ oz/15 g) minced fresh chervil or chives

1 teaspoon salt

Preheat the oven to 375°F (190°C). Lightly coat a 9-by-5-inch (23-by-13-cm) terrine mold or loaf pan with vegetable oil spray.

In a blender or food processor, combine all the ingredients until emulsified. Spoon into the prepared pan or mold and bake in the preheated oven for 6 to 8 minutes, or until set. Let cool. Refrigerate for at least 4 hours, or until well chilled.

Just before serving, run a knife around the edges of the mousse. Unmold by dipping the pan or mold into a bowl of hot water, then inverting it on a plate. Cut into 6 slices with a knife that has been dipped in hot water. Arrange a slice on each of 6 plates and serve.

*Makes 6 servings*

PER SERVING

*Calories 120 • Carbohydrates 1 g • Cholesterol 45 mg • Fat 4.5 g • Protein 18 g • Sodium 480 mg*

# Seared Duck Breasts with Green Peppercorns and Mâche

*Marinade*

> ¹/₂ cup (4 fl oz/125 ml) white port
>
> ¹/₂ onion, sliced very thin
>
> 6 black peppercorns
>
> 1 bay leaf
>
> 1 carrot, sliced very thin
>
> 4 duck breast halves, skinned and trimmed of fat

*Green Peppercorn Sauce*

> 2 cups (16 fl oz/500 ml) white port
>
> 2 to 3 bay leaves
>
> 2 tablespoons minced shallot
>
> 2 cups (16 fl oz/500 ml) duck or chicken stock (see Basics) or canned low-salt chicken broth
>
> ¹/₂ to 1 tablespoon green peppercorns
>
> ¹/₂ cup (¹/₂ oz/15 g) shredded mâche
>
> ¹/₂ red onion, sliced very thin
>
> 1 tablespoon white wine vinegar or sherry vinegar
>
> 4 cups (4 oz/125 g) mâche
>
> 1 cup (1 oz/30 g) arugula

To make the marinade: Combine all the ingredients in a glass baking dish. Place the duck breasts in the baking dish and turn to coat with the marinade. Cover and refrigerate for 2 hours.

Remove the duck breasts from the marinade (reserve the marinade) and let sit at room temperature for 30 minutes. Preheat the oven to 400°F (200°C).

Heat a large sauté pan or skillet over medium-high heat until very hot. Sear the duck breasts briefly on each side. Return the duck to the baking dish with the marinade and bake in the preheated oven for 15 minutes, or until medium-rare. The breasts will cook very fast, so watch them closely.

176

To make the green peppercorn sauce: In a medium saucepan, combine the port, bay leaves, and shallot. Bring to a boil and cook to reduce the liquid by two-thirds. Pour in the stock or broth and continue cooking until reduced by half. Add the peppercorns and mâche. Pour any pan juices from the baked duck into the sauce. Strain the sauce through a fine-meshed sieve and set aside.

Lightly coat a large sauté pan or skillet with vegetable oil spray and heat over medium heat. Sauté the red onion for 5 minutes, or until soft. Add the vinegar, mâche, and arugula and sauté until slightly wilted.

Arrange the mâche mixture in the center of each of 4 plates. Thinly slice the duck breasts on a bias and fan them out over the mâche. Drizzle each serving with about 2 tablespoons of the green peppercorn sauce.

*Makes 4 servings*

PER SERVING

*Calories 270 • Carbohydrates 11 g • Cholesterol 110 mg • Fat 7 g • Protein 31 g • Sodium 105 mg*

# Glazed Turnips

4 small turnips, about 1 pound (500 g), peeled and quartered

1/2 cup (4 fl oz/125 ml) chicken stock (see Basics)
   or canned low-salt chicken broth

2 teaspoons minced shallot

2 teaspoons honey

1/2 teaspoon ground mace or nutmeg

Cook the turnips in salted boiling water for 15 minutes, or until almost tender when pierced with a fork. Drain the turnips of all but 1/2 cup (4 fl oz/125 ml) of their cooking water. Add the remaining ingredients to the turnips. Cook over medium-low heat until almost all the liquid evaporates and a glaze forms.

*Makes 4 servings*

PER SERVING

*Calories 45 • Carbohydrates 10 g • Cholesterol 0 mg • Fat 0 g • Protein 1 g • Sodium 80 mg*

# Chocolate Cake

*Although you won't taste the pumpkin purée in this easy-to-make recipe, it keeps this dense-flavored cake moist.*

³/₄ cup (7 oz/220 g) canned or homemade pumpkin purée (see Basics)

2 eggs, beaten

¹/₂ cup (4 fl oz/125 ml) canola oil

1 cup (8 oz/250 g) sugar

2 cups (10 oz/315 g) unbleached all-purpose flour

¹/₂ teaspoon baking soda

¹/₂ teaspoon baking powder

¹/₂ teaspoon salt

1 cup (3 oz/90 g) unsweetened cocoa powder

³/₄ cup (6 fl oz/185 ml) low-fat milk

Preheat the oven to 375°F (190°C). Lightly coat an 8-inch (20-cm) square cake pan with vegetable oil spray.

In a large bowl, combine the pumpkin purée, eggs, canola oil, and sugar and stir until well mixed.

In a medium bowl, stir the flour, baking soda, baking powder, salt, and cocoa powder together. Stir the flour mixture into the pumpkin mixture. Gradually stir in the milk until well blended.

Pour the batter into the prepared pan and bake in the preheated oven for 40 minutes, or until a knife inserted in the center comes out clean.

*Makes one 8-inch (20-cm) cake*

PER SERVING (each 2-by-2-inch/5-by-5-cm piece)

*Calories 190 • Carbohydrates 28 g • Cholesterol 30 mg • Fat 9 g • Protein 4 g • Sodium 135 mg*

# MENU

*Spa Chef's Salad*

❖

*Pacific Halibut with Citrus and Basil*

❖

*Chilled California Berries Soup*

# Meadowood Napa Valley

### St. Helena, California

*Meadowood . . . recalls the grand old resorts of the early 1900s
with its gabled lodges overlooking the manicured croquet lawn and
golf course . . . and [the spa] epitomizes the Napa Valley lifestyle:
easy informality and superb taste.*

**—Fodor's Healthy Escapes**

## ✦ PROFILE ✦

Meadowood is located in the heart of the Napa Valley, about an hour-and-a-half drive north of San Francisco. Once an exclusive private club, today it is a country resort of refined comfort featuring a full-service health spa, a nine-hole golf course, seven tennis courts, and two competition croquet lawns, complete with all the necessary equipment and a world-class professional for personal croquet lessons! A wine-lover's delight, Meadowood also offers tours of local vineyards, an extraordinary cellar, a Friday-night wine reception, and classes with John Thoreen, who will help you develop personal insight into wines and confidence in your palate. The resort has been named Best of the Year "Weekend at a Resort" by *Bon Appétit* and is a member of Relais & Chateaux.

## ✦ CUISINE ✦

The Restaurant at Meadowood serves fresh Wine Country cuisine (a Vintner's Tasting Menu is available) and offers a view of the resort's lush lawns and wooded hillsides. The Grill at Meadowood features bistro food served in a more casual atmosphere. During summer months, the Poolside Cafe is also open. The resort's spa menu draws inspiration from California's bounty of produce and seafood in its selection of light, healthy dishes. The following delicious recipes were created by chefs Didier Lenders and Maria del Pilar Sanchez.

## ❖ SETTING ❖

Located on 250 wooded acres dotted with old stone fences, Meadowood contains eighty-five luxurious rooms and suites in country-traditional lodges complete with white dormers and furnished porches. The rooms feature fieldstone fireplaces, high ceilings, gabled windows, watercolor prints, radiant heat, and large tile bathrooms. A variety of cultural events, such as concerts, lectures, and seminars, are held year-round at the resort, which is a favorite gathering place for the wine-making community. Meadowood also hosts such events as the Napa Valley Wine Auction and the Meadowood Croquet Classic.

## ❖ ACTIVITIES, TREATMENTS, AND FACILITIES ❖

Spa programs at Meadowood range from à la carte to day spas to a week's worth of pampering treatments and physical challenges—all with the goal of returning your body to "its perfect balanced state." The health spa offers two sun-filled gyms, state-of-the-art weight equipment, an Olympic-size swimming pool, a whirlpool, saunas, and steam rooms. There are also bicycles to rent and a shaded three-mile hiking trail on the grounds. At Meadowood, you can participate in exercise classes such as yoga, step, and aqua aerobics and benefit from private consultations in nutrition, physiology, and fitness. There is a complete range of luxurious treatments, including ayurvedic massages, reflexology, facials, a rehydrating aloe body wrap, a mineral-rich salt scrub, and massages with the resort's own soothing Chardonnay lotion, made from Napa Valley Chardonnay grapes, seaweed, vitamin E, sweet almond and sesame oils, and extracts of chamomile, calendula, lavender, sweet melissa, and orange.

## Spa Chef's Salad

3 tablespoons walnut oil

1 tablespoon white wine vinegar

Salt and freshly ground pepper to taste

Leaves from $1/2$ head butter lettuce

Leaves from $1/2$ head romaine lettuce

Leaves from $1/2$ head red leaf lettuce

$1/2$ bunch watercress

1 cup baby spinach leaves

Leaves from 1 Belgian endive

4 green onions, sliced (white part only)

2 ounces (60 g) shiitake mushrooms, stemmed and sliced

2 ounces (60 g) oyster mushrooms, sliced

10 radishes, sliced

1 Red Delicious apple, peeled, cored, and thinly sliced

1 avocado, peeled, pitted, and thinly sliced

$1/2$ cup chopped walnuts

In a small bowl, whisk the oil and vinegar together; add salt and pepper. Wash the lettuce, pat dry, and tear into bite-sized pieces. Wash and dry the watercress, leaving the whole stem.

In a large bowl, combine the lettuce, watercress, and the remaining ingredients. Add the dressing and toss lightly until mixed. Divide the salad evenly among each of 4 plates.

*Makes 4 servings*

### PER SERVING

*Calories 330 • Carbohydrates 21 g • Cholesterol 0 mg • Fat 28 g • Protein 6 g • Sodium 35 mg*

# Pacific Halibut with Citrus and Basil

8 small new potatoes, preferably purple, peeled and diced

3 tablespoons butter

Salt and freshly ground pepper to taste

Low-fat milk, warmed (optional)

2 tablespoons canola oil

Four 6-ounce (180-g) halibut fillets

2 navel oranges, peeled and cut into sections

2 pink grapefruits, peeled and cut into sections

2 seedless tangerines, peeled and cut into sections

4 tablespoons finely shredded fresh basil

6 tablespoons extra-virgin olive oil

Cook the potatoes in salted boiling water for 10 to 15 minutes, or until tender. Drain and pass the potatoes through a food mill or mash with a potato masher. In a medium bowl, stir the potatoes and butter together until the butter is completely melted. Add salt to taste. (Note: Purple potatoes are naturally creamy, so it is not necessary to add any milk. However, if you prefer creamier potatoes, add a little warm milk.)

In a large nonstick sauté pan or skillet over medium heat, heat the canola oil. Salt and pepper both sides of the halibut fillets. Carefully add the fish to the hot pan and cook for about 4 minutes on one side. Meanwhile, in a medium bowl, toss the citrus sections, basil, olive oil, and a pinch of salt together until mixed. Turn the fish over and cook for 3 to 4 minutes more, or until the fillets are lightly browned on both sides and opaque throughout. Transfer the fish to paper towels and pat dry on both sides.

Spoon the potato purée into the center of each of 4 plates. Arrange the citrus sections around the potatoes. Place the fish on top of the potatoes and serve immediately.

*Makes 4 servings*

PER SERVING

*Calories 730 • Carbohydrates 55 g • Cholesterol 80 mg • Fat 40 g • Protein 41 g • Sodium 190 mg*

# Chilled California Berries Soup

1 cup (5 oz/155 g) fresh strawberries, hulled

1 cup (5 oz/155 g) fresh raspberries

1 cup (5 oz/155 g) fresh blueberries

1 cup (8 fl oz/250 ml) apple juice

$1/2$ cup (4 fl oz/125 ml) nonfat milk

4 papaya halves, seeded (optional)

4 fresh mint sprigs or berries for garnish

In a blender or food processor, purée the berries, apple juice, and milk until smooth. Pour the soup into 4 chilled cups, glass bowls, or papaya halves. Garnish with a mint sprig or a few whole berries and serve immediately.

*Makes 4 servings*

## PER SERVING

*Calories 90 • Carbohydrates 20 g • Cholesterol 0 mg • Fat 0.5 g • Protein 2 g • Sodium 20 mg*

# MENU

*Crabmeat and Baby Spinach Salad*

❖

*Vegetable and Egg-White Frittata*
*or*
*Pan-Seared Chicken with Crisp Baked Potatoes*

❖

*Frozen Yogurt Crunch with Strawberry Sauce*

# The Peaks at Telluride

Telluride, Colorado

*While there are other places to ski, nowhere else can you . . . ski from
the hotel to the lifts, return for a spa lunch, then . . . don a Frette robe and
slippers and let the treatments begin.*

—Town & Country

## ✦ PROFILE ✦

A luxurious mountain resort catering to both spa-lovers and outdoors enthusiasts, The Peaks at Telluride is located 9,500 feet up in the Colorado Rockies. An ultramodern ski/spa sanctuary, it is complete with panoramic views, spectacular slopes, roaring fires, and a unique treatment program that includes Southwest and Native American healing practices. Customized spa programs help guests to relax, lose weight, introduce exercise and healthy eating into their lives, achieve peak sports performance, or realize a combination of goals. The Peaks' comfortable accommodations and professional staff make it "a winner solidly entrenched in the Reader's Choice Top 10 U.S. Spas list" according to *Condé Nast Traveler*, and *Snow Country* ranked the Telluride Ski Area number one for scenery in North America. For young guests, KidSpa offers day-long adventures, so parents can truly unwind (and kids can truly enjoy themselves!).

## ✦ CUISINE ✦

The resort's restaurant, Legends of the Peaks, features breathtaking views, an outdoor sundeck, and creative regional fare for health-conscious guests. The delicious entrées on the spa menu—called Performance Cuisine—are made with the highest quality produce and a minimum of fat and salt. These energy-boosting, low-calorie dishes provide guests with the fuel they need to enjoy the resort's recreational opportunities, and are served for breakfast, lunch, and dinner alongside the regular menu, Ranchlands Cuisine. Both menus focus on classic American dishes with a distinctive Colorado style.

## ✦ SETTING ✦

This ten-story mountain hideaway is set in the San Juan range of the Rocky Mountains, surrounded by dramatic views of 14,000-foot peaks and featuring ski-in/ski-out access. Attention to detail and comfort is evident throughout: the welcoming lobby is furnished with Navajo rugs and mammoth leather couches; the spa waiting room offers Harney & Sons teas; and the 181 plush guest rooms and suites feature marble bathrooms, VCRs, and private balconies looking out onto the mountains. In addition to great downhill and cross-country skiing, The Peaks also offers more adventurous pursuits like helicopter skiing, dogsled rides, snowmobiling, and ice climbing. In the summer, guests can hike or bike on mountain trails, visit hot springs, river raft, golf on a championship course, play tennis, or explore the area on horseback.

## ✦ ACTIVITIES, TREATMENTS, AND FACILITIES ✦

The spa at The Peaks features a wide range of classes, treatments, and activities, from Ayurvedic healing practices to cardiofunk aerobics to special therapeutic baths in guests' own rooms. Covering an entire acre, the facilities contain forty-four treatment rooms, an Olympic-sized lap pool connected by water slide to a lower indoor-outdoor pool, a cardiovascular deck and Cybex weight room, squash and racquetball courts—even an indoor climbing wall. To begin the day, you can enjoy sunrise yoga in a glass-walled studio, or Native American–inspired chanting, drumming, and dancing to awaken the spirit. Or perhaps you'd prefer the Purification Ritual: a steam, sauna, and whirlpool circuit that helps adjust the body's water levels to high altitude. The Peaks' special organic-based body and facial treatments use ingredients found locally, such as alpine wildflowers, wild strawberries, evergreen oils, and clay from Alamosa, Colorado. Also available are a variety of massage techniques and hydrotherapy sessions that detoxify, rejuvenate, and soothe muscles après ski. Spa treatments are available à la carte, or as three- and five-night packages.

188

# Crabmeat and Baby Spinach Salad

*Pickled Red Onions*

   1/2 cup (2 oz/60 g) sliced red onion
   1/4 cup (2 fl oz/60 ml) balsamic vinegar
   1/2 tablespoon fresh lemon juice

*Ancho-Citrus Vinaigrette*

   2 tablespoons *each* fresh lemon and lime juice
   1/4 cup (2 fl oz/60 ml) grapefruit juice
   2 tablespoons finely chopped red onion
   1/2 teaspoon chopped fresh cilantro
   1/2 ancho chili, roasted, seeded (see Basics), and deribbed
   1 small garlic clove, minced
   1/2 cup (4 fl oz/125 ml) rice wine vinegar

   2 handfuls baby spinach leaves
   10 baby green beans, blanched
   4 ounces (125 g) fresh lump crabmeat, picked over for shell pieces
   6 grapefruit segments

Preheat the oven to 375°F (190°C). In a glass baking dish, combine the red onion, vinegar, and lemon juice. Cover the pan with aluminum foil and bake in the preheated oven for 30 minutes. Remove from heat and let the onion cool. Meanwhile, make the vinaigrette: In a small saucepan, combine all the ingredients and cook over medium heat for 20 minutes, or until the liquid is reduced by half. Transfer to a blender or food processor and purée. Strain through a fine-meshed sieve.

In a large bowl, toss the spinach, green beans, and crabmeat with some of the vinaigrette. Divide the salad between 2 plates, arrange the grapefruit segments on top, and scatter with half of the pickled red onions.

*Makes 2 servings*

PER SERVING

*Calories 120 • Carbohydrates 16 g • Cholesterol 35 mg • Fat 1 g • Protein 12 g • Sodium 190 mg*

189

# Vegetable and Egg-White Frittata

Olive oil for sautéing (optional)
1/2 small red pepper, diced
1/2 cup (1 oz/30 g) chopped portobello mushroom
1/2 cup (1 oz/30 g) broccoli florets, chopped
2/3 cup (5 fl oz/160 ml) liquid egg substitute, or 5 egg whites
Salt and freshly ground pepper to taste
1/4 cup (2 fl oz/60 ml) Roasted-Tomato Salsa (recipe follows)
Grilled red onion slices for garnish (optional)

Lightly coat a sauté pan with olive oil or vegetable oil spray and heat over medium heat. Sauté the red pepper, mushroom, and broccoli for 5 minutes; set aside.

Preheat the broiler. Lightly coat an ovenproof omelette pan with vegetable oil spray and place over medium heat. Add the egg substitute or egg whites, the cooked vegetables, and salt and pepper. Place under the preheated broiler and cook until set and lightly browned, about 3 minutes. Cut in half.

Cover each of 2 serving plates with 2 tablespoons salsa and place one-half of the frittata on top. Garnish with grilled red onions, if desired, and serve immediately.

*Makes 2 servings*

PER SERVING

*Calories 100 • Carbohydrates 5 g • Cholesterol 0 mg • Fat 3 g • Protein 13 g • Sodium 160 mg*

## Roasted-Tomato Salsa

**6 Roma (plum) tomatoes**
**$^1/_2$ serrano or 1 jalapeño chili**
**1 tablespoon finely chopped onion**
**$^1/_2$ teaspoon minced garlic**
**$^1/_2$ poblano chili, roasted, seeded, and peeled (see Basics)**
**1 tablespoon chopped fresh cilantro**
**Salt and freshly ground pepper to taste**

Preheat the broiler and broil the tomatoes and serrano or jalapeño chili for 7 minutes, or until lightly blackened. Let cool. Chop the tomatoes and seed the chili.

Lightly coat a small, heavy saucepan with vegetable oil spray and heat over medium heat. Sauté the onion for 5 minutes, or until soft, then add the garlic and sauté for 1 minute longer. Stir in all the remaining ingredients and simmer for 20 minutes. Transfer to a blender or food processor and purée. The salsa can be stored in an airtight container in the refrigerator for up to 5 days.

*Makes 1$^1/_2$ cups (12 fl oz/375 ml)*

### PER TABLESPOON

*Calories 5 • Carbohydrates 1 g • Cholesterol 0 mg • Fat 0 g • Protein 0 g • Sodium 0 mg*

# Pan-Seared Chicken with Crisp Baked Potatoes

*Crisp Baked Potatoes*

> 1 unpeeled baking potato, cut into $1/4$-inch-thick (6-mm) slices
> Salt and freshly ground pepper to taste

> Two 4-ounce (125-g) boneless, skinless chicken breast halves
> Salt and freshly ground pepper to taste
> $1/2$ cup (2 oz/60 g) green beans
> $1/2$ cup (2 oz/60 g) yellow wax beans
> Sweet Red Onions (recipe follows)
> $1/2$ cup (4 fl oz/125 ml) Mustard Sauce (recipe follows)

Preheat the oven to 375°F (190°C). In a baking dish with shallow sides, arrange the potatoes in a single layer and season with salt and pepper. Bake in the preheated oven for 30 minutes, or until crisp.

Season the chicken with salt and pepper. Lightly coat a nonstick sauté pan or skillet with vegetable oil spray and heat over medium-high heat. Sauté the chicken for about 5 minutes on each side, or until opaque throughout. Remove from heat and let cool. Slice thinly.

In a large pot of salted boiling water, cook the green and wax beans for 3 minutes, or until crisp-tender. Drain, rinse under cold water, and drain again. In a sauté pan or skillet, combine the beans and red onions. Cook over medium heat until heated through.

To serve, spread $1/4$ cup (2 fl oz/60 ml) mustard sauce on each of 2 plates and top with the beans and onions. Arrange the potatoes on top of the beans and finish with the sliced chicken.

*Makes 2 servings*

PER SERVING

*Calories 270 • Carbohydrates 29 g • Cholesterol 65 mg • Fat 3.5 g • Protein 27 g • Sodium 240 mg*

THE PEAKS AT TELLURIDE

## Sweet Red Onions

$^{1}/_{2}$ cup (4 oz/125 g) sliced red onion
$^{1}/_{4}$ cup (2 fl oz/60 ml) raspberry vinegar
1 teaspoon sugar

In a small nonstick sauté pan or skillet, combine all the ingredients and cook over low heat for 15 minutes, or until the onion has softened.

*Makes $^{1}/_{2}$ cup (2 oz/60 g)*

PER $^{1}/_{4}$ CUP (1 oz/30 g)

*Calories 40 • Carbohydrates 11 g • Cholesterol 0 mg • Fat 0 g • Protein 0 g • Sodium 0 mg*

## Mustard Sauce

1 cup (8 fl oz/250 ml) chicken stock (see Basics)
    or canned low-salt chicken broth
$^{1}/_{4}$ cup (2 fl oz/60 ml) dry sherry
4 teaspoons stone-ground whole-grain mustard

In a medium saucepan over high heat, combine all the ingredients and cook until reduced by half.

*Makes about $^{1}/_{2}$ cup (4 fl oz/125 ml)*

PER TABLESPOON

*Calories 10 • Carbohydrates 1 g • Cholesterol 0 mg • Fat 0 g • Protein 0.5 g • Sodium 45 mg*

# Frozen Yogurt Crunch with Strawberry Sauce

*Prepare the Strawberry Sauce at least 1 hour before serving.*

> 4 small scoops (about 2 oz/60 g each) frozen low-fat vanilla yogurt
>
> 3/4 cup (7 oz/220 g) low-fat granola
>
> 4 fresh strawberries, hulled
>
> 12 fresh blueberries
>
> 12 fresh raspberries
>
> 1/4 cup (2 fl oz/60 ml) Strawberry Sauce (recipe follows)

Roll the scoops of frozen yogurt in the granola to coat lightly. Place 2 scoops in the center of each of 2 plates. Surround with the strawberries, blueberries, and raspberries and drizzle with the strawberry sauce. Serve immediately.

*Makes 2 servings*

### PER SERVING

*Calories 430 • Carbohydrates 87 g • Cholesterol 10 mg • Fat 5 g • Protein 14 g • Sodium 190 mg*

# Strawberry Sauce

> 3/4 cup (3 oz/90 g) fresh strawberries, hulled
>
> 2 tablespoons sugar

In a blender or food processor, purée the strawberries and sugar. Strain the sauce through a fine-meshed sieve. Cover and refrigerate for at least 1 hour or up to 4 days.

*Makes about 1/2 cup (4 fl oz/125 ml)*

### PER TABLESPOON

*Calories 15 • Carbohydrates 4 g • Cholesterol 0 mg • Fat 0 g • Protein 0 g • Sodium 0 mg*

# The Phoenician
## Centre for Well-Being
### Scottsdale, Arizona

*Besides great spa food, any kind of beauty treatment you
can think of, yoga, and meditation, there is a well-developed
spiritual program . . . in a beautiful desert location.*
—**Condé Nast Traveler**

❖ PROFILE ❖

An all-purpose spa within a luxury resort, the Centre for Well-Being at
The Phoenician provides a soothing refuge in the Sonoran Desert.
"People have been coming to the desert to heal for a long time," notes one
manager, and the spa today continues to place a special focus on physical and
spiritual healing. Since 1992, the Centre has more than doubled its space and
greatly expanded its offerings. Attention to detail is evident throughout:
Washcloths in eucalyptus-scented ice water await when you step from your
sauna; soothing music provides a gentle background in the treatment rooms;
and a cheerful staff anticipates every need. The year-round children's camp
guarantees that both kids and parents will have the vacation they want, and the
resort is a recipient of the Mobil Five-Star Award.

❖ CUISINE ❖

The following recipes were created by chef de cuisine Kevin Gay for The
Terrace Dining Room, the largest of The Phoenician's eight restaurants. With
an emphasis on Mediterranean food, the restaurant serves both a regular menu
and a spa menu called "Choices Cuisine" that is flavorful and filling but low in
fat, salt, and calories. At the Centre for Well-Being, a Choices Cuisine bar
offers juice, fruit, bottled waters from eight countries, and delicious spa lunches. To learn more about personal dietary needs and healthy eating at home,
guests can meet with the Centre's dietician for a consultation.

## ✤ SETTING ✤

The Phoenician's Southwestern-inspired architecture is set in a spectacular cactus garden up against Camelback Mountain. Guests stay in suites and large rooms with imported Italian linen, Berber carpeting, private balconies, original art, and oversized marble bathrooms. (Homelike casitas are located nearest to the spa.) Surrounded by 250 acres of gorgeous desert terrain in the Valley of the Sun, the resort offers a championship golf course, tennis courts, and nine swimming pools in addition to its spa facilities.

## ✤ ACTIVITIES, TREATMENTS, AND FACILITIES ✤

The Centre for Well-Being promotes a healthful and balanced lifestyle with an array of services and treatments including skin care, massage and body therapies, and professional consultations and lectures in the areas of nutrition, fitness, and life management. The workout facilities of the Centre cover 22,000 square feet: twenty-four treatment rooms, weight and cardiovascular equipment, an aerobics studio, saunas, steam rooms, whirlpools, and Swiss showers. The Meditation Atrium is a skylit yoga and relaxation area with a fountain flowing at one end, comfortable seats, soft music, and the scent of lavender. Many of the skin treatments and body wraps here were inspired by Native American therapeutic traditions and use desert plants and minerals such as jojoba, Sedona mud, aloe vera, sage, juniper, and Ayate cactus. Also available are shiatsu massages, Ayurvedic treatments, hikes up Camelback Mountain, and a complete fitness assessment and training consultation by an exercise physiologist. Services at the Centre can be chosen à la carte or as part of a wellness program ranging from four to eight days.

# MENU

*Classic Gazpacho with a Twist*

❖

*Penne with Grilled Eggplant and Green Beans*
*or*
*Pan-Seared Salmon with New Potatoes*
*and Shaved-Vegetable Salad*

❖

*Strawberry-Ricotta Trifle*

197

# Classic Gazpacho with a Twist

*The zing of lime gives this classic soup its twist.*

1¹/₂ pounds (750 g) tomatoes, peeled, seeded (see Basics), and diced

1 English (hothouse) cucumber, peeled and cut into 1/4-inch (6-mm) dice

¹/₂ green bell pepper, seeded, deribbed, and finely diced

¹/₂ red bell pepper, seeded, deribbed, and finely diced

¹/₂ jalapeño, seeded, deribbed, and finely diced

¹/₂ lime

¹/₂ bunch fresh cilantro, stemmed and coarsely chopped

2 cups (16 fl oz/500 ml) tomato juice, or to taste

Extra-virgin olive oil to taste

Salt and freshly ground pepper to taste

In a large bowl, combine the tomatoes, cucumber, bell peppers, and jalapeño.

Using a large, sharp knife, slice off the top and bottom of the lime down to the flesh. Set the lime on end and cut off the peel down to the flesh. Slice the lime crosswise, then cut into fine dice. Stir the lime and cilantro into the tomato mixture. Stir in enough tomato juice to make a soupy consistency. Stir in the olive oil, salt, and pepper. Refrigerate the gazpacho for at least 2 hours. Serve chilled.

*Makes 6 servings*

PER SERVING

*Calories 50 • Carbohydrates 13 g • Cholesterol 0 mg • Fat 0.5 g • Protein 2 g • Sodium 310 mg*

# Penne with Grilled Eggplant and Green Beans

1 small globe eggplant, sliced into $1/2$-inch (12-mm) rounds

1 cup (4 oz/125 g) green beans, trimmed

3 cups (12 oz/375 g) penne (quill-shaped pasta)

1 tablespoon olive oil

2 teaspoons minced garlic

2 tablespoons minced fresh parsley

Salt and freshly ground pepper to taste

Light a fire in a charcoal grill or preheat a gas grill or boiler. Grill or broil the eggplant slices until they are soft and have distinct grill marks on both sides. Let cool and cut into $1/2$-inch-thick (12-mm) strips.

In a large pot of salted boiling water, blanch the green beans for 3 minutes, or until just crisp-tender. Drain, run under cold water, and drain again.

In a large pot of salted boiling water, cook the pasta until al dente, about 10 minutes. Drain, reserving $1/4$ cup (2 fl oz/60 ml) of the pasta water.

In a large sauté pan or skillet over medium heat, heat the olive oil and sauté the garlic for 2 minutes. Stir in the eggplant strips, green beans, cooked pasta, reserved pasta water, parsley, salt, and pepper. Toss over high heat until the water is evaporated. Serve immediately.

*Makes 4 servings*

### PER SERVING

*Calories 370 • Carbohydrates 68 g • Cholesterol 0 mg • Fat 5 g • Protein 12 g • Sodium 5 mg*

# Pan-Seared Salmon with New Potatoes and Shaved-Vegetable Salad

12 ounces (375 g) new potatoes, sliced (about 2 cups)

1 tablespoon extra-virgin olive oil

2 teaspoons fresh lemon juice

1/4 cup (1/3 oz/10 g) minced fresh flat-leaf parsley

1 carrot, peeled and thinly sliced

2 asparagus spears, steamed until crisp-tender and thinly sliced

4 radishes, thinly sliced

1/4 cup (1 oz/30 g) *each* thinly sliced fennel and celery

Four 4-ounce (125-g) salmon fillets, boned

Salt and freshly ground pepper to taste

1 tablespoon olive oil

4 slices crusty Italian or French bread for serving

In a large pot of salted boiling water, cook the potatoes for 12 to 15 minutes, or until tender. Drain and transfer to a colander; set aside and let cool to room temperature.

In a small bowl, whisk together the extra-virgin olive oil, lemon juice, and parsley to make a vinaigrette. In a large bowl, combine the carrot, asparagus, radishes, fennel, and celery. Add the vinaigrette to the vegetables and toss to thoroughly combine.

Season the salmon fillets with salt and pepper on both sides. In a large sauté pan or skillet over high heat, heat the olive oil and sear the fillets for 2 minutes on each side, or until opaque on the outside but translucent at the very center.

Arrange the vegetables on each of 4 plates and place a salmon fillet on top, with the new potatoes on the side. Serve immediately, with slices of crusty Italian or French bread.

*Makes 4 servings*

PER SERVING

*Calories 350 • Carbohydrates 33 g • Cholesterol 60 mg • Fat 12 g • Protein 27 g • Sodium 270 mg*

# Strawberry-Ricotta Trifle

*Begin preparing this recipe, by chef pâtissier Richard Ruskell, the day before you plan to serve it.*

> 4 cups (1 lb/1 kg) strawberries, hulled and quartered
> 1 cup (8 oz/250 g) sugar
> 2 cups (16 oz/500 g) low-fat ricotta cheese
> Nonfat milk, as needed
> 1 angel food cake (see Basics)
> Fresh strawberries for garnish

In a medium bowl, sprinkle the strawberries with ½ cup (4 oz/125 g) of the sugar. Cover and refrigerate overnight.

In a blender or food processor, combine the ricotta and remaining sugar; process until smooth. If the mixture is too thick, add a little nonfat milk to make it creamy.

Cut the angel food cake into ½-inch-thick (12-mm) slices. Place the slices around the bottom and sides of a pretty 4-cup (1-l) glass bowl. Spoon some of the strawberries over the cake and then spread about one-fourth of the ricotta cheese mixture over the berries. Cover with more cake slices. Repeat with the remaining ricotta, strawberries, and cake, ending with ricotta. Cover the trifle with plastic wrap and refrigerate for at least 3 hours before serving.

Just before serving, remove the plastic wrap and decorate the top of the trifle with fresh strawberries.

*Makes 6 servings*

### PER SERVING

*Calories 420 • Carbohydrates 77 g • Cholesterol 25 mg • Fat 7 g • Protein 13 g • Sodium 530 mg*

# MENU

## *BREAKFAST*

*Garden Eggs Ranchero with Curried Tofu*

❖

*Breakfast Bread with Cranberries and Apricots*

## *LUNCH*

*Roasted Red and Yellow Bell Pepper Soup*

❖

*Bill's Mexican Tuna and Corn Tostada*

❖

*Biscotti with Seasonal Fruit*

## *DINNER*

*Mexican Corn Soup with Chipotle-Cilantro Pesto*

❖

*Blue Corn Tomale with Feta*

❖

*Postres del Sol*

# Rancho La Puerta

Tecate, Baja California, Mexico

*Rancho La Puerta is heaven on earth. It will save your life, make you young again, . . . and make you beautiful, brilliant, rich, successful and fulfilled. At least I left Rancho La Puerta feeling so.*

—Denver Post

## ❖ PROFILE ❖

Sister spa to the elegant Golden Door in California (see pages 88 to 100), Rancho La Puerta is more informal—a "camp for grown-ups" says *Town & Country*—but still offers all the amenities of a destination resort. Established over fifty-five years ago by Deborah and Edmond Szekely, it was the first North American fitness spa, and hundreds of thousands of guests have come to experience the founders' belief that a healthy life includes good nutrition, regular exercise, and recognizing the interdependence of mind, body, and spirit. Rancho La Puerta has grown from a cluster of tents on ranchland into a paradise complete with handsome casitas and villas, swimming pools, tennis courts, men's and women's health centers, libraries, eight gyms, and fifty acres of landscaped gardens. A place for renewal and retreat, it offers "simple luxuries" for 150 guests—people who wish to step out of their lives for a week, eat well, work out, and restore mind and body. In fact, over 60 percent of guests return here, drawn by the gentle year-round climate and beautiful gardens, the caring and knowledgeable staff, and the warm companionship.

## ❖ CUISINE ❖

The menu at Rancho La Puerta is largely vegetarian, with fish served twice a week and an emphasis on grains, legumes, and produce picked daily from the spa's bountiful garden. Flavorful and highly satisfying dishes emphasize low-fat, high-fiber foods often enlivened by zesty Sonora-style cooking. Breakfast and lunch are served cafeteria-style, while dinner is served in the art-filled dining room. One of the spa's favorite activities is the garden breakfast hike, a tour of the six-acre organic vegetable garden that concludes with an unforgettable buffet served at chef Bill Wavrin's country kitchen. Chef Bill's cooking classes are among the most popular events at the spa.

## ❖ SETTING ❖

Forty miles southeast of San Diego, Rancho La Puerta is set on three hundred acres of rolling countryside at the foot of imposing Mount Kuchumaa, and is home to hawks, quail, hummingbirds, coyotes, and rabbits. The spa itself is a romantic villagelike compound of Spanish Colonial–influenced buildings and casitas with red-tile roofs, winding paths, and lovely gardens. The accommodations, ranging from single rooms to villas, are built with locally fired bricks, quarried stone, and hand-painted tiles and are decorated with hand-woven bedspreads and fine Mexican arts and crafts. The rooms don't have televisions or phones, but most include a fireplace and each has its own private patio and garden.

## ❖ ACTIVITIES, TREATMENTS, AND FACILITIES ❖

Based on a self-starter philosophy that encourages balance and progression, activities at Rancho La Puerta begin with sunrise mountain hikes amid scents of sage and camphor. As at the Golden Door, a typical schedule alternates between invigorating movement periods and delightfully relaxing ones, adjusted for each individual's level of ability. The many fitness options include hikes (from an hour to a day), circuit training, tennis, volleyball, Pilates, back strengthening, women's self-defense, aqua aerobics, and funk, jazz, and Latin dancing. Quiet interludes include yoga, massage, a wide range of beauty treatments with Golden Door products, herbal wraps, meditation, and perhaps napping in a hammock in the shade or relaxing sore muscles in a heated whirlpool. After the day is done and a delicious dinner enjoyed, there are evening programs such as crafts classes, lectures, movies, and concerts. A haven for relaxation and renewal, Rancho La Puerta offers a seven-day program, Saturday to Saturday.

# Garden Eggs Ranchero with Curried Tofu

*These scrambled eggs are low in fat, have no cholesterol, and are picantito (a little spicy). At Rancho La Puerta, they're served with vegetables picked fresh from the organic garden. The curry powder gives the egg whites the yellow color of whole eggs.*

1 teaspoon olive oil

¼ onion, finely diced

½ small zucchini, finely diced

¼ small carrot, peeled and diced

1 Swiss chard leaf, chopped

½ small tomato, finely diced

½ jalapeño chili, minced

2 garlic cloves, minced

¼ teaspoon *each* minced fresh oregano, thyme, and lavender

2 ounces (60 g) firm tofu, crumbled (about ½ cup)

¼ teaspoon curry powder

Freshly ground pepper to taste

8 egg whites

4 corn tortillas, warmed

Rosie's Tomatillo Salsa for serving (recipe follows)

In a large sauté pan or skillet over medium-high, heat the olive oil and sauté the onion, zucchini, carrot, and chard for 3 minutes. Add the tomato, jalapeño, garlic, oregano, thyme, and lavender and sauté for 2 minutes. Sprinkle the tofu over the vegetables and sprinkle the curry powder and pepper on top.

Reduce heat to low and stir in the egg whites. Continue to cook and stir for 8 to 10 minutes, or until the eggs are cooked to your liking. For each person, serve one-fourth of the eggs with a warm tortilla and pass the salsa at the table.

*Makes 4 servings*

### PER SERVING

*Calories 140 • Carbohydrates 17 g • Cholesterol 0 mg • Fat 3.5 g • Protein 10 g • Sodium 190 mg*

## Rosie's Tomatillo Salsa

*Rosie Wavrin, chef Bill Wavrin's wife, is famous for many salsas; tomatillos add a wonderfully tart dimension to this one. The salsa is delicious over eggs, grilled chicken, or fish, and of course, most Mexican dishes.*

1/2 teaspoon olive oil

1/2 onion, chopped

1 arbol chili,* stemmed and seeded

2 ancho chilies,* stemmed and seeded

10 fresh tomatillos,** husked, rinsed, and chopped

1/2 cup (4 fl oz/125 ml) water

2 garlic cloves, minced

1/4 teaspoon ground cumin

2 tablespoons chopped fresh cilantro

Salt to taste

In a medium saucepan over medium heat, heat the olive oil and sauté the onion and chilies for about 2 minutes, or until the chilies are toasted. Remove the chilies and add the tomatillos, water, and garlic; cook for 15 minutes, stirring occasionally.

Transfer the onion mixture to a blender or food processor. Add the chilies, tomatillo mixture, cumin, cilantro, and salt. Blend for 10 seconds, or until still slightly chunky. The salsa will keep, covered, in the refrigerator for up to 1 week.

*Makes about 3 cups (24 fl oz/750 ml)*

### PER TABLESPOON

*Calories 5 • Carbohydrates 1 g • Cholesterol 0 mg • Fat 0 g • Protein 0 g • Sodium 0 mg*

---

*\*Arbol chilies are slim, bright red dried Mexican pods. Their flavor is close to cayenne in heat and flavor; cayenne pepper to taste may be substituted. Ancho chilies are dried poblano chilies, and are available in Hispanic markets or specialty foods stores.*

*\*\*Tomatillos resemble green tomatoes and are cousins of the gooseberry. They are available in the produce section of many supermarkets and in Hispanic markets.*

# Breakfast Bread with Cranberries and Apricots

*This quick, wholesome bread is delicious for breakfast or as a dessert. It's low in fat and calories and full of nutrients and fiber. To vary the recipe, substitute other dried fruits.*

1$\frac{1}{8}$ cups (5$\frac{1}{2}$ oz/170 g) whole-wheat flour

2$\frac{1}{2}$ tablespoons wheat bran

$\frac{1}{2}$ teaspoon *each* baking soda and baking powder

3 teaspoons ground cinnamon

Pinch of ground ginger

2$\frac{1}{2}$ tablespoons nonfat plain yogurt

3$\frac{1}{2}$ tablespoons apple juice

2 tablespoons vanilla extract

1$\frac{1}{2}$ teaspoons canola oil

2 tablespoons honey

2 egg whites

$\frac{1}{2}$ carrot, grated

$\frac{1}{4}$ cup (1 oz/30 g) dried cranberries

$\frac{1}{4}$ cup (1$\frac{1}{2}$ oz/45 g) dried apricots, chopped

Preheat the oven to 350°F (180°C). Lightly coat a 9-by-5-inch (23-by-13-cm) loaf pan with vegetable oil spray and set aside. In a medium bowl, combine the flour, wheat bran, baking soda, baking powder, cinnamon, and ginger.

In a large bowl, mix all the remaining ingredients together until well blended. Fold the flour mixture into the yogurt mixture until just blended; do not overmix, or the bread will be tough. Pour the batter into the prepared pan and bake in the center of the preheated oven for 45 minutes, or until a knife inserted in the center comes out clean. Turn out onto a wire rack to cool for 15 minutes before slicing.

*Makes one 9-by-5-inch (23-by-13-cm) loaf; 16 slices*

### PER SLICE

*Calories 60 • Carbohydrates 13 g • Cholesterol 0 mg • Fat 0.5 g • Protein 2 g • Sodium 55 mg*

# Roasted Red and Yellow Bell Pepper Soup

*This savory soup is a popular way that chef Wavrin uses the many varieties of bell peppers grown in Rancho La Puerta's organic garden.*

2 red bell peppers, roasted and seeded (see Basics)

2 yellow bell peppers, roasted and seeded (see Basics)

1 teaspoon olive oil

1 onion, chopped

2 garlic cloves, minced

1/2 new potato, chopped

2 Roma (plum) tomatoes, chopped

1 tablespoon minced fresh oregano

1/2 teaspoon minced fresh sage, plus 6 fresh sage sprigs for garnish

4 cups (32 fl oz/1 l) vegetable stock (see Basics)
   or canned low-salt vegetable broth

1 dried Thai chili, toasted and crumbled, or cayenne pepper to taste

1 tablespoon balsamic vinegar

Salt and freshly ground pepper to taste

Dice 1 red and 1 yellow roasted bell pepper and reserve.

In a large saucepan over medium heat, heat the olive oil and sauté the onion for 5 minutes, or until golden. Add the 2 whole roasted bell peppers, the garlic, and potato and sauté for 5 minutes. Add the tomatoes, oregano, sage, and stock or broth and simmer for 15 minutes. Stir in the Thai chili or cayenne and the balsamic vinegar.

Transfer the soup to a blender or food processor and process until smooth. Return the soup to the saucepan. Add the reserved diced peppers and season with salt and pepper. Bring to a simmer. Ladle the soup into 6 bowls and garnish each with a sage sprig.

*Makes 6 servings*

PER SERVING

*Calories 60 • Carbohydrates 11 g • Cholesterol 0 mg • Fat 1 g • Protein 3 g • Sodium 25 mg*

# Bill's Mexican Tuna and Corn Tostada

1 ear fresh corn

$1/2$ red onion, sliced

12 ounces (375 g) canned tuna packed in water, drained

3 small romaine lettuce leaves, cut into $1/4$-inch (6-mm) shreds

1 green onion, sliced

1 garlic clove, minced

1 teaspoon chopped fresh oregano

$1/4$ cup ($1^1/2$ oz/45 g) diced red bell pepper

Juice of 1 lime

$1/2$ cup (4 fl oz/125 ml) plain nonfat yogurt

$1/4$ cup (2 oz/60 g) capers, rinsed and drained

$1/2$ teaspoon toasted arbol chili, or cayenne pepper to taste

Salt to taste

6 corn tortillas

6 fresh cilantro sprigs and 2 limes, cut into wedges, for garnish

Preheat the oven to 350°F (180°C). Coat a baking sheet with vegetable oil spray. Heat a dry medium sauté pan or skillet over medium-high heat. Toast the ear of corn evenly until the kernels are golden brown. Remove from heat, slice the kernels from the cob, and set them aside. Lightly coat a medium sauté pan or skillet with vegetable oil spray and heat over medium heat. Sauté the red onion for 5 minutes.

In a large bowl, mix together the toasted corn kernels, sautéed red onion, tuna, lettuce, green onion, garlic, oregano, bell pepper, lime juice, yogurt, capers, chili or cayenne, and salt. Place the tortillas on the prepared pan and bake in the preheated oven for about 15 minutes, or until they begin to crisp. Turn the tortillas, return to the oven, and crisp on the other side for 4 to 5 minutes. Place a tortilla in the center of each of 6 plates and top with a scoop of the tuna and corn mixture. Garnish each serving with a sprig of cilantro and lime wedges.

*Makes 6 servings*

PER SERVING

*Calories 170 • Carbohydrates 23 g • Cholesterol 15 mg • Fat 1.5 g • Protein 19 g • Sodium 470 mg*

# Biscotti with Seasonal Fruit

*These crisp cookies are a low-fat, delicious answer to feeding a sweet tooth. Serve as a snack or dessert with fresh seasonal fruit or fruit butter.*

2 cups (10 oz/315 g) unbleached all-purpose flour

$^1\!/_4$ teaspoon salt

2 teaspoons baking powder

5 egg whites

$^1\!/_2$ cup (3$^1\!/_2$ oz/105 g) plus 2 tablespoons packed brown sugar

1 teaspoon vanilla extract

1 teaspoon almond extract

2 tablespoons canola oil

1 tablespoon fennel seed or aniseed, toasted (see Basics)

$^1\!/_4$ cup (1 oz/30 g) almonds, ground

1 tablespoon grated orange zest (see Basics)

1 tablespoon ground cinnamon

Sliced fresh seasonal fruit, for serving

Preheat the oven to 325°F (165°C). Lightly coat 2 baking sheets with vegetable oil spray.

In a large bowl, stir together the flour, salt, and baking powder. In another large bowl, beat the egg whites until soft peaks form. Gradually beat in the $^1\!/_2$ cup (3$^1\!/_2$ oz/105 g) brown sugar until stiff, glossy peaks form. Fold in the vanilla and almond extracts, canola oil, fennel or anise seeds, ground almonds, and orange zest until blended. Fold the egg white mixture into the flour mixture until blended.

Turn the dough out onto a well-floured work surface and divide it into 2 equal pieces. With floured hands, roll the dough into cylinders approximately 3 inches (7.5 cm) in diameter. Flatten the cylinders into logs about 1 inch (2.5 cm) high. Place the logs on the prepared baking sheets. With a knife, cut a thin line about $^1\!/_4$ inch (6 mm) deep down the center of each log.

In a small bowl, mix the 2 tablespoons brown sugar with the cinnamon and sprinkle evenly over the top of each roll.

Bake in the preheated oven for 30 minutes. Remove from the oven and let cool for 5 minutes. Raise the oven temperature to 375°F (190°C).

Cut each log diagonally into $^3/_4$-inch-thick (2-cm) slices. Return the cookies to the baking sheets, cut side up, and bake for 5 minutes. Turn the biscotti over and bake for 5 minutes. Transfer the cookies to wire racks to cool completely. (The biscotti can be stored in an airtight container for up to 1 week.) Serve with fresh fruit.

*Makes 20 biscotti*

PER BISCOTTI (without fruit)

*Calories 100 • Carbohydrates 16 g • Cholesterol 0 mg • Fat 2.5 g • Protein 3 g • Sodium 70 mg*

# Mexican Corn Soup with Chipotle-Cilantro Pesto

*Toasting some of the corn kernels adds a wonderful flavor to this soup.*

3 cups (18 oz/560 g) fresh corn kernels (from about 6 ears)

$^1/_2$ teaspoon olive oil

1 onion, chopped

1 *each* celery stalk and carrot, chopped

$^1/_2$ new potato, scrubbed and chopped

3 garlic cloves, minced

1 tablespoon minced fresh oregano

4 cups (32 fl oz/1 l) vegetable stock (see Basics)
   or canned low-salt vegetable broth, plus more as needed

Salt and freshly ground pepper to taste

Juice of 1 lime, or to taste

6 tablespoons (3 fl oz/90 ml) Chipotle-Cilantro Pesto (recipe follows)

6 fresh cilantro sprigs for garnish

Heat a dry sauté pan or skillet over medium-high heat. Add 1 cup (6 oz/185 g) of the corn kernels and toast, stirring constantly, until the kernels are evenly golden brown. Remove from heat and set aside.

In a large saucepan over medium heat, heat the olive oil and sauté the onion, celery, and carrot for 5 minutes. Add the potato, garlic, the remaining 2 cups (12 oz/375 g) corn kernels, and oregano and sauté for 5 minutes. Pour in the stock or broth and simmer for 10 minutes, or until the potato is soft.

Transfer the soup to a blender or food processor and blend, in batches if necessary, until smooth. Return the soup to the saucepan and bring to a low simmer. If the soup is too thick, add a bit more stock or broth. Stir in the toasted corn kernels and season with salt, pepper, and lime juice. To serve, ladle the soup into 6 soup bowls and place a tablespoonful of the cilantro pesto in the center of each bowl. Garnish with a sprig of cilantro.

*Makes 6 servings*

PER SERVING

*Calories 120 • Carbohydrates 21 g • Cholesterol 0 mg • Fat 2.5 g • Protein 5 g • Sodium 80 mg*

## Chipotle-Cilantro Pesto

*Tarragon, rosemary, sun-dried tomatoes, roasted bell peppers, or roasted egg-plant can be added to this pesto. Have fun experimenting with different flavors.*

3 garlic cloves, minced

2 cups (3 oz/90 g) chopped fresh cilantro

1 chipotle chili in adobo,\* drained

2 cups (2 oz/60 g) packed spinach leaves, chopped

¼ cup (⅓ oz/10 g) chopped fresh parsley

1 tablespoon minced fresh oregano

2 tablespoons grated Parmesan cheese

¼ cup (1 oz/30 g) hulled pumpkin seeds, toasted (see Basics)

1 tablespoon fresh lime juice

4 teaspoons olive oil

In a blender or food processor, combine the garlic, cilantro, chili, spinach, parsley, oregano, Parmesan cheese, and pumpkin seeds. Pulse to blend. Add the lime juice and olive oil and blend for 15 to 20 seconds. Transfer to a bowl, cover, and refrigerate until ready to use. The pesto will keep in the refrigerator for 3 to 4 days.

*Makes about 1¼ cups (10 fl oz/310 ml)*

### PER TABLESPOON

*Calories 15 • Carbohydrates 1 g • Cholesterol 0 mg • Fat 1.5 g • Protein 1 g • Sodium 40 mg*

---

*\*Chipotles in adobo are smoked dried jalapeño chilies packed in a spicy sauce. They can be found in Latino markets and many supermarkets. They are medium hot and have a rich aroma and deep smoky flavor. If you are a chili lover, add the entire chipotle; if not, add just a little.*

# Blue Corn Tamale with Feta

*This dish is really a layered casserole rather than a corn husk–wrapped tamale. Serve it with puréed parsnips, steamed spinach, or spiced sweet potato purée. If blue cornmeal is unavailable, substitute yellow cornmeal.*

1 onion, sliced

4 garlic cloves, minced

1 jalapeño chili, seeded, deribbed, and minced

1 carrot, peeled and cut into julienne

8 ounces (250 g) mushrooms, sliced

1/2 teaspoon minced fresh oregano

1 zucchini, julienned

2 cups (8 oz/250 g) plain low-fat yogurt

6 egg whites

1 tablespoon ground cumin

3 cups (18 oz/560 g) fresh corn kernels (from about 6 ears)

Low-salt soy sauce to taste

1 teaspoon freshly ground pepper

1/2 cup (4 oz/125 g) grated part-skim mozzarella cheese

3 ounces (90 g) feta cheese, crumbled (about 1/2 cup)

1 cup (5 oz/155 g) blue or yellow cornmeal

8 fresh Anaheim chilies, roasted, peeled, and seeded (see Basics),
   or 8 whole canned Ortega chilies, drained

6 tablespoons (1/2 oz/15 g) chopped fresh cilantro

Rosie's Tomatillo Salsa (recipe on page 206)

Preheat the oven to 375°F (190°C). Lightly coat a 9-by-13-inch (23-by-33-cm) baking pan or casserole dish with vegetable oil spray.

Lightly coat a sauté pan with vegetable oil spray and place over medium-high heat. Sauté the onion for 3 minutes, or until soft. Add the garlic, jalapeño, and carrot and sauté for 3 to 4 minutes. Add the mushrooms, oregano, and zucchini and sauté 2 minutes longer. Transfer the vegetables to a large bowl and set aside.

In a blender or food processor, combine the yogurt, egg whites, cumin, corn, and soy sauce and blend until smooth. Pour into the bowl with the sautéed vegetables. Add the pepper, mozzarella, feta, and cornmeal and stir to combine well.

Line the bottom of the prepared baking pan or casserole dish with the roasted Anaheim chilies. Pour the vegetable-yogurt mixture gently into the casserole, smoothing to even the top. Cover the casserole with aluminum foil and bake in the preheated oven for 55 to 60 minutes. Uncover, return to the oven, and bake until golden brown. Remove from the oven and let cool for 10 minutes before cutting into 8 equal servings. Sprinkle with cilantro and serve with the salsa.

*Makes 8 servings*

PER SERVING (with 2 tablespoons salsa)

*Calories 300 • Carbohydrates 46 g • Cholesterol 15 mg • Fat 7 g • Protein 16 g • Sodium 260 mg*

# Postres del Sol

*This dessert is a Ranch favorite. Postre del Sol means "pastry of the sun," and these cookies are so named because they resemble little suns.*

3/4 cup (6 oz/185 g) packed brown sugar

6 tablespoons (3 oz/90 g) canola margarine

1 egg white

1/2 cup (2 1/2 oz/45 g) whole-wheat flour

1 1/2 cups (12 oz/375 g) unbleached all-purpose flour

*Filling*

1/2 cup (4 oz/125 g) part-skim ricotta cheese

1 teaspoon packed brown sugar

Dash of ground cinnamon

1/2 teaspoon vanilla extract

2 cups (16 fl oz/500 ml) mango pureé (see Basics)

25 fresh mint leaves, for garnish

Preheat the oven to 350°F (180°C). In a medium bowl, beat the brown sugar and margarine together until fluffy. Beat in the egg white until well blended. Gradually add the flours and stir until blended. Form 2 tablespoons of the dough into a ball and press into fluted brioche cups or a sun-shaped cookie mold. Repeat to use the remaining dough. Bake in the preheated oven for 15 to 20 minutes, or just until the cookies are golden brown. Unmold and let cool completely on a wire rack. Store the cookies in an airtight container for up to 1 week or wrap in plastic wrap and freeze for up to 3 months.

To make the filling: In a medium bowl, whip together the ricotta, brown sugar, cinnamon, and vanilla. Transfer the cheese mixture to a pastry bag with a star tip and form a 1/2-teaspoon-size ricotta star in the center of each cookie. Fill the rest of each cookie shell with 2 tablespoons mango purée. Garnish with a mint leaf.

*Makes about 25 cookies*

PER COOKIE

*Calories 100 • Carbohydrates 16 g • Cholesterol 0 mg • Fat 3.5 g • Protein 2 g • Sodium 45 mg*

# Sonoma Mission Inn & Spa

### Sonoma, California

*[At] one of the prettiest retreats in Northern California's wine country, . . .
guests have many options for pampering themselves, from long soaks in
mineral baths to facials and massages, [while] dining at The Grille . . .
can be an indulgence of another sort.*

**—San Francisco Chronicle**

## ❖ PROFILE ❖

Built in 1927 as an architectural reproduction of a Spanish mission, Sonoma Mission Inn & Spa is adjacent to the healing subterranean springs of the Sonoma Valley, where the coastal Miwok tribe located their sweat lodges. The bubbling springs lured fashionable San Franciscans in the 1920s, who traveled forty miles—in those days quite a distance—to "take the waters." Today, the spa draws overstressed individuals and vacationing romantics from around the Bay Area and throughout the United States who want to get away to the California countryside and relax. Casually elegant and unpretentious, Sonoma Mission Inn is perfect for a vacation retreat, offering a wide variety of spa services; fresh, sophisticated food; leisurely bicycle rides through scenic vineyards; and the highest level of personal comfort and attention. The Inn has been awarded four stars by Mobil and four diamonds by AAA and was named Best Resort Spa in the World by *Gourmet*.

## ❖ CUISINE ❖

At Sonoma Mission Inn, The Cafe, a casual bistro, serves superb American regional cuisine throughout the day, while the more elegant Grille is reserved for candlelight dinners and Sunday brunch. Both menus emphasize healthy, locally produced ingredients prepared with simplicity and flair, and the acclaimed Grille has an excellent wine list, taking advantage of the proximity of some of the world's best wineries. A special spa menu offers dishes that are lower in calories and cholesterol. *Gourmet* calls the food "the best of the new Wine Country," and *Condé Nast Traveler* says "it's worth a special trip just to eat here." Head chef Jeffrey Jake and pastry chef Steve Fischer created the following delicious recipes.

## ✦ SETTING ✦

Sonoma Mission Inn & Spa is situated on ten acres in the heart of California's sunny wine country, surrounded by eucalyptus groves and vineyards as far as the eye can see. The distinctive earthy pink mission-style building, complete with bell tower, arcade, and red tile roof, is nestled in lushly planted grounds with fountains, tennis courts, and lighted pathways. Two hundred spacious rooms and thirty luxury suites—many with fireplaces and terraces—are decorated in soft terra-cotta and salmon shades, and feature plush robes, billowy pillows, and marble bathrooms.

## ✦ ACTIVITIES, TREATMENTS, AND FACILITIES ✦

The Spa at Sonoma Mission Inn is European style with a California twist. Intended to soothe, beautify, and revitalize, there are more than forty treatments: a full repertoire of massages, facials, fragrant herbal wraps, and holistic practices from different cultures. You can let your cares melt away during a 105-minute scalp-to-toe Ayurvedic "rejuvenation" complete with a linen wrap, or wake up your skin with the stimulating citrus scrub, in which tangerine, orange, and grapefruit oils are misted onto your skin, which is then exfoliated with sea salt. The coed facilities include a large aerobics studio, sauna, steam room, and variety of cardiovascular equipment, and you can also enjoy the benefits of bathing in naturally hot mineral water, as the two outdoor pools and whirlpools are filled from artesian springs located directly beneath the Inn. Fitness classes include tai chi, yoga, aquatics, aerobics, stretch, and body sculpting, and you can also sign up for hikes with a naturalist, image consultations, guided meditation, one-on-one fitness training, and personal sessions on nutrition and stress management. The Spa offers a variety of packages: à la carte, day spa, weekend stays, and tailored personalized programs that include meals.

# MENU

*BREAKFAST*

*Egg White Cassolette*

*LUNCH*

*Crab and Spinach Salad with Asian Vinaigrette*

❖

*Angel Hair Pasta with Wild Mushrooms,
Roasted Garlic, Tomato, and Basil*

*DINNER*

*Artichokes Stuffed with Bay Shrimp*

❖

*Mediterranean Vegetable Bisque*

❖

*Swordfish with Risotto and Roasted-Tomato Broth*

❖

*Lemon Chiffon with Strawberry Sauce*

219

SONOMA MISSION INN & SPA

# Egg White Cassolette

1/2 teaspoon extra-virgin olive oil

1/4 cup (2 oz/60 g) sliced onions

1/4 cup (2 oz/60 g) sliced roasted red bell pepper (see Basics)

1 shiitake mushroom (2 oz/60 g), sliced

1/4 cup (2 oz/60 g) low-fat herb cream cheese

8 egg whites

Salt and freshly ground pepper to taste

2 tablespoons grated Asiago cheese

Preheat the oven to 400°F (200°C). Lightly coat an 8-inch (20-cm) square gratin dish with vegetable oil spray.

In a sauté pan or skillet over medium-low heat, heat the olive oil and cook the onions, stirring frequently, for 15 minutes, or until they begin to caramelize. Raise heat to high, stir in the bell pepper and mushrooms and sauté for 10 minutes, or until the peppers are soft. Remove from heat and set aside.

In a deep bowl, beat the egg whites until stiff, glossy peaks form. Fold the vegetable mixture into the beaten whites. Stir in the herb cream cheese until blended.

Pour the mixture into the prepared dish, sprinkle with the salt, pepper, and cheese, and bake in the preheated oven for 10 minutes, or until the egg whites are firm.

*Makes 4 servings*

PER SERVING

*Calories 100 • Carbohydrates 5 g • Cholesterol 12.5 mg • Fat 4 g • Protein 10 g • Sodium 165 mg*

# Crab and Spinach Salad with Asian Vinaigrette

*Asian Vinaigrette*

> 1 teaspoon light soy sauce
>
> 2 tablespoons rice wine vinegar
>
> 1/4 teaspoon wasabi paste*
>
> 1/4 teaspoon Asian (toasted) sesame oil
>
> 1/4 teaspoon minced fresh ginger
>
> 1/4 teaspoon minced garlic
>
> 2 ounces (60 g) fresh lump crabmeat
>
> 3 cups (3 oz/90 g) packed spinach leaves

In a small bowl, whisk together the vinaigrette ingredients. In a medium bowl, toss the spinach and vinaigrette together. Arrange the crabmeat on top of the salad and serve.

*Makes 2 servings*

### PER SERVING

*Calories 45 • Carbohydrates 2 g • Cholesterol 20 mg • Fat 1 g • Protein 8 g • Sodium 290 mg*

---

*Wasabi paste can be found in specialty foods stores, Asian markets, and some grocery stores.

# Angel Hair Pasta with Wild Mushrooms, Roasted Garlic, Tomato, and Basil

4 ounces (125 g) angel hair pasta

2 teaspoons extra-virgin olive oil

1 teaspoon roasted garlic (see Basics)

4 ounces (125 g) mixed wild mushrooms, sliced

1 ¼ cups (8 oz/250 g) diced tomato

½ teaspoon minced fresh basil

¼ cup (2 fl oz/60 ml) chicken stock (see Basics)
  or canned low-salt chicken broth

Salt and freshly ground pepper to taste

In a large pot of salted boiling water, cook the pasta until al dente. Drain.

Meanwhile, in a medium sauté pan or skillet over medium heat, heat the olive oil and sauté the garlic, mushrooms, and tomato for 7 minutes. Add the basil and stock or broth and cook for 20 minutes. In a large bowl, toss the sauce and pasta together. Season with salt and pepper and serve immediately.

*Makes 2 servings*

PER SERVING

*Calories 240 • Carbohydrates 40 g • Cholesterol 0 mg • Fat 6 g • Protein 10 g • Sodium 210 mg*

# Artichokes Stuffed with Bay Shrimp

**2 large artichokes**

**Juice of ½ lemon, plus ¼ cup (2 fl oz/60 ml) fresh lemon juice**

**6 ounces (90 g) bay shrimp**

**2 tablespoons finely diced celery**

**2 tablespoons finely diced apple**

**¼ cup (2 fl oz/60 ml) fresh lemon juice**

**2 teaspoons chopped fresh cilantro**

**Baby lettuce leaves, tomato wedges, and sprouts for garnish**

Using scissors, cut off the tips of the artichoke leaves. Cut off the stems of the artichokes with a knife. Add the juice of ½ lemon to a pot of boiling water and cook the artichokes until tender, about 40 minutes. Using a slotted spoon, transfer to a colander and drain upside down.

Meanwhile, toss the shrimp, celery, apple, ¼ cup (2 fl oz/60 ml) lemon juice, and cilantro together in a medium bowl. Using a tablespoon, remove the choke from each artichoke and spoon half the shrimp mixture into the center. Arrange the artichokes on each of 2 plates and garnish with a few lettuce leaves, tomato wedges, and sprouts.

*Makes 2 servings*

### PER SERVING

*Calories 220 • Carbohydrates 33 g • Cholesterol 130 mg • Fat 2 g • Protein 25 g • Sodium 300 mg*

# Mediterranean Vegetable Bisque

6 tomatoes

2 red bell peppers, seeded and deribbed

3 zucchini

3 yellow summer squash

1 eggplant, cut into $1/2$-inch-thick (12-mm) slices

$1/2$ red onion, quartered

1 Yukon gold potato

$1/2$ fennel bulb

3 tablespoons olive or canola oil, or a blend of the two

3 garlic cloves, minced

$1/2$ teaspoon ground allspice

Salt and freshly ground pepper to taste

4 $3/4$ cups (38 fl oz/1.2 ml) vegetable stock (see Basics),
    canned low-salt vegetable broth, or water, as needed

$1/2$ cup cooked couscous, toasted Israeli couscous* preferred

Preheat the boiler. Cut 1 each of the tomatoes, red bell peppers, zucchini, and squash in half. On a baking sheet, arrange the following, skin side up: half of the eggplant slices, the red onion, and the halved vegetables. Broil for 5 minutes, turn over the eggplant slices, and broil 5 minutes longer, or until the skins are blistered.

Meanwhile, cut all the remaining vegetables, including the potatoes and fennel, into $1/2$-inch (12-mm) dice. Remove the roasted vegetables from heat and cut into $1/2$-inch (12-mm) dice; set aside.

In a soup pot over medium heat, heat the oil and sauté the eggplant, fennel, and garlic for 5 minutes. Add all the remaining vegetables, the allspice, salt, and pepper and sauté for 7 minutes. Add 4 cups (32 fl oz/1 l) of the stock, broth, or water and simmer until the vegetables are tender.

In a medium saucepan, bring the remaining $3/4$ cup (6 fl oz/180 ml) stock, broth, or water just to a boil. Stir in the couscous and cover the pan. Remove from heat and let stand for 5 minutes. Lightly fluff the couscous with a fork.

Transfer the soup to a blender or food processor and purée in batches, if necessary. To serve, ladle the soup into each of 8 shallow soup bowls and garnish with a spoonful of cooked couscous.

*Makes 8 servings*

PER SERVING

*Calories 150 • Carbohydrates 21 g • Cholesterol 0 mg • Fat 6 g • Protein 5 g • Sodium 40 mg*

*\*Israeli couscous, a toasted couscous, is a relatively new product in the United States. It can be found in some natural foods stores and international markets.*

# Swordfish with Risotto and Roasted-Tomato Broth

12 cherry tomatoes

Olive oil for coating

Salt to taste

Four 3-ounce (90-g) swordfish steaks

1 cup (8 fl oz/250 ml) Roasted-Tomato Broth (recipe follows)

1 cup (6 oz/180 g) cooked risotto (see Basics)

8 pieces broccoli rabe, blanched

2 tablespoons tapenade

Preheat the the broiler. Lightly coat the cherry tomatoes with olive oil and sprinkle with salt. Arrange the tomatoes on a sheet pan and place under the broiler for 10 minutes, or until the skin blisters and turns slightly black; set aside.

Broil the swordfish steaks until just cooked through, about 3 minutes per side. Spoon ¼ cup (2 fl oz/60 ml) of the roasted-tomato broth on each of 4 plates. Arrange the swordfish, risotto, and 2 pieces of broccoli rabe on each plate. Top each serving with a little tapenade and 3 charred cherry tomatoes.

*Makes 4 servings*

### PER SERVING

*Calories 320 • Carbohydrates 19 g • Cholesterol 45 mg • Fat 18 g • Protein 22 g • Sodium 1,340 mg*

## Roasted-Tomato Broth

3 tablespoons virgin olive oil

2 tablespoons diced yellow onion

1 teaspoon roasted garlic (see Basics)

1/2 teaspoon herbes de Provence (optional)

3 ripe tomatoes, roasted, seeded, and peeled (see Basics)

2 teaspoons kosher salt

1 teaspoon freshly ground pepper

2 cups (16 fl oz/500 ml) vegetable stock (see Basics),
    canned low-salt vegetable broth, or water

In a large skillet or sauté pan over medium heat, heat the oil and sauté the onion for 5 minutes, or until soft. Add the remaining ingredients and simmer for 20 minutes. Taste and adjust the seasoning.

*Makes about 3 cups (24 fl oz/750 ml)*

PER 1 CUP (8 fl oz/250 ml)

*Calories 160 • Carbohydrates 7 g • Cholesterol 0 mg • Fat 14 g • Protein 3 g • Sodium 1,310 mg*

# Lemon Chiffon with Strawberry Sauce

2 tablespoons water

1 teaspoon grated lemon zest (see Basics)

1 envelope (1 tablespoon) plain gelatin

2 tablespoons fresh lemon juice

2 eggs

1/4 cup (2 oz/60 g) sugar, or to taste

3/4 cup (6 oz/185 g) plain low-fat yogurt

*Strawberry Sauce*

1 cup (4 oz/125 g) fresh strawberries, hulled and sliced

1 tablespoon fructose or sugar, or to taste

2 tablespoons *each* water and dry white wine

In a small saucepan, combine the water and lemon zest and simmer for a few minutes. Remove from heat and strain through a fine-meshed sieve into a bowl. Add the gelatin to the lemon essence, stir in the lemon juice, and let sit for about 5 minutes, or until dissolved. Heat the mixture slightly if necessary to completely dissolve the gelatin.

In a medium bowl, beat the eggs and sugar until pale and thick. Stir in the gelatin mixture. Fold the yogurt into the mixture until well blended. Pour into 4 individual molds and refrigerate until set, at least 2 or 3 hours.

Meanwhile, make the strawberry sauce: In a medium saucepan, combine all the ingredients and heat until the strawberries are soft. Strain through a fine-meshed sieve, pushing the berries through with the back of a large spoon. Adjust the sweetness if necessary.

To serve, immerse the bottom of each mold in hot water until the chiffon slides out easily. Place each chiffon on an individual dessert plate and spoon the strawberry sauce around it.

*Makes 4 servings*

PER SERVING

*Calories 150 • Carbohydrates 22 g • Cholesterol 110 mg • Fat 3.5 g • Protein 7 g • Sodium 70 mg*

# The Spa at Doral

*Our goal is to provide an environment in which anyone can explore
innovative ways to address physical and emotional needs, rejuvenate
their bodies and spirits, and learn to cope with stress, in an atmosphere of
five-star luxury and pampering.*

—*Jossie Feria, Director*

## ✤ PROFILE ✤

Catering to body and mind in a luxurious setting, the Spa at Doral is an intimate hotel nestled within the world-class Doral Golf Resort. Guests from around the globe come to renew their senses, refresh their spirits, and reward their bodies with exercise and beauty treatments, while they relax in delightful surroundings and dine on delicious spa cuisine. An oasis of serenity, the spa offers fitness, beauty, and "integrated wellness" regimens. Its services, products, and wide variety of classes make use of cutting-edge innovations and medical discoveries and are distinguished by an elegant European flair. The Spa at Doral has been ranked by Zagat as one of the top spas in the country and is on the Gold List.

## ✤ CUISINE ✤

The award-winning spa cuisine of executive chef George Patrick Goins highlights the flavors of South Florida and Asia. A truly delectable dining experience, his menu changes with the seasons, emphasizing foods at their freshest and maximizing vitamins, minerals, and other nutrients. Through cooking demonstrations, recipe cards, and nutritional counseling, The Spa teaches guests how to choose and cook food, and inspires them to turn their stay into a long-term commitment to healthy eating.

## ✦ SETTING ✦

The Spa at Doral blends "gracious Tuscan villa" with "luxurious Florida resort." Overlooking formal gardens with Mediterranean-style statuary and splashing fountains, its forty-eight guest suites feature private Jacuzzis, wet bars, balconies, and video entertainment centers. Spa guests can also stay in the resort lodges, which are situated next to the golf courses (resort guests can book spa services on a daily basis). The resort itself has nearly seven hundred rooms and is set on 650 acres richly landscaped with papaya, banana, and orange trees, flowers, and other tropical plants. Facilities include eighty-one holes of golf, including the famous Blue Monster course; the fifteen-court Arthur Ashe Tennis Complex; six restaurants; and, of course, the Spa.

## ✦ ACTIVITIES, TREATMENTS, AND FACILITIES ✦

Whether you want a day-spa workout, a week-long package, or just some flexible daily regimens, there are fitness, nutrition, stress-relief, and beauty programs for everyone. Appealing to both women and men, classes emphasize jazzy low-impact workouts and include dance classes, boxercise, yoga, tai chi, chi kung, morning power walks, weight lifting, and aqua aerobics. For superfit spa-goers, the "Boot Camp" program provides a demanding workout of aerobics, plyometrics, and abdominal exercises. Body and skin-care treatments include gommage, total-body fango, a passionfruit body glow, a soothing aloe vera body wrap, an anti-cellulite program, and a variety of massage therapies. Other facilities include cascading waterfalls for hydromassage, indoor and outdoor pools, hot and cold plunge pools, saunas, a whirlpool, private women's and men's sun decks, and a full-service beauty salon.

# MENU

## *BREAKFAST*

*Whole-Wheat Banana Pancakes with Fruit Sauce*

## *LUNCH*

*Carrot-Ginger Soup*

❖

*Lime-Marinated Shrimp Kabobs with Bulgur Wheat*

## *DINNER*

*Spring Rolls with Sesame-Soy Dipping Sauce*

❖

*Lobster Tail Fra Diablo Over Capellini*

❖

*Key Lime Cannoli*

THE SPA AT DORAL

# Whole-Wheat Banana Pancakes with Fruit Sauce

*Fruit Sauce*

> $^1/_2$ cup (4 oz/125 g) all-fruit preserves of choice
> $^3/_4$ cup (6 fl oz/185 ml) unsweetened apple juice
> $^3/_4$ cup (6 fl oz/185 ml) water
>
> $1^1/_2$ cups ($4^1/_2$ oz/140 g) rolled oats
> 1 cup (5 oz/155 g) whole-wheat flour
> 1 tablespoon thawed apple juice concentrate
> 1 tablespoon baking powder
> $1^1/_2$ teaspoons vanilla extract
> 2 egg whites, lightly beaten
> 2 ripe bananas, mashed

To make the fruit sauce: In a medium saucepan, stir all the ingredients together and bring to a boil. Reduce heat to low and simmer for 10 minutes, or until reduced by half. Keep warm.

To make the pancakes: In a medium bowl, combine the oats, flour, apple juice concentrate, and baking powder and blend thoroughly.

In another medium bowl, beat the vanilla, egg whites, and bananas together. Stir the banana mixture into the flour mixture and mix until just combined. Lightly coat a griddle or large skillet with vegetable oil spray and place over medium heat. When hot, drop the batter by heaping tablespoons onto the griddle or skillet and cook until bubbles appear evenly on the surface, about 1 minute. Turn and cook for 1 minute on the other side, or until golden. Serve the pancakes immediately, with warm fruit sauce.

*Makes about sixteen 6-inch (15-cm) pancakes*

PER PANCAKE (with 1 tablespoon fruit sauce)

*Calories 95 • Carbohydrates 21 g • Cholesterol 0 mg • Fat 0.5 g • Protein 3 g • Sodium 50 mg*

# Carrot-Ginger Soup

  2 pounds (1 kg) carrots, peeled (about 10 carrots)
  12 ounces (375 g) red onions, diced
  $^1/_2$ potato, peeled and diced
  1 tablespoon grated fresh ginger
  6 cups (48 fl oz/1$^1/_2$ l) water
  2 tablespoons honey
  $^3/_4$ cup (6 fl oz/185 ml) evaporated nonfat milk
  $^1/_4$ teaspoon salt
  Ground white pepper to taste
  Chopped fresh parsley for garnish

Cut 1 of the carrots into fine dice and reserve; thinly slice the remaining carrots. Cook the sliced carrots in salted boiling water until tender, about 15 minutes; drain.

Lightly coat a large, heavy saucepan with vegetable oil spray and heat it over medium heat. Sauté the red onions for 5 minutes, or until golden brown. Add the potato and ginger. Stir in the carrots and water and bring to a boil.

Reduce heat to low, cover, and simmer for 10 minutes. Transfer the soup to a blender or food processor in batches and purée.

Return the soup to the saucepan and stir in the reserved diced carrot, honey, milk, salt, and pepper. Bring to a boil, reduce heat, and simmer for 10 minutes, or until the diced carrot is tender.

To serve, ladle the soup into shallow soup bowls and garnish with parsley.

*Makes 12 servings*

### PER SERVING

*Calories 60 • Carbohydrates 14 g • Cholesterol 0 mg • Fat 0 g • Protein 2 g • Sodium 95 mg*

# Lime-Marinated Shrimp Kabobs with Bulgur Wheat

1/4 cup (2 fl oz/60 ml) fresh lime juice
2 tablespoons low-salt soy sauce
1/4 teaspoon olive oil
3 garlic cloves, minced
3 tablespoons chopped fresh parsley
8 ounces (250 g) medium shrimp, shelled and deveined with tails intact
1 cup (4 oz/120 g) bulgur wheat
2 cups (16 fl oz/500 ml) water
Lime wedges for garnish

In a medium bowl, combine the lime juice, soy sauce, olive oil, garlic, and parsley. Add the shrimp and toss to coat. Cover and refrigerate for 30 minutes.

Light a fire in a charcoal grill, or preheat a gas grill or broiler. Soak the 4 wooden skewers in water to cover.

In a medium saucepan, combine the bulgur wheat and water, cover, and bring to a boil. Reduce heat to low and simmer for 15 minutes. Set aside.

Drain the shrimp, reserving the marinade. Thread the shrimp onto the skewers.

Lay the skewers on the grill or under the broiler and cook for 4 to 5 minutes, turning and basting, until pink and opaque. Serve on a bed of bulgur wheat and garnish with lime wedges.

*Makes 4 servings*

### PER SERVING

*Calories 140 • Carbohydrates 18 g • Cholesterol 85 mg • Fat 1.5 g • Protein 15 g • Sodium 180 mg*

# Spring Rolls with Sesame-Soy Dipping Sauce

2 teaspoons minced garlic

$^1/_2$ cup ($2^1/_2$ oz/75 g) shredded carrot

$^1/_2$ cup (2 oz/60 g) finely chopped onion

$^1/_2$ cup ($2^1/_2$ oz/75 g) *each* finely diced celery and green bell pepper

$^1/_2$ cup ($1^1/_2$ oz/45 g) shredded cabbage

$^1/_2$ teaspoon low-salt soy sauce

8 wonton wrappers

*Sesame-Soy Dipping Sauce*

2 tablespoons low-salt soy sauce

$^1/_2$ cup (4 fl oz/125 ml) rice wine vinegar

$^1/_2$ tablespoon minced fresh ginger

6 tablespoons (3 fl oz/90 ml) water

Preheat the oven to 375°F (190°C). Lightly coat a baking sheet with vegetable oil spray. Lightly coat a nonstick pan or skillet with vegetable oil spray and heat over medium heat. Sauté the garlic for 3 minutes. Add all the vegetables and sauté for 1 or 2 minutes, or just until the vegetables are crisp-tender. Stir in the soy sauce, remove from heat, and let cool.

Lay a wonton wrapper on a work surface and mound one-eighth of the vegetables along one edge. Fold in the 2 sides and roll up the wrapper. Repeat to use the remaining wrappers and filling. Transfer the rolls to the prepared pan, seam sides down. Lightly mist the tops of the rolls with vegetable oil spray and bake in the preheated oven for about 15 minutes, or until crisp and just golden.

In a small bowl, whisk all the dipping sauce ingredients together. Serve the spring rolls with the dipping sauce.

*Makes 8 spring rolls; serves 4*

PER SERVING (with 2 tablespoons dipping sauce)

*Calories 220 • Carbohydrates 42 g • Cholesterol 10 mg • Fat 1 g • Protein 8 g • Sodium 535 mg*

# Lobster Tail Fra Diablo Over Capellini

1/2 tablespoon olive oil

1/4 cup (1 oz/30 g) chopped onion

1 tablespoon minced garlic

2 tablespoons chopped red bell pepper

1/4 cup (2 fl oz/60 ml) dry white wine

1/2 cup (4 fl oz/125 ml) tomato sauce

1 pound (500 g) Roma (plum) tomatoes, diced (about 4 cups)

1/4 teaspoon ground pepper

1/4 teaspoon cayenne pepper

1/2 teaspoon chopped fresh cilantro

12 ounces (375 g) cooked lobster tail meat, cut into 1-inch (2.5-cm) pieces

12 ounces (375 g) capellini (angel hair pasta)

In a large, heavy saucepan over medium heat, heat the olive oil and sauté the onion for 3 minutes, or until soft. Add the garlic and sauté for 2 minutes. Add the bell pepper and sauté for 5 minutes, or until the pepper is slightly soft. Pour in the wine and cook for 5 minutes. Add the tomato sauce, tomatoes, ground pepper, cayenne, and cilantro, raise the heat to high, and bring to a boil. Reduce heat and simmer for 30 minutes.

In a large pot of salted boiling water, cook the pasta until al dente, about 8 minutes. Drain.

Divide the capellini evenly among 6 plates and top each with 1/2 cup (4 fl oz/125 ml) sauce. Arrange one-sixth of the lobster on top of each serving and serve immediately.

*Makes 6 servings*

### PER SERVING

*Calories 310 • Carbohydrates 47 g • Cholesterol 45 mg • Fat 4 g • Protein 19 g • Sodium 480 mg*

# Key Lime Cannoli

## Cannoli Shells

3 tablespoons flour

$1/2$ cup (4 oz/125 g) sugar

3 tablespoons quick-cooking rolled oats

2 tablespoons finely chopped almonds

1 tablespoon unsweetened cocoa powder

$1/8$ teaspoon salt

2 tablespoons butter, melted

$1/2$ teaspoon vanilla extract

$1/4$ teaspoon almond extract

3 egg whites, beaten until frothy

## Key Lime Filling

$1/2$ cup (4 oz/125 g) low-fat cream cheese, at room temperature

3 tablespoons sugar

1 tablespoon fresh key lime or regular lime juice

$1 1/2$ teaspoons grated lime zest (see Basics)

$1/4$ cup (2 oz/60 g) low-fat ricotta cheese

$1/2$ cup (4 fl oz/125 ml) Raspberry Coulis (see page 250)

Fresh raspberries and 8 thin lime slices for garnish

To make the shells: Preheat the oven to 350°F (180°C). Line a baking sheet with parchment paper and lightly coat with vegetable oil spray. In a medium bowl, combine the flour, sugar, oats, almonds, cocoa, and salt and stir until well blended. In another medium bowl, beat together the butter, vanilla, almond extract, and egg whites. Add the flour mixture to the butter mixture and mix until thoroughly blended.

Drop 1 tablespoonful of the batter onto the prepared baking sheet. Using a spatula, spread the batter into a thin circle. Repeat to make 8 circles; if necessary, bake in batches. Bake in the preheated oven for 8 to 10 minutes, or until set but still slightly flexible. Remove from the oven and immediately roll into 1-inch-diameter (2.5-cm) cylinders. Let cool until crisp.

To make the filling: In a medium bowl, beat the cream cheese, sugar, lime juice, and lime zest together until smooth. Beat in the ricotta. Cover and refrigerate at least 2 hours, or until chilled and firm.

Just before serving, fill each cylinder with 2 tablespoons filling. Spread 1 tablespoon raspberry coulis on each of 8 plates and top with 1 cannoli. Garnish each plate with 5 raspberries and a twisted lime slice.

*Makes 8 servings*

PER SERVING

*Calories 190 • Carbohydrates 27 g • Cholesterol 20 mg • Fat 8 g • Protein 5 g • Sodium 140 mg*

# Topnotch at Stowe

Stowe, Vermont

*Perched in Vermont's Green Mountains, Topnotch is a classic country inn that caters to sports enthusiasts and weary urbanites seeking escape from civilization.*

**—Fodor's Healthy Escapes**

## ❖ PROFILE ❖

Opened in 1958 as a small summer and ski resort, Topnotch at Stowe was refurbished over the years and began to be known as a luxury retreat in the early 1980s; its spa facilities were completed in 1989. Making the most of its wholesome mountain environment, Topnotch offers exceptional vacations that are both restful and invigorating. The homey, comfortable resort features some of the finest cuisine in New England, gracious service and amenities, glorious panoramic views, excellent tennis facilities, and a 23,000-square-foot, state-of-the-art spa. A consistent award-winner, Topnotch has received four stars from the Mobil travel guide for eighteen straight years and four diamonds from AAA, and is on the *Condé Nast Traveler* Gold List.

## ❖ CUISINE ❖

Maxwell's, the main restaurant at Topnotch, serves both gourmet spa and superb American country cuisine. The restaurant offers a spectacular view of Mt. Mansfield, and during the summer, lunch is available outside on the patio terrace or poolside. Showcasing the best of Vermont's locally grown foods, the spa menu's culinary selections are innovative, balanced, and healthy. Executive chef Edward St. Onge created the following recipes.

## ❖ SETTING ❖

Located at the base of Mt. Mansfield, Vermont's highest peak, Topnotch at Stowe covers 120 acres in the heart of the Green Mountain range. You will experience the rustically elegant comfort of the place as soon as you enter the lobby, with its floor-to-ceiling windows looking out on the lush Vermont countryside, walk-around fireplace, and wood and stone interior typical of the rest of the resort. Guests have their choice of ninety spacious rooms and suites, and twenty town houses featuring fireplaces, saunas, whirlpools, and sundecks. Accommodations offer a variety of pool, garden, and mountain views and are individually decorated with antique furnishings, libraries, and original works of art. At Topnotch, activities vary with the seasons: in the winter, excellent downhill and cross-country skiing, as well as ice skating on a pond; in the summer, horseback riding (there is an equestrian center for lessons and trail rides), golf, and mountain biking. Tennis and swimming are available year-round.

## ❖ ACTIVITIES, TREATMENTS, and FACILITIES ❖

The spa at Topnotch offers a full range of personal treatments and services to help guests look and feel their best. Staffed with caring professionals, its facilities include a twelve-foot whirlpool with cascading hydromassage waterfall; a sixty-foot indoor exercise pool; a heated outdoor pool; twenty treatment and therapy rooms; fully equipped exercise/weight studios; and lounge areas with saunas, steam rooms, and fireplaces. Among the treatments are a variety of massages, aromatherapy, facials, hydrotherapy, dosha balancing, herbal wraps, and salt-glow loofah scrubs. Fitness classes include aerobics, circuit weight training, stretching, upper and lower body shaping, lower-back strengthening, jazz dance, yoga, and water volleyball. Personal consultations are available, as are seminars on stress reduction and guided mountain hikes. Guests can choose a fully structured two- to seven-day spa program, spend a special "Day at the Spa," or select spa services on a daily basis.

# MENU

*BREAKFAST*

**Cornmeal-Buttermilk Waffles with Blueberry-Orange Syrup**

*LUNCH*

**Chicken Enchiladas with Black Beans**

*DINNER*

**Wild Mushroom and Chèvre Strudel**

❖

**Steamed Sea Bass Tower with Portobello Mushrooms
and White Truffle–Spinach Vinaigrette**

❖

**Chilled Melon Balls with Warm Ginger Sauce**

241

# Cornmeal-Buttermilk Waffles with Blueberry-Orange Syrup

1 egg, beaten

2 cups (16 fl oz/500 ml) buttermilk

1/2 cup (4 oz/125 g) yellow cornmeal

2 tablespoons sugar

1 tablespoon baking powder

1/2 teaspoon baking soda

1/2 cup (4 oz/125 g) unsalted butter, melted

1 tablespoon molasses

2 egg whites

Blueberry-Orange Syrup (recipe follows)

In a medium bowl, beat the egg and buttermilk together. Stir in the cornmeal, sugar, baking powder, and baking soda until smooth. Stir in the melted butter and molasses.

In a large bowl, beat the egg whites until stiff, glossy peaks form. Stir one-fourth of the egg whites into the cornmeal mixture, then fold in the remaining whites until blended.

Lightly coat a nonstick waffle iron with vegetable oil spray and heat. Pour in the batter and cook the waffles until golden brown. Serve with the blueberry-orange syrup.

*Makes 6 servings*

PER SERVING (with 2 tablespoons syrup)

*Calories 285 • Carbohydrates 27 g • Cholesterol 80 mg • Fat 17 g • Protein 6 g • Sodium 340 mg*

## Blueberry-Orange Syrup

**2 cups (8 oz/250 g) fresh or frozen blueberries**
**¼ cup (2 fl oz/60 ml) orange juice**
**1 cinnamon stick**
**2 tablespoons honey**

In a medium, heavy saucepan, combine all the ingredients and bring to a boil. Reduce heat and simmer for 20 minutes. Remove the cinnamon stick. Transfer the syrup to a blender or food processor and purée.

*Makes about 1½ cups (12 fl oz/375 ml)*

### PER TABLESPOON

*Calories 13 • Carbohydrates 4 g • Cholesterol 0 mg • Fat 0 g • Protein 0 g • Sodium 0 mg*

# Chicken Enchiladas with Black Beans

1 tablespoon olive oil

Six 6-ounce (185-g) boneless, skinless chicken breast halves

3 red bell peppers, seeded, deribbed, and sliced

3 green bell peppers, seeded, deribbed, and sliced

12 corn tortillas

$^1/_2$ cup (4 fl oz/125 ml) Red Chili Sauce (recipe follows)

2 cups (14 oz/440 g) cooked black beans (recipe follows),
   or canned low-salt black beans, rinsed and drained

$^3/_4$ cup (6 oz/185 g) nonfat sour cream

1 bunch cilantro, chopped

Preheat the oven to 350°F (180°C). In a large sauté pan or skillet over medium heat, heat the olive oil and sauté the chicken breasts for 5 minutes on each side, or until opaque throughout; set aside. Steam the peppers for 1 minute and let cool.

Dip a corn tortilla in the red chili sauce. Place one-sixth of the sliced chicken and peppers along the edge of the tortilla and roll up. Transfer the enchilada to a 7-by-11-inch (18-by-28-cm) baking pan. Repeat to dip and fill the remaining tortillas. Bake in the preheated oven for 5 to 8 minutes, or until heated through.

Heat the black beans if necessary and place $^1/_3$ cup (2$^1/_2$ oz/75 g) beans in the center of each of 6 plates. With a ladle, spoon a circle of red chili sauce around the beans. Using a spatula, place 2 enchiladas on top of the black beans and ladle a little sauce over to coat the tortillas. Top each tortilla with a dollop of sour cream and sprinkle with chopped cilantro. Serve immediately.

*Makes 6 servings*

PER SERVING

*Calories 470 • Carbohydrates 53 g • Cholesterol 95 mg • Fat 9 g • Protein 45 g • Sodium 190 mg*

## Red Chili Sauce

> 1 tablespoon olive oil
> 1/2 onion, chopped
> 2 ounces (60 g) ancho chilies, seeded and stemmed
> 2 garlic cloves, chopped
> 1 cup (8 fl oz/250 ml) apple juice
> Vegetable stock (see Basics) or canned low-salt vegetable broth, as needed

In a medium, heavy saucepan over medium heat, heat the olive oil and sauté the onion, chilies, and garlic for 5 minutes. Pour in the apple juice and simmer for 20 minutes. Transfer the sauce to a blender or food processor and purée. Add enough stock or broth to achieve a thin sauce consistency. Strain the sauce through a fine-meshed sieve.

*Makes 1³/4 cups (14 fl oz/430 ml)*

### PER TABLESPOON

*Calories 15 • Carbohydrates 2 g • Cholesterol 0 mg • Fat 0.5 g • Protein 0 g • Sodium 0 mg*

## Black Beans

> ²/3 cup (5 oz/155 g) dried black beans
> 1 small bay leaf
> 1 garlic clove

Rinse and pick over the beans. Soak the beans overnight in water to cover by 2 inches (5 cm). Drain. In a large saucepan, combine the beans and water to cover by 2 inches (5 cm). Add the bay leaf and garlic. Bring to a boil, then reduce the heat to low. Cover and simmer for 1 hour, or until the beans are tender. Remove and discard the bay leaf.

*Makes about 2 cups (14 oz/440 g)*

### PER ¹/3 CUP (2¹/4 oz/67 g)

*Calories 70 • Carbohydrates 13 g • Cholesterol 0 mg • Fat 0 g • Protein 5 g • Sodium 0 mg*

# Wild Mushroom and Chèvre Strudel

2 tablespoons unsalted butter

1/4 cup (2 oz/60 g) minced shallots

5 garlic cloves, minced

1 pound (500 g) wild mushrooms, such as porcini, cremini, stemmed shiitakes, diced

1/2 cup (4 fl oz/125 ml) dry white wine

2 ounces (60 g) chèvre cheese, crumbled (about 1/2 cup)

2 tablespoons minced fresh herbs, such as chives, tarragon, and/or parsley

6 sheets frozen phyllo dough, thawed

In a large sauté pan or skillet, melt 1 tablespoon of the butter over medium heat and sauté the shallots and garlic for 3 minutes, or until translucent. Add the mushrooms and continue to sauté until the liquid released by the mushrooms has cooked away. Pour in the wine and cook until the mixture is fairly dry. Remove from heat and let cool completely.

In a large bowl, combine the chèvre, mixed herbs, and cooled mushroom mixture. Preheat the oven to 350°F (180°C). Lightly coat a baking sheet with vegetable oil spray. Melt the remaining 1 tablespoon butter.

Stack 3 sheets of phyllo dough on a work surface. Cover the remaining 3 sheets with a damp towel. Lightly brush the top sheet in the stack with half the melted butter and mound half the mushroom filling along the long edge of the stack; roll up tightly. Repeat with the remaining sheets and filling. Tuck the ends of each strudel under and place, seam side down, on the prepared pan. Score the top of each strudel to indicate cutting lines for portions.

Bake in the preheated oven for 10 minutes, or until golden brown. Remove from the oven and let cool on wire racks for 15 minutes before serving. Slice carefully with a large, sharp knife.

*Makes 4 servings*

### PER SERVING

*Calories 240 • Carbohydrates 26 g • Cholesterol 20 mg • Fat 11 g • Protein 8 g • Sodium 220 mg*

# Steamed Sea Bass Tower with Portobello Mushrooms and White Truffle–Spinach Vinaigrette

4 tomatoes, cut into $1/4$-inch-thick (6-mm) crosswise slices

2 zucchini, cut into $1/4$-inch-thick (6-mm) lengthwise slices

1 globe eggplant, cut into $1/4$-inch-thick (6-mm) crosswise slices

6 portobello mushrooms, stemmed and cut into $1/4$-inch-thick (6-mm) slices

Six 5-ounce (155-g) sea bass fillets

Salt and freshly ground pepper to taste

White Truffle-Spinach Vinaigrette (recipe follows)

Fresh herb sprigs for garnish

Light a fire in a charcoal grill or preheat a gas grill or the broiler. Grill or broil the tomato, zucchini, and eggplant slices until soft and lightly browned on both sides. Place in a low oven to keep warm.

In a covered pot, steam the mushrooms over boiling water for 1 minute. Remove from steamer basket and place in the oven to keep warm. Season the sea bass with salt and pepper, add to steamer basket, and steam for 5 minutes, or until opaque throughout. Carefully remove from the steamer basket.

Alternate the vegetables in a stack in the center of each of 6 plates. Place a sea bass fillet on top of each vegetable stack and ladle $1/4$ cup (2 fl oz/60 ml) of the truffle-spinach vinaigrette around the outside edge of each plate. Garnish with fresh herbs and serve.

*Makes 6 servings*

PER SERVING

*Calories 230 • Carbohydrates 14 g • Cholesterol 60 mg • Fat 6 g • Protein 30 g • Sodium 140 mg*

## White Truffle–Spinach Vinaigrette

**8 ounces (250 g) fresh spinach, stemmed**
**6 tablespoons (3 fl oz/90 ml) rice vinegar**
**1 tablespoon white truffle oil**
**Salt and freshly ground pepper to taste**

Wash the spinach and place it, still wet, in a large covered pan. Cook over high heat for 3 to 4 minutes, or until wilted. Place in a sieve and press with the back of a large spoon to drain the excess liquid.

Transfer the spinach to a blender or food processor. Add the rice vinegar, truffle oil, salt, and pepper and purée.

*Makes about 1¹/₂ cups (12 fl oz/375 ml)*

### PER TABLESPOON

*Calories 8 • Carbohydrates 0.5 g • Cholesterol 0 mg • Fat 0.5 g • Protein 0.5 g • Sodium 8 mg*

# Chilled Melon Balls with Warm Ginger Sauce

**1 large honeydew melon, halved and seeded**

**2 cantaloupes, halved and seeded**

*Ginger Sauce*

**4 tablespoons finely diced fresh ginger**

**4 cups (32 fl oz/1 l) fresh orange juice**

**2 tablespoons raspberry vinegar**

**1 teaspoon fresh lemon juice**

**2 teaspoons honey**

**Julienned fresh mint and basil for garnish**

Using a melon baller, scoop out the flesh of the honeydew and cantaloupes to make melon balls.

To make the ginger sauce: In a medium, heavy saucepan, combine the ginger, orange juice, vinegar, lemon juice, and honey, bring to a simmer, and cook to reduce the liquid to about 1 cup (8 fl oz/250 ml). Set the sauce aside and keep warm.

To serve: Divide the melon balls among 6 plates. Drizzle 2 tablespoons of the ginger sauce in a lace pattern over each serving and garnish with mint and basil.

*Makes 6 servings*

### PER SERVING

*Calories 120 • Carbohydrates 29 g • Cholesterol 0 mg • Fat 0.5 g • Protein 2 g • Sodium 10 mg*

# BASICS

## Angel Food Cake

   1³/₄ cups (9 oz/270 g) cake flour, sifted
   2 cups (16 oz/500 g) sugar
   16 egg whites
   2 tablespoons vanilla extract
   1 teaspoon cream of tartar
   1 teaspoon salt

Preheat the oven to 375°F (190°C). In a medium bowl, stir the flour and 1¹/₂ cups (12 oz/375 g) of the sugar together; set aside.

In a very large bowl, beat the egg whites and vanilla until soft peaks form. Gradually beat in the cream of tartar, salt, and remaining sugar until stiff, glossy peaks form. Gently fold in the flour mixture until blended. Pour the batter into an ungreased 10-inch (25-cm) tube pan, cutting vertically through the batter several times with a rubber spatula to pop any air bubbles. Smooth the top with the rubber spatula.

Bake the cake in the preheated oven for about 30 minutes, or until it's spongy and a thin wooden skewer inserted in the center of the cake comes out clean. Invert the pan and let the cake cool completely. Remove the cake from the mold.

*Makes one 10-inch (25-cm) cake*

## Berry Coulis

   4 cups (16 oz/500 g) fresh berries
   ¹/₄ cup (2 oz/60 g) sugar or fructose
   Juice of 1/2 lemon

In a blender or food processor, combine the berries and sugar or fructose and blend until smooth. Stir in the lemon juice and strain through a fine-meshed sieve. Store in an airtight container in the refrigerator for 3 to 4 days.

*Makes 4 cups (32 fl oz/1 l)*

## Butternut Squash or Pumpkin Purée

Canned pumpkin purée can be used in recipes calling for squash or pumpkin purée, or you can make your own: Pierce the skin of a 11/2-pound (750-g) butternut squash or sugar (pie) pumpkin in several places with a sharp knife or metal skewer. Place on a baking sheet and bake in a preheated 350°F (180°C) oven for 1 hour, or until soft. Remove from the oven and let cool. Halve the squash or pumpkin and scoop out the seeds and strings. Scoop out the pulp and purée in a blender or food processor. Makes about 3 cups (24 oz/750 g).

## Chicken or Fish Velouté

> 1 cup (8 fl oz/250 ml) homemade chicken or fish stock
>    or canned low-salt chicken or clam broth
> 1 cup (8 fl oz/250 ml) evaporated skim milk
> 1/4 teaspoon salt
> 1/8 teaspoon ground white pepper
> 2 tablespoons arrowroot mixed with 2 tablespoons water

In a heavy saucepan, combine the stock or broth, evaporated milk, salt, and pepper and bring to a boil. Add the arrowroot mixture to the boiling milk mixture and stir constantly until it thickens. Reduce heat to low and simmer for about 5 minutes.

*Makes 2 cups (16 fl oz/500 ml)*

## Citrus Zest

Using a zester, vegetable peeler, or sharp paring knife, cut thin strips of the colored part (the zest) of the citrus peel; don't include the white pith underneath, which is apt to be bitter.

## Mango Purée

Peel 2 large mangoes and cut the flesh away from the pit. In a blender or food processor, blend the flesh to a smooth purée. Makes about 2 cups (16 fl oz/500 ml).

## Pastry Cream

> 2 tablespoons sugar or fructose
> 1½ tablespoons cornstarch or arrowroot powder
> 1 egg yolk
> ¾ cup (6 fl oz/180 ml) low-fat milk
> 1 teaspoon vanilla extract

In a medium bowl, stir the sugar or fructose and cornstarch or arrowroot together. Whisk in the egg yolk until smooth.

In a small saucepan, heat the milk over medium-high heat until bubbles form around the edges of the pan. Gradually whisk the hot milk into the egg mixture in a thin stream. Return the mixture to the saucepan and bring to a boil over medium heat, whisking constantly. Reduce heat to a simmer and whisk until the mixture thickens enough to coat the back of a spoon.

Remove from heat and stir in the vanilla. Cover with plastic wrap by pressing the plastic directly onto the surface of the pastry cream. Let cool completely before using. Pastry cream can be stored in the refrigerator for up to 3 days.

*Makes about 1 cup (8 fl oz/250 ml)*

## Risotto

> 3 to 4 cups (24 to 32 fl oz/750 ml to 1 l) homemade chicken stock (see page 254) or canned low-salt chicken broth
> 1 tablespoon olive oil
> ¾ cup (4 oz/125 g) finely chopped onion
> 1 cup (7 oz/220 g) Arborio rice
> ½ cup (4 fl oz/125 ml) dry white wine
> Salt and freshly ground pepper to taste

In a small saucepan, bring the stock or broth to a boil; reduce heat and keep it at a simmer.

In a heavy, medium saucepan over medium heat, heat the olive oil and sauté the onion until soft, about 5 minutes. Add the rice and cook for 3 minutes, stirring constantly.

Gradually add ½ cup (4 fl oz/125 ml) of the hot stock or broth to the rice; stir constantly until the stock or broth is absorbed. Repeat twice. Add the wine and stir until it is absorbed. Continue adding the remaining stock, ½ cup (4 fl oz/125 ml) at a time, stirring constantly each time until it is absorbed, until the rice is creamy and al dente, 25 to 30 minutes. Season with salt and pepper and serve at once.

*Makes 4 servings*

## Roasting Peppers and Chilies

Char whole peppers or chilies over a gas flame until the skin is blackened all over. Or, for peppers, cut into fourths, core, seed, and devein, press to flatten, and char under a preheated broiler. Using tongs, transfer the peppers or chilies to a paper or plastic bag, close it, and let the peppers or chilies cool for 10 to 15 minutes. Remove from the bag, peel off the skin with your fingers or a small, sharp knife, and core and seed the peppers or chilies if charred whole. Be sure to wear gloves when working with hot chilies such as jalapeño, serrano, chili de arbol, and habanero.

## Peeling and Seeding Tomatoes

Cut out the cores from the tomatoes and cut an X in the opposite end. Drop the tomatoes into a pot of rapidly boiling water for about 10 seconds, or until the skin by the X peels away slightly. Transfer the tomatoes to a bowl of cold water; the skin should slip off easily. To seed, cut the tomatoes in half crosswise, hold each half upside down over the sink, and gently squeeze and shake to remove the seeds.

# Stocks

Stocks make soups, sauces, and gravies more nutritious and savory without adding salt or many calories. You may add any vegetables to the stock that you like, with the exception of members of the cabbage family (broccoli, cauliflower, etc.), which tend to impart a strong flavor and can make stock bitter. The following stock recipes (except the duck and lamb stocks) are from Cal-a-Vie.

## Low-fat Chicken Stock

2 pounds (1 kg) chicken bones
1 pound (500 g) skinless chicken, cubed
2 unpeeled onions, quartered
2 carrots, peeled and coarsely chopped
2 celery stalks, coarsely chopped
4 unpeeled garlic cloves
6 parsley sprigs
1 teaspoon minced fresh thyme
1 or 2 bay leaves
1 gallon (4 l) water

In a large stockpot, combine all the ingredients and bring to a boil. Reduce heat to low and simmer for 4 to 6 hours. Strain the stock through a fine-meshed sieve. Refrigerate overnight. Lift off and discard the congealed fat. Cover and store in the refrigerator for up to 3 days. To keep longer, bring to a boil every 3 days, or freeze.

*Makes 4 quarts (4 l)*

## Low-fat Duck Stock

3 pounds (1.5 kg) duck bones and trimmings, all fat and skin removed
1 cup (8 fl oz/250 ml) dry red wine
1 onion, chopped
1 large carrot, peeled and chopped
1 celery stalk, chopped
1 leek, including some of the green leaves, cleaned and chopped
9 fresh parsley sprigs
Salt and freshly ground black pepper to taste (optional)

Preheat the oven to 450°F (230°C). Rinse the bones and trimmings and place them in a roasting pan. Bake in the preheated oven, turning once or twice, for 30 minutes, or until deep brown. Transfer the bones to a large stockpot and drain the fat from the baking pan.

Set the baking pan over medium heat and pour in the wine. Stir to scrape up any browned bits on the bottom of the pan. Add this liquid to the stockpot, along with the onion, carrot, celery, leek, and parsley. Add water to cover by 1 inch (2.5 cm) and bring to a boil over high heat. Skim the surface to remove any foam that rises to the top. Reduce heat to low and cook, uncovered, for 3 to 4 hours, adding water as needed to keep the ingredients covered. Add salt and pepper if you like.

Strain the stock through a fine-meshed sieve. Cover and refrigerate overnight. Remove and discard the congealed fat. Cover and store in the refrigerator for up to 3 days. To keep longer, bring to a boil every 3 days or freeze for up to 3 months.

*Makes about 6 cups (48 fl oz/1.5 l)*

## Fish Stock

   1 pound (500 g) fish bones and trimmings of any white fish, chopped
   1 cup (3$^{1}/_{2}$ oz/105 g) sliced onion
   $^{1}/_{2}$ cup (4 fl oz/125 ml) dry white wine
   2 tablespoons fresh lemon juice
   3 to 4 cups (24 to 32 fl oz/750 ml to 1 l) water

In a large saucepan, combine all the ingredients and bring to a boil. Skim any foam that rises to the surface. Reduce heat and simmer for 30 minutes. Strain the stock through a fine-meshed sieve. Cover and store in the refrigerator for up to 3 days. To keep longer, bring to a boil every 3 days, or freeze for up to 3 months.

*Makes 8 cups (64 fl oz/2 l)*

## Lamb Stock

   Uncooked bones and trimmings from a boned leg of lamb
   1 carrot, peeled and chopped
   1 onion, chopped
   1 cup (8 fl oz/250 ml) water
   1 celery stalk, chopped
   2 garlic cloves, crushed
   1 bay leaf
   $^{1}/_{4}$ teaspoon minced fresh rosemary
   Salt and freshly ground black pepper to taste (optional)

Preheat the oven to 425°F (220°C). In a roasting pan, combine the bones and trimmings, carrot, and onion. Bake in the preheated oven, turning occasionally, for 30 to 40 minutes, or until browned. Transfer the bones and vegetables to a stockpot and drain the fat from the roasting pan.

Set the roasting pan over medium heat and add the water. Stir to scrape up the browned bits from the bottom of the pan. Pour the pan liquid into the pot with the bones. Add water to cover the ingredients by 1 inch (2.5 cm) and bring to a boil. Skim off any foam that rises to the surface. Reduce heat to low. Add the chopped celery, garlic, bay leaf, and rosemary. Cover and simmer for 3 to 4 hours, adding water as needed to keep the ingredients covered.

Strain through a fine-meshed sieve. Refrigerate overnight. Remove and discard the congealed fat. Cover and store in the refrigerator for up to 3 days. To keep longer, bring to a boil every 3 days, or freeze for up to 3 months.

*Makes about 8 cups (64 fl oz/2 l)*

## Vegetable Stock

1 cup (5 oz/155 g) coarsely chopped carrot
1 cup (5 oz/155 g) chopped celery
2 unpeeled onions, quartered, or 2 leeks, cleaned and chopped
1 cup (5 oz/155 g) peeled and chopped parsnip
1 cup (5 oz/155 g) peeled and chopped rutabaga or turnip
2 cups (10 oz/315 g) vegetable scraps
2 or 3 fresh parsley sprigs
1 or 2 bay leaves
$1/2$ teaspoon minced fresh thyme
$1/2$ teaspoon ground pepper
8 cups (64 fl oz/2 l) water, or more as needed

In a large stockpot, combine all the ingredients and bring to a boil. Reduce heat to low and simmer for 2 to 3 hours. Remove from heat and strain through a fine-meshed sieve.

Cover and refrigerate for up to 3 days. To keep longer, bring the stock to a boil every 3 days, or freeze for up to 3 months.

*Makes about 8 cups (64 fl oz/2 l)*

## Toasting Nuts and Seeds

*Toasting intensifies the flavor of nuts and seeds.*

Preheat the oven to 350°F (180°C). Spread the nuts or seeds on a baking sheet and bake, stirring once or twice, for 5 to 10 minutes, or until fragrant and very lightly browned.

# Nutritional Data

The nutritional composition of each of the recipes in this cookbook was calculated by registered dietitian Karen Duester at the Food Consulting Company of San Diego, California.

When a recipe gives a choice of ingredients, the first choice is the one used to determine the nutritional data. Optional ingredients and those listed without a specific quantity (such as salt and pepper to taste) are not included in the calculations. When a range of ingredient amounts or serving sizes is given, the smaller amount or portion is used to calculate the nutritional profile.

# CONVERSION CHARTS

## Weight Measurements

| Standard U.S. | Ounces | Metric |
|---|---|---|
| 1 ounce | 1 | 30 g |
| $^1/_4$ pound | 4 | 125 g |
| $^1/_2$ pound | 8 | 250 g |
| 1 pound | 16 | 500 g |
| $1^1/_2$ pounds | 24 | 750 g |
| 2 pounds | 32 | 1 kg |
| $2^1/_2$ pounds | 40 | 1.25 kg |
| 3 pounds | 48 | 1.5 kg |

## Oven Temperatures

| Fahrenheit | Celsius | Gas Mark |
|---|---|---|
| 250° | 120° | $^1/_2$ |
| 275° | 135° | 1 |
| 300° | 150° | 2 |
| 325° | 165° | 3 |
| 350° | 180° | 4 |
| 375° | 190° | 5 |
| 400° | 200° | 6 |
| 425° | 220° | 7 |

## Volume Measurements

| Standard U.S. | Fluid Ounces | Metric |
|---|---|---|
| 1 tablespoon | $^1/_2$ | 15 ml |
| 2 tablespoons | 1 | 30 ml |
| 3 tablespoons | $1^1/_2$ | 45 ml |
| $^1/_4$ cup (4 T) | 2 | 60 ml |
| $^1/_3$ cup ($5^1/_3$ T) | 3 | 80 ml |
| 6 tablespoons | 3 | 90 ml |
| $^1/_2$ cup (8 T) | 4 | 125 ml |
| $^3/_4$ cup | 6 | 180 ml |
| 1 cup | 8 | 250 ml |
| 1 pint (2 cups) | 16 | 500 ml |
| 4 cups | 32 | 1 l |
| 1 quart (8 cups) | 64 | 2 l |

## Conversion Factors

*Ounces to grams:* Multiply the ounce figure by 28.3 to get the number of grams.

*Pounds to grams:* Multiply the pound figure by 453.59 to get the number of grams.

*Pounds to kilograms:* Multiply the pound figure by 0.45 to get the number of kilograms.

*Ounces to milliliters:* Multiply the ounce figure by 30 to get the number of milliliters.

*Cups to liters:* Multiply the cup figure by 0.24 to get the number of liters.

*Fahrenheit to Celsius:* Subtract 32 from the Fahrenheit figure, multiply by 5, then divide by 9 to get the Celsius figure.

Note: For ease of use, measurements in this book have been rounded off.

# LIST OF CONTRIBUTORS

**Cal-a-Vie Health Resort**
2249 Somerset Road
Vista, CA 92084
Tel. (760) 945-2055
Fax (760) 630-0074
www.cal-a-vie.com

**Canyon Ranch in the Berkshires**
Bellefontaine, 165 Kemble Street
Lenox, MA 01240
Tel. (413) 637-4100
Fax (413) 637-0057
www.canyonranch.com

**Canyon Ranch Tucson**
8600 East Rockcleff Road
Tucson, AZ 85750
Tel. (520) 749-9000/(800) 742-9000
Fax (520) 749-1646
www.canyonranch.com

**Château Élan**
100 Rue Charlemagne
Braselton, GA 30517
Tel. (770) 932-0900/(800) 233-9463
Fax (770) 271-6000
www.chateauelan.com

**Givenchy Hotel & Spa**
4200 East Palm Canyon Drive
Palm Springs, CA 92264-5230
Tel. (760) 770-5000/(800) 276-5000
Fax (760) 324-6104
www.desertresorts.com/givenchy

**Golden Door**
P.O. Box 463077
Escondido, CA 92046
Tel. (760) 744-5777/(800) 424-0777
Fax (760) 471-2393
www.goldendoor.com

**Grand Wailea Resort, Spa Grande**
3850 Wailea Alanui Drive
Wailea, Maui, HI 96753
Tel. (808) 875-1234
Fax (808) 874-2424
www.grandwailea.com

**The Greenhouse**
P.O. Box 1144
Arlington, TX 76004
Tel. (817) 640-4000
Fax (817) 649-0422

**The Hills Health Ranch**
Box 26, 108 Mile Ranch
British Columbia
V0K 2Z0  Canada
Tel. (250) 791-5225
Fax (250) 791-6384
www.GRT-Net.com/thehills

**Hilton Head Health Institute**
P.O. Box 7138
Hilton Head Island, SC 29938
Tel. (803) 785-7292/(800) 292-2440
Fax (803) 686-5659

**Ihilani Resort & Spa**
92-1001 Olani Street
Kapolei, HI 96707
Tel. (808) 679-0079 / (800) 626-4446
Fax (808) 679-0080
www.ihilani.com

**The Inn at Manitou**
McKellar, Ontario P0G 1C0
Canada
Tel. (705) 389-2171/(800) 571-8818
Fax (705) 389-3818

**La Costa Resort and Spa**
Costa Del Mar Road
Carlsbad, CA 92009
Tel. (760) 438-9111/(800) 854-5000
Fax (760) 931-7559
www.lacosta.com

**The Lodge at Skylonda**
16350 Skyline Boulevard
Woodside, CA 94062
Tel. (650) 851-6625/(800) 851-2222
Fax (650) 851-5504
www.skylondalodge.com

**Meadowood Napa Valley**
900 Meadowood Lane
St. Helena, CA 94574
Tel. (707) 963-3646/(800) 458-8080
Fax (707) 963-3532

**The Peaks at Telluride**
136 Country Club Drive
Telluride, CO 81435
Tel. (970) 728-6800/(800) 789-2220
Fax (970) 728-6175

**The Phoenician Centre
for Well-Being**
6000 East Camelback Road
Scottsdale, AZ 85251
Tel. (602) 941-8200/(800) 888-8234
Fax (602) 947-4311
www.thephoenician.com

**Rancho La Puerta**
P.O. Box 463057
Escondido, CA 92046
Tel. (760) 744-4222/(800) 443-7565
Fax (760) 744-5007
www.rancholapuerta.com

**Sonoma Mission Inn & Spa**
P.O. Box 1447
Sonoma, CA 95476
Tel. (707) 938-9000/(800) 862-4945
Fax (707) 938-4250
www.sonomamissioninn.com

**The Spa at Doral**
8755 Northwest 36th Street
Miami, FL 33178
Tel. (305) 593-6030/(800) 331-7768
Fax (305) 591-9266
www.doralgolf.com

**Topnotch at Stowe**
4000 Mountain Road
P.O. Box 1458
Stowe, VT 05672
Tel. (802) 253-8585/(800) 451-8686
Fax (802) 253-9263
www.topnotch-resort.com/spa

# SPA RESOURCES

To find the ideal spa getaway, you can read the individual descriptions of the spas in this book and contact them directly (see page 260 to 261 for listings), or get further information from the resources listed below.

## Travel Agencies

**All Destinations Travel**
2091 Springdale Road, Suite 16
Cherry Hill, NJ 08003
Tel. (609) 751-6767/(800) 755-1718
Fax (609) 751-1247
www.alltravel.com

**Custom Spa Vacations**
1318 Beacon Street
Brookline, MA 02146
Tel. (617) 566-5144/(800) 443-7727
Fax (617) 731-0599
www.spatours.com

**Spa Connection**
1780 South Bellaire Street, Suite 506
Denver, CO 80222
Tel. (303) 756-9939/(888) 580-8388
Fax (303) 758-8862

**Spa-Finders Travel Arrangements, Ltd.**
*SpaFinder Magazine*
91 Fifth Avenue
New York, NY 10003
Tel. (212) 924-6800/(800) 255-7727
Fax (212) 924-7240
www.spafinders.com

**Spas & Salons USA**
1131 Central Avenue
Wilmette, IL 60091
Tel. (847) 256-6523/(800) 467-2566
www.gosalon.com

**Spa Traveler**
15246 NW Greenbrier Parkway
Beaverton, OR 97006
Tel. (800) 300-1565
Fax (503) 645-7088
www.spatraveler.com

**Spa Trek Travel**
475 Park Avenue South, 34th Floor
New York, NY 10016
Tel. (212) 779-3480/(800) 272-3480
Fax (212) 779-3471

## Publications

*Fodor's Healthy Escapes:*
*Spas, Fitness Resorts, Cruises*
Fodor's Travel Publications,
Random House
201 East 50th Street
New York, NY 10022
Tel. (212) 751-2600
www.fodors.com

*Condé Nast Traveler*
P.O. Box 52470
Boulder, CO 80321
Tel. (800) 777-0700
Fax (800) 666-5629
www.condenet.com

*Spa Magazine*
5305 Shilshole Avenue NW, Suite 200
Seattle, WA 98107
Tel. (206) 789-6506/(800) 835-2722
Fax (206) 789-9193
www.spamagazine.com

*Town & Country*
1700 Broadway
New York, NY 10019
Tel. (800) 289-8696

*Travel & Leisure*
P.O. Box 2094
Harlan, IA 51593
Tel. (800) 888-8728
Fax (515) 246-1020
www.travelandleisure.com

*Online*

*The Spa Gateway*
www.spamagazine.com

*Spa Lifestyle*
www.spa-resort.com

*World Spas*
www.worldspas.com

*Associations*

**ClubSpa USA, The Day Spa Association**
P.O. Box 5232
West New York, NJ 07093
Tel. (201) 865-2065
Fax (201) 865-3961
www.clubspausa.com

**International Spa and Fitness Association (I/SPA)**
546 East Main Street
Lexington, KY 40508
Tel. (888) 651-4772
Fax (606) 226-4424
www.gotravel.com/ispa

# ACKNOWLEDGMENTS

I would like to thank the many people who made this volume possible.

My deepest gratitude to the proprietors and chefs of the spas who generously contributed menus and recipes to the cookbook: Marlene Power, Steve Pernetti, Joanie Laib, Yvonne Nienstadt, and Deborah Zie from Cal-a-Vie; Mel Zuckerman, Jona Liebrecht, and John Luzader from Canyon Ranch; Barry Correia from Canyon Ranch in the Berkshires; Nancy Panoz and Yves Samake from Chateau Élan; Rose Narva and Luis Garcia from Givenchy Hotel & Spa; Deborah Szekely, Michel Stroot, Rachel Caldwell, and Mary-Elizabeth Gifford from the Golden Door; Greg Kostering, Darrell Marsden, Adrian Aina, and Glen Tolosko from Grand Wailea Resort; Lee Katzoff, Leopoldo Gonzales, and Shirley Ogle from The Greenhouse; Patrick Corbett from The Hills Health Ranch; Ken Whitaker and Erich Striegel from Hilton Head Health Institute; Robert McEleney and Mark Adair from the Ihilani Resort & Spa; Sheila and Ben Wise, Julia Eaton, and Scott Wilshaw from the Inn at Manitou; John Peto and Joseph Lageder from La Costa Resort and Spa; Larry Callahan, Sue Chapman, and Lisa Henry from The Lodge at Skylonda; Bill Harlan, Didier Lenders, and Maria del Pilar from Meadowood Napa Valley; Ken Humes from The Peaks; Alan Fuerstman from The Phoenician; Bill Wavrin and Phyllis Pilgrim from Rancho La Puerta; Charles Henning, Jeffrey Jake, and Steve Fischer from Sonoma Mission Inn; Joel Paige and George Goins from The Spa at Doral; Robert Boyle and Edward St. Onge from Topnotch at Stowe. Thanks also to the staffs at the spas for their prompt assistance. Special thanks to my dear friend, Marlene Power of Cal-a-Vie, for my first spa experience— I will remember it always. Thanks also to everyone at Rancho La Puerta.

I am forever grateful to pianists François-Joël Thiollier and Idil Biret for their exquisite performances. Thanks once again to George Horn at Fantasy Studios, Berkeley, for the digital mastering. Heartfelt appreciation to Sharilyn Hovind for excellent writing and generous good advice. Once again, my warmest thanks to Carolyn Miller for her thoughtful editing, expert guidance, and attention to detail. Brenda Rae Eno of Brenda Eno Design and Brent Beck of Fifth Street Design deserve thanks for their wonderful design and enthusiastic support of this project. Thanks to Karen Duester, M.S., R.D., of the Food Consulting Company for the nutritional data. Grateful acknowledgments are due to Sarah Creider for numerous contributions; and to Sharlene Swacke, Ned Waring, Tim Forney, Mike Coykendall, Connie Wood, and the rest of the staff at Menus and Music.

And as always, to my daughters, Claire and Caitlin, and my husband, John, for their love and for their great support during the many hours of work this project required.

ACKNOWLEDGMENTS

# INDEX

Adapting recipes, 17

Almond Ricotta Torte with Cocoa-Kahlúa Sauce, 55

Appetizers

    Artichokes Stuffed with Bay Shrimp, 223

    Roast Tomatoes Filled with Pine Nuts, Couscous, and Chanterelles, 156

    Salmon Mousse with Orange and Chervil, 175

    Shrimp Salad with Japanese Rice Rolls, 76

    Spa California Rolls, 168

    Spring Rolls with Sesame-Soy Dipping Sauce, 235

    Wild Mushroom and Chèvre Strudel, 246

Apple(s)

    Baked, with raisins, 160

    and Apricots Gratin with Cal-a-Vie Granola, 49

    Butter, 166

    -Carrot Muffins, 116

    Crisp, 111

    Empanadas, 63

    Strudels with Cinnamon Sauce, 133

Aromatherapy, 32

Artichoke(s)

    Mushroom, and Sun-Dried Tomato Phyllo Pouches, 169

    Stuffed with Bay Shrimp, 223

Asparagus

    Grilled, Salad with Sherry Vinaigrette, 53

    Grilled, with Grilled Portobello Mushrooms, Couscous, and Pepper Coulis, 93

Barley and Chicken "Risotto," 71

Baths, 34

Bean(s)

    Black, 245

    Black, Soup with Fresh Tomato Salsa, 128

    Spicy Black, Salad in Papayas, 105

Berry(ies)

    Blackberry-Orange Cobbler, 72

    Soup, Chilled California, 185

Beverages

    Aveda Pear-Ginger Smoothie, 21

    Cal-a-Vie Revitalizer, 20

Biscotti with Seasonal Fruit, 210

Blueberry-Orange Syrup, 243

Body scrubs, 34

Bread

    Breakfast, with Cranberries and Apricots, 207

    Butternut Squash and Cranberry, with Yogurt Cheese, 91

Breakfast, 19

Breakfast and brunch dishes

    Apple-Carrot Muffins, 116

    Breakfast Bread with Cranberries and Apricots, 207

    Butternut Squash and Cranberry Bread with Yogurt Cheese, 91

    Cornmeal-Buttermilk Waffles with Blueberry-Orange Syrup, 242

    Egg White Cassolette, 220

    Energizer Cereal with Apple Butter, 165

    Fluffy Spinach and Sweet Pepper Omelette, 115

    French Toast with Blueberry Syrup, 137

    Garden Eggs Ranchero with Curried Tofu, 205

    Granola, Cal-a-Vie, 50

    Gratin of Apples and Apricots with Cal-a-Vie Granola, 49

    Tofu-and-Vegetable Hash, 104

    Whole-Wheat Banana Pancakes with Fruit Sauce, 232

Butternut Squash

    and Cider Soup, 68

    and Cranberry Bread with Yogurt Cheese, 91

    Purée, 251

    Sorbet, 52

Cake
    Angel Food, 250
    Chocolate, 179
Cal-a-Vie, 47
California Rolls, 168
Canyon Ranch, 57
Canyon Ranch in the Berkshires, 65
Carrot
    -Apple Muffins, 116
    -Ginger Soup, 233
Cereal, Energizer, with Apple Butter, 165
Château Élan, 73
Chicken
    and Barley "Risotto," 71
    Breasts with English Peas, French Style, 78
    Enchiladas with Black Beans, 244
    and Feta Roulades with Red Lentil
        Ragout, 109
    Pan-Seared, with Crisp Baked Potatoes, 192
    Poached, with Cheese, Spinach, and Red
        Pepper Coulis, 130
    Stock, 254
    Tandoori with Stir-Fried Vegetables, 117
    with Tarragon-Walnut Wild Rice Salad, 51
    Velouté, 251
    and Wild Rice Chowder, 138
Chili Soup with Tortilla Strips, 60
Chocolate Cake, 179
Chopin, Frédéric, 43
Cobbler, Blackberry-Orange, 72
Cooking light, 15
Corn
    Chips, Spa, 167
    -Roasted Salsa, 62
    Soup with Chipotle-Cilantro Pesto, 212
    Tamale with Feta, 214
Coulis
    Berry, 250
    Mango, 170
    Raspberry, 170
    Red Pepper, 131

    Two-Pepper, 95
Crab and Spinach Salad with Asian
    Vinaigrette, 221
Crabmeat and Baby Spinach Salad, 189
Cranberry
    and Butternut Squash Bread, 91
    Breakfast Bread with Apricots, 207
    Ketchup, 70
Cucumber Relish, 141

Debussy, Claude, 43
Desserts
    Almond Ricotta Torte with Cocoa-Kahlúa
        Sauce, 55
    Apple Crisp, 111
    Apple Empanadas, 63
    Apple Strudels with Cinnamon Sauce, 133
    Baked Apples with Raisins and Cinnamon-
        Vanilla Ice Cream, 160
    Biscotti with Seasonal Fruit, 210
    Blackberry-Orange Cobbler, 72
    Chilled California Berries Soup, 185
    Chocolate Cake, 179
    Frozen Yogurt Crunch with Strawberry
        Sauce, 194
    Fruit Tabbouleh with Mango and Raspberry
        Coulis, 170
    German Pear Strudel, 143
    Key Lime Cannoli, 237
    Lemon Chiffon with Strawberry Sauce, 228
    Mango-Banana Sorbet, 100
    Mango Yogurt Flan with Almond Crisps
        and Tropical Fruit, 151
    Melon Balls, Chilled, with Warm Ginger
        Sauce, 249
    Oatmeal Cookies, 99
    Pear-Polenta Soufflés, 124
    Pineapple Parfait, 79
    Postres del Sol, 216
    Roasted Pear Elegante, 87
    Strawberry-Ricotta Trifle, 201
    Strawberry-Tofu Sherbet, 119
Dinner and dessert, 21

Duck Breasts, Seared, with Green Peppercorns and Mâche, 176

Eggplant and Green Beans with Penne, 199
Eggs
 Egg White Cassolette, 220
 Fluffy Spinach and Sweet Pepper Omelette, 115
 Ranchero with Curried Tofu, 205
 Vegetable and Egg-White Frittata, 190
Enchiladas, Chicken, with Black Beans, 244
European spas, 9
Eye care, 30

Facial
 scrubs, 24
 steaming, 25
 toning, 27
Facials, 23
Fish
 Ahi Tuna Napoleon with Sake-Lime Vinaigrette, 106
 Ahi Tuna, Seared, with Couscous Salad, 149
 Halibut, Pacific, with Citrus and Basil, 184
 Salmon, Baked, in a Garlic Crust with Cucumber Relish, 140
 Salmon Mousse with Orange and Chervil, 175
 Salmon, Pan-Seared, with New Potatoes and Shaved-Vegetable Salad, 200
 Salmon with Potatoes and Cabbage Cream Sauce, 158
 Sea Bass, Poached, with Salmon Mousseline, 122
 Sea Bass Tower, 247
 Swordfish, Grilled, with Papaya-Kiwi Salsa, 97
 Swordfish with Risotto and Roasted-Tomato Broth, 226
 Velouté, 251
Foot care, 28
French Toast with Blueberry Syrup, 137
Fruit Tabbouleh with Mango and Raspberry Coulis, 170

Gazpacho
 Classic, with a Twist, 198
 with Poached Scallops, 147
Givenchy Hotel & Spa, 81
Golden Door, 89
Grand Wailea Resort, 101
Granola, Cal-a-Vie, 50
Gratin of Apples and Apricots with Cal-a-Vie Granola, 49
The Greenhouse, 113

Hair care, 31
Halibut, Pacific, with Citrus and Basil, 184
Hand and nail care, 28
The Hills Health Ranch, 125
Hilton Head Health Institute, 135

Ihilani Resort & Spa, 145
The Inn at Manitou, 153

Jicama Slaw, 121

Key Lime Cannoli, 237

La Costa Resort & Spa, 163
Lamb Loins with Port Wine Sauce, 54
Lasagna, Grilled-Vegetable, 85
Lemon Chiffon with Strawberry Sauce, 228
Lentil Ragout, Red, 109
Lime Cannoli, 237
Lobster Tail Fra Diablo Over Capellini, 236
The Lodge at Skylonda, 173
Lunch, 19

Mango
 -Banana Sorbet, 100
 Purée, 251
 Yogurt Flan with Almond Crisps and Tropical Fruit, 151
Manicure, 28
Masks, 25
Massage, 40
Meadowood Napa Valley, 181

Meditation, 39

Melon Balls, Chilled, with Warm Ginger Sauce, 249

Moisturizing, 27

Muffins, Apple-Carrot, 116

Mushroom, Wild, and Chèvre Strudel, 246

North American historical spas, 9

Nuts and seeds, toasting, 258

Oatmeal Cookies, 99

Omelette, Spinach and Sweet Pepper, 115

Onions

    Pickled Red, 189

    Sweet Red, 193

Pancakes, Whole-Wheat Banana, with Fruit Sauce, 232

Pasta

    Angel Hair Pasta with Wild Mushrooms, Roasted Garlic, Tomato, and Basil, 222

    Grilled-Vegetable Lasagnas, 85

    Lobster Tail Fra Diablo Over Capellini, 236

    Penne with Grilled Eggplant and Green Beans, 199

Pastry Cream, 252

The Peaks, 187

Pear

    Strudel, German, 143

    -Polenta Soufflés, 124

    Roasted, Elegante, 87

Pedicure, 28

Pepper(s)

    Coulis, 95

    Roasting, 253

    Soup, Roasted Red and Yellow Bell, 208

    and Spinach Omelette, 115

Pesto, Chipotle-Cilantro, 213

The Phoenician, 195

Phyllo Pouches, Artichoke, Mushroom, and Sun-Dried Tomato, 169

Pineapple

    Parfait, 79

    Risotto, 107

Polenta-Pear Soufflés, 124

Portobello Mushrooms, Grilled, with Couscous, Pepper Coulis, and Grilled Asparagus, 93

Potatoes, Crisp Baked, 192

Pumpkin Purée, 251

Quinoa with Parsley, 98

Rancho La Puerta, 203

Ravel, Maurice, 45

Relish, Cucumber, 141

Rice; see also Wild Rice

    Japanese Rolls with Shrimp, 76

    Orange, 142

Ricotta Almond Torte with Cocoa-Kahlúa Sauce, 55

Risotto, 252

    Barley and Chicken, 71

    Pineapple, 107

Roman baths, 8

Roasting peppers and chilies, 253

Salad

    Asparagus, Grilled, with Sherry Vinaigrette, 53

    Chef's, Spa, 183

    Couscous, with Seared Ahi Tuna, 149

    Crab and Spinach, with Asian Vinaigrette, 221

    Crabmeat and Baby Spinach, 189

    Hearts of Lettuce with Sherry Dressing, 120

    Jicama Slaw, 121

    Niçoise, 139

    Shrimp, with Japanese Rice Rolls, 76

    Southwestern Taco, 167

    Spicy Black Bean, in Papayas, 105

    Wild Rice, Tarragon-Walnut, with Chicken, 51

Salad Dressing(s); see also Vinaigrette

    Ancho-Citrus Vinaigrette, 189

    Asian Vinaigrette, 221

    Ginger Vinaigrette, 84

Sherry Dressing, 121
Sherry Vinaigrette, 53
Sake-Lime Vinaigrette, 108
Salmon
    Baked, in a Garlic Crust with Cucumber
        Relish, 140
    Mousse, with Orange and Chervil, 175
    Pan-Seared, with New Potatoes and
        Shaved-Vegetable Salad, 200
    with Potatoes and Cabbage Cream
        Sauce, 158
Salsa
    Fresh Tomato, 129
    Papaya-Kiwi, 97
    Roasted-Corn, 62
    Roasted-Tomato, 191
    Rosie's Tomatillo, 206
Satie, Erik, 44
Sauce; *see also* Salsa *and* Coulis
    Dipping, Sesame-Soy, 235
    Fruit, 232
    Ginger, 249
    Mustard, 193
    Pesto, Chipotle-Cilantro, 213
    Red Chili, 245
    Roasted-Tomato Broth, 227
    Strawberry, 194, 228
Scallops, Poached, with Gazpacho, 147
Sea Bass
    Poached, with Salmon Mousseline, 122
    Tower with Portobello Mushrooms and
        Truffle-Spinach Vinaigrette, 247
Sherry
    Dressing, 121
    Vinaigrette, 53
Shopping lean, 13
Shrimp
    Bay, Artichokes Stuffed with, 223
    Kabobs with Bulgur Wheat, Lime-
        Marinated, 234
    in Kataifi with Artichoke Hearts and
        Ginger Vinaigrette, 83

Salad with Japanese Rice Rolls, 76
Slaw, Jicama, 121
Snacks, 20
Sonoma Mission Inn, 217
Sorbet
    Butternut Squash, 52
    Mango-Banana, 100
    Strawberry-Tofu Sherbet, 119
Soup
    Berries, Chilled California, 185
    Black Bean with Fresh Tomato Salsa, 128
    Butternut Squash and Cider, 68
    Carrot-Ginger, 233
    Chili, with Tortilla Strips, 60
    Classic Gazpacho with a Twist, 198
    Gazpacho with Poached Scallops, 147
    Mediterranean Vegetable Bisque, 224
    Mexican Corn, with Chipotle-Cilantro
        Pesto, 212
    Roasted Red and Yellow Bell Pepper, 208
    Watermelon Gazpacho with Cucumber, 96
    Wild Rice and Chicken Chowder, 138
Southwestern Taco Salad, 167
Spa
    California Rolls, 168
    Chef's Salad, 183
    Corn Chips, 167
    cuisine, 12
The Spa at Doral, 229
Spinach
    and Crabmeat Salad, 189
    and Crab Salad with Asian Vinaigrette, 221
    and Sweet Pepper Omelette, 115
Spring Rolls with Sesame-Soy Dipping
    Sauce, 235
Stir-Fried Vegetables, 118
Stock
    Chicken, 254
    Duck, 255
    Fish, 256
    Lamb, 256

Vegetable, 257
Strawberry
    -Ricotta Trifle, 201
    Sauce 194, 228
    -Tofu Sherbet, 119
Stress reduction, 38
Swordfish
    Grilled, with Papaya-Kiwi Salsa, 97
    with Risotto and Roasted-Tomato Broth, 226

Tabbouleh, Fruit, with Mango and Raspberry
    Coulis, 170
Taco Salad, Southwestern, 167
Tamale, Blue Corn, with Feta, 214
Toasting nuts and seeds, 258
Tofu
    and Vegetable Hash, 104
    -Strawberry Sherbet, 119
Tomato(es)
    Salsa, Fresh, 129
    peeling and seeding, 253
    Roast, Filled with Pine Nuts, Couscous,
        and Chanterelles, 156
    Roasted, Broth, 227
Topnotch at Stowe, 239
Tostadas
    Bill's Mexican Tuna and Corn, 209
    Vegetarian with Roasted-Corn Salsa, 61
Tuna
    Ahi, Napoleon with Sake-Lime
        Vinaigrette, 106
    Ahi, Seared, with Couscous Salad, 149
    and Corn Tostada, Bill's Mexican, 209
Turkey Burgers with Cranberry
    Ketchup, 69
Turnips, Glazed, 178

Vegetable(s); see also specific vegetables
    Bisque, Mediterranean, 224
    and Egg-White Frittata, 190
    Lasagna, Grilled, 85
    Stir-Fried, 118
    Stock, 257

Vegetarian main dishes
    Angel Hair Pasta with Wild Mushrooms,
        Roasted Garlic, Tomato, and Basil, 222
    Artichoke, Mushroom, and Sun-Dried
        Tomato Phyllo Pouches, 169
    Blue Corn Tamale with Feta, 214
    Chili Soup with Tortilla Strips, 60
    Grilled-Vegetable Lasagnas, 85
    Penne with Grilled Eggplant and
        Green Beans, 199
    Portobello Mushrooms, Grilled, with
        Couscous, Pepper Coulis, and Grilled
        Asparagus, 93
    Spicy Black Bean Salad in Papayas, 105
    Tarragon-Walnut Wild Rice Salad with
        Seitan, 51
    Vegetable and Egg-White Frittata, 190
    Vegetarian Tostadas with Roasted-Corn
        Salsa, 61
    Wild Mushroom and Chèvre Strudel, 246
Vinaigrette
    Ancho-Citrus, 189
    Asian, 221
    Ginger, 84
    Sherry, 53
    Sake-Lime, 108
    White Truffle-Spinach, 248

Waffles, Cornmeal-Buttermilk, with
    Blueberry-Orange Syrup, 242
Watermelon Gazpacho with Cucumber, 96
Weight loss, 22
Wild Rice
    and Chicken Chowder, 138
    with Lemon, 132
    Salad, Tarragon-Walnut, with Chicken, 51

Yogurt
    Cheese, 92
    Frozen, with Strawberry Sauce, 194
    Mango, Flan with Almond Crisps and
        Tropical Fruit, 151

Zest, citrus, 251

Sharon O'Connor is a musician, cook, and author of thirteen books in the Menus and Music series, which combines her love of music, food, and travel. Founder of the San Francisco String Quartet, she was educated at the University of California, Berkeley and the Amsterdam Conservatory of Music. She now lives in the San Francisco Bay Area with her husband and two daughters.